Manage Your **Money** and **Investments**

with Microsoft® **Excel**

Peter G. Aitken

800 E. 96th Street
Indianapolis, Indiana 46240

Manage Your Money and Investments with Microsoft® Excel

Copyright © 2006 by Que Publishing

International Standard Book Number: 0-7897-3428-1

Library of Congress Catalog Card Number: 2005922654

Printed in the United States of America

First Printing: July 2005

09   08   07   4   3

Trademarks

Warning and Disclaimer

Bulk Sales

Que Publishing offers excellent discounts on this book when ordered in quantity for bulk purchases or special sales. For more information, please contact

U.S. Corporate and Government Sales
1-800-382-3419
corpsales@pearsontechgroup.com

For sales outside of the U.S., please contact

International Sales
international@pearsoned.com

Associate Publisher
Greg Wiegand

Acquisitions Editor
Todd Green

Development Editor
Greg Perry

Managing Editor
Charlotte Clapp

Project Editor
Dan Knott

Production Editor
Heather Wilkins

Indexer
Erika Millen

Technical Editor
Michael Kitces

Publishing Coordinator
Sharry Lee Gregory

Multimedia Developer
Dan Scherf

Designer
Anne Jones

Page Layout
Eric S. Miller

Contents

III FINANCING YOUR HOME AND CAR

IV MANAGING YOUR INVESTMENTS

APPENDICES

About the Author

Peter Aitken was writing about computers and software before the first version of Excel was released. Since then he has written more than 40 books and innumerable magazine and Web articles on topics ranging from office applications and personal finance to application development and digital photography. Peter is also the proprietor of PGA Consulting, providing application development and technical writing services to clients since 1996. You can learn more about Peter's books at www.pgacon.com/books.htm.

Dedication

To my dear wife Maxine, for all your love and support.

Acknowledgments

A book might have just one listed author, but it's a group effort in so many ways. I am most grateful for the able and essential contributions made by the following people: Todd Green, acquisitions editor; Dan Knott, project editor; Greg Perry, development editor; Michael E. Kitces; technical editor; and Heather Wilkins, production editor. Thanks everyone!

We Want to Hear from You!

As the reader of this book, *you* are our most important critic and commentator. We value your opinion and want to know what we're doing right, what we could do better, what areas you'd like to see us publish in, and any other words of wisdom you're willing to pass our way.

As an associate publisher for Que Publishing, I welcome your comments. You can email or write me directly to let me know what you did or didn't like about this book—as well as what we can do to make our books better.

Please note that I cannot help you with technical problems related to the topic of this book. We do have a User Services group, however, where I will forward specific technical questions related to the book.

When you write, please be sure to include this book's title and author as well as your name, email address, and phone number. I will carefully review your comments and share them with the author and editors who worked on the book.

Email: feedback@quepublishing.com

Mail: Greg Wiegand
           Associate Publisher
           Que Publishing
           800 East 96th Street
           Indianapolis, IN 46240 USA

For more information about this book or another Que Publishing title, visit our website at www.quepublishing.com. Type the ISBN (excluding hyphens) or the title of a book in the Search field to find the page you're looking for.

Introduction

Benjamin Franklin said, "A penny saved is a penny earned." It's true, too—although we are not too concerned with pennies these days, each dollar, or ten dollars, or fifty dollars that you save is just like having that much more in your paycheck. I'm not talking about the kind of saving that results from denying yourself the pleasures or even some necessities of life. No, what this book is about is the savings you can realize by taking charge of your finances.

People start working with personal finance at an early age. You might start with just an allowance and then maybe in high school move onto a part-time job and a small savings account. Eventually you find yourself on your own with a job, a checking account, and maybe a family to help support. Car loans, credit cards, and a mortgage come soon enough for many of us. All these aspects of personal finance seem to be an unavoidable part of modern life.

How you approach your personal finances can have a big impact on your life. Some people seem to just muddle through from week to week while others make an effort to learn the ins and outs of personal finance so they can take charge of their own situation. Is it worth the effort? You bet it is! Let me explain.

First of all, when you don't master your own finances, you are almost sure to be paying out a lot in unnecessary fees and interest. I am always amazed to hear how much profit banks and credit card companies make from overdraft and late fees, interest, and other avoidable charges to the consumer. This money is coming out of your pocket! When you take charge of your finances, you can eliminate or at least greatly reduce these unnecessary payments. That means more money in your pocket to spend or save as you see fit.

Second, many of life's major goals require some financial planning. Buying your first house, saving for Junior's college education, affording that fishing boat you have always wanted, looking forward to a secure retirement—these are some of the more important examples. Without planning, such goals might remain forever beyond your grasp.

My goal in writing this book is to provide you with the information and tools you need to take charge of your finances. It's not always the easiest thing to do—after all, bad financial habits can die hard—but it is very worthwhile.

Why Excel?

Why did I focus this book on using the Excel spreadsheet program? Aren't there some specialized personal finance programs available? Please let me explain.

There are several sophisticated personal finance programs on the market, the best known being Quicken and Microsoft Money. They are excellent programs, but—and this is a big but—they try to provide every possible feature any user could conceivably want. As a result, these programs are unavoidably complex. And—unavoidably as well—you must buy them.

Excel, in contrast, is a general purpose data manipulation program that includes many tools for working with finances. Most importantly, it is already installed on millions of computers. Chances are that when you bought your computer, it had Excel already installed as a free extra. Or you might have installed Excel yourself for your personal or business use. Either way, there are millions of people around the world who can use the Excel templates provided with this book without any additional expense.

Who This Book Is For

The people who want to take charge of their finances come from all walks of life, and not all of them are computer experts. That's why I wrote this book to be understandable and usable by almost anyone. As long as you know the basics of using your computer and Excel, you will do just fine.

The only requirement is that you have Excel installed on your computer. The templates that come with this book work with any of the recent versions of Excel, including Excel 2000, Excel XP, and Excel 2003.

Each workbook is provided in two versions. The one with Example in the name (for example, Check Register Example.xls) contains sample data that you can use to experiment with and see how the workbook functions. The one without Example in the name (for example, Check Register.xls) is empty and ready for you to start entering your own data.

More Information and Updates

The publisher maintains a website for this book at http://www.quepublishing.com/title/0789734281. You can visit this site for more information about the book, to place orders, and to find links to Que's other publications. I maintain my own site for this book at http://www.pgacon.com/Books/ManageMoneyExcel.htm. Visit my site if you want to send me a comment and to check for corrections in the text and templates. Please note that even though I love to hear from readers, I can respond only to matters that are directly related to the book.

Peter Aitken
Chapel Hill, North Carolina
April 2005

Understanding the Basics of Financial Calculations

Taking Control of Your Finances

If you ask people what they do not have enough of, the most common answer is likely to be "money." No matter how hard you work, no matter how good your job is, it can be a struggle to make ends meet while maintaining the standard of living you want. Can you do anything about this situation? Yes, you can! One approach is to bring in more money, but that's not something I can help you with. The other is to take control of your finances, and that's something I definitely *can* help you with! In fact, that is the whole point of this book.

Facing the Problem

Before getting down to details, it is a good idea to look at the problems facing many people today when it comes to their finances. The majority of Americans are financially illiterate. If you fall into this category, don't blame yourself—after all, personal finance classes are not offered in most high schools or colleges and, even when they are, they are usually a low priority for most students. People are expected to somehow absorb all the intricacies of personal finance on their own, and, in my opinion, that's asking a lot.

Some people are hesitant to admit they do not know much about personal finance. In our society, competence is valued and you might feel embarrassed to admit you don't know much about the topic. That's exactly the wrong attitude! Competence comes from learning, and the first step in learning is admitting you *need* to learn. Getting this book was a good first step.

Another source of problems is that some people equate finances with investing. There is undoubtedly something very alluring about the stock market and the chance to see your investments grow over the months and years. Investing is, in fact, important, and several chapters of this book are devoted to it. But investing is only part of the personal finance picture.

Setting Goals

As you embark on the task of getting your personal finances in order, it's helpful to have some goals. Of course, if you do not yet know what's wrong with your finances, it might not be easy to set these goals—not yet, anyway. But the fact that you are reading this suggests you think something is not as it should be. As you work through the chapters in this book, keep the thought of goals in mind and formulate them as you go along.

For many people, financial goals are centered on saving money. America has one of the lowest saving rates of any developed country, so a lot of people are in this boat. You might want to save for something major, the most common things being to buy a house, to pay for your children's college, and to fund your retirement. Perhaps you just want to build up a reserve against emergencies. Many financial planners recommend you have enough savings to live off of for six months in the event of a job loss. Very few people have this cushion.

It's interesting to note that Americans' personal debt ratio has not increased significantly in decades. This means that on average we are not borrowing more relative to our income. But we are still borrowing, and those payments are still due regardless of a job loss or other hardship. This is one reason the low personal savings rate is worrysome. With a decent cushion of savings, you will be able to continue your loan payments through a period of decreased or no income. Without that cushion, you will find creditors knocking at your door.

Whatever your goals, the first step in achieving them is to take control of your finances. What exactly do I mean by taking control of your finances? There are three parts to this as I see it.

First, you need to avoid unnecessary expenditures. No, I don't mean that set of Elvis CDs you bought off late-night TV. After all, I am not here to tell you how to spend your money. I mean *really* unnecessary expenditures, such as checking account overdraft fees and excessive credit card interest payments. These are the sorts of outlays you really need to avoid because they are a total waste—you get nothing in return. With some planning (and this book), you should be able to avoid them entirely. Every dollar you do not spend on these unnecessary fees is another dollar in your pocket to be spent on something more important and enjoyable.

Don't believe that these little fees can add up to much? Then look at this hypothetical but realistic example. We have Jane Q. Careless who

- Does not pay attention to her checkbook balance, so she bounces an average of one check a month. The bank charges $25 per bounced check and the typical merchant bounced check fee is $15. That's (25 + 15) × 12 or $480 per year wasted.

- Withdraws $100 twice a month from an ATM that does not belong to her bank, incurring a 2.5% charge each time. That's 100 × 2.5% × 24 equalling $60 a year down the drain.

- Maintains a $3,500 balance on a credit card that charges 21.99% interest. She pays $61.14 in interest each month for a yearly total of $769.

- Forgets to pay her credit card bill on time four times a year. The late fee charge is $35 (never mind the extra interest!) for $140 a year.

Are you ready for the result? All those unnecessary charges add up to close to $1,450 a year for Jane. I know that I have a lot of better things to do with that kind of money, and I'll bet you do, too.

Second, you need to be a wise consumer of financial products and services. Pretty much everyone is going to have a checking account and one or more credit or debit cards. Many also have mortgages, home equity loans, investment accounts (whether stocks or mutual funds), one or more retirement accounts, consumer loans, and money market accounts. Knowing how to evaluate and compare these products can make a big difference in your financial picture.

Finally, you need to be savvy about how things work in the world of money. Many people make bad financial decisions, not because they are lazy or stupid, but because they just do not have the information necessary to make the right choices. Unfortunately, in our society financial education is almost always left up to chance, and most people enter the adult world poorly equipped to handle the financial challenges that lie ahead. This book provides the required information about the world of finance and the tools you need to make informed decisions.

What Excel Can Do for You

Excel is Microsoft's spreadsheet program. It is not a home finance program, so why am I using it in this book? Excel is a very flexible program that has applications in many different areas, and one of them is finance. Excel might not be designed specifically for personal finance, but it certainly has the tools you need. Let's take a look at the fundamentals of Excel. If you already have some familiarity with Excel, you might want to skim or skip this section.

At the heart of Excel is the concept of a *worksheet*. You can think of a worksheet as an electronic form of a page from a ledger book that is ruled into rows and columns. A worksheet is larger than any real book, however, having 65,536 rows and 256 columns. The rows are numbered sequentially starting at the top, and the columns are identified by letters. The first 26 columns are A through Z, and subsequent columns are assigned double letters, starting with AA, AB, and so on up to IV. You rarely use all the rows and columns in a worksheet, but it's nice to know they are there if you need them.

At the intersection of each row and column is a *cell*. Each cell is identified by its column and row. For example, cell B3 is located where the second column and third row intersect. A cell can contain one of three things:

- Text
- A number
- A formula

It's the third item, formulas, that gives Excel its power. With formulas, you can perform calculations on data in the worksheet. These can be simple calculations, such as adding the numbers in two cells together and displaying the result in a third cell, or complex calculations, such as determining depreciation for tax purposes. Figure 1.1 shows a simple worksheet that illustrates the basic components of a worksheet.

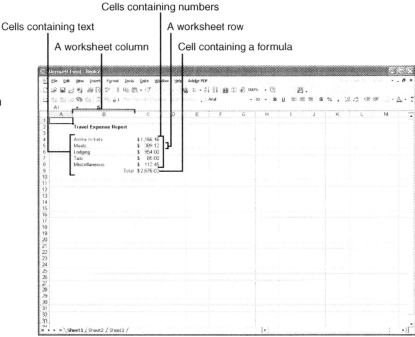

Cells containing numbers

Cells containing text

A worksheet row

A worksheet column

Cell containing a formula

Figure 1.1

The fundamental components of an Excel worksheet.

Worksheets are organized into *workbooks* that can contain one or more individual worksheets. Each worksheet in a workbook has a tab at the bottom of the screen, and you can display a worksheet by clicking its tab. The workbook is the unit saved to disk in an Excel file.

Excel can also display charts based on data in a worksheet. Visual representations of data are a powerful way to view and interpret information.

But enough about Excel! This is not a book intended to teach you about Excel, and the included templates have been carefully designed so anyone can use them, regardless of their level of experience with Excel.

Why Excel and Not Quicken or Money?

As you probably know, several specialized home finance programs are on the market, the best known being Quicken and Microsoft Money.

Why would you want to use Excel for your finances instead of one of these programs? That's a good question, so read on.

Most basically, these programs are not free—although they occasionally are provided free as part of some promotion. Excel is not free either, of course, but many people already have Excel as part of a software bundle that came with a new computer and they can start using these templates without any extra expense.

Another consideration is that the dedicated home finance programs are very complex. This is unavoidable when you try to include every possible feature in a single program. With checking accounts, mutual funds, budgets, stocks, taxes, retirement planning, and who knows what else crammed into one program, there's just no way you can have a simple and easy to use program. Don't get me wrong, I think these programs are great for some people, but if you want clarity and simplicity, they might not be the way to go.

The final factor is flexibility. Although Quicken and Microsoft Money are powerful programs, they do not offer any flexibility. You have to do things the program's way, or not at all. What if you cannot get the report you need or display your financial information in the way you want? Too bad, you are out of luck. With Excel, you have essentially unlimited flexibility to do things your way. If the templates provided with this book do not suit you, you can change them as needed.

Excel Versions

Excel is updated every year or so by Microsoft. As of this writing, the latest version is Excel 2003. However, many people have older versions. If you are one of these people, how does an older version affect the use of the book's templates?

Not to worry. Microsoft has made a concerted effort to retain compatibility between Excel versions. In other words, a workbook created with one version of Excel can be opened and used with another version of Excel. You do not need the latest version to use these templates. In fact, they were not created with the latest version but with Excel XP, which is one version back.

Using the Worksheet Templates

The heart of this book is a series of Excel worksheet templates you can use to help you with various aspects of your finances. Each of these templates is explained in detail in the corresponding chapter. In this section, I will provide an overview of how you go about using these tools. Each template is an Excel workbook, an XLS file, that contains all the formulas and other elements you need. All you have to do is enter your own data to get your results. Figure 1.2 shows an example; this is the net worth calculator from Chapter 4, "Tracking Your Net Worth."

Figure 1.2

Each template automatically calculates the results based on information you enter.

Type data into the template...

...and Excel automatically calculates the results

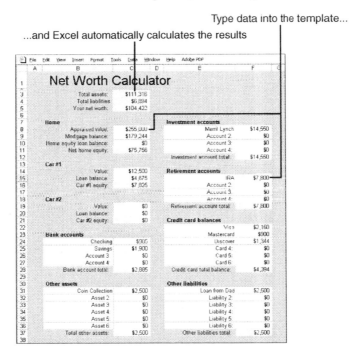

What Is a Template?

A *template* is nothing more than an Excel workbook that already has some data and formulas in it. When you open a template, you can add your own personal data as needed.

The first step is to install the templates from the CD-ROM and save them on your local hard disk. Please refer to "What's on the CD-ROM" at the back of the book for instructions on how to do this.

After the templates are installed on your computer, follow these steps to use a specific template:

1. Select the File, Open command in Excel or click the Open button on the toolbar.
2. Navigate to the folder where you saved the templates.
3. Select the desired template and click the Open button.

At this point you have the template open and ready for use. To avoid overwriting the original template workbook—after all, you might want to use it again—you need to save it with a new name or in a new location (or both) before you enter any data or make any other changes. Here's how:

1. Select File, Save As from the Excel menu to display the Save As dialog box (shown in Figure 1.3).
2. In the Save As Type drop-down list, make sure Microsoft Excel Workbook (*.xls) is selected.
3. Enter a descriptive name for the workbook in the File Name box.
4. If necessary, navigate to the folder where you want the workbook saved.
5. Click the Save button.

Figure 1.3

You must use the Save As command to save the Excel template as a workbook with a different name.

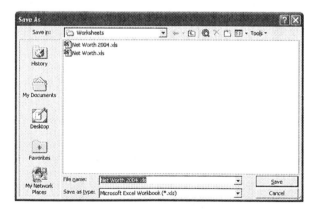

Did You Overwrite a Template by Mistake?

It's easy to forget to save the template with a new name or in a different folder. Not to worry, you can always download the original template again as described in "What's on the CD-ROM."

Now you are ready to start entering data and using the template. I'll explain the details for each template as we come to it in later chapters.

Template Conventions

All of the templates have been designed using certain conventions that make it easier for you to get the most out of them.

Each worksheet has an active area displayed with a light gray background. All the active parts of the worksheet are contained in this area—there is no need for you to scroll outside this area looking for something you think you might have missed. If the workbook has multiple worksheets, each has its own active area as described here.

Although some templates use only a single worksheet, others use more than one. In this case, each worksheet is clearly identified by the name on its tab at the bottom of the Excel window.

Cells that contain money values are formatted with Excel's currency format, with the option selected to display negative numbers in parentheses. Although this is standard accounting practice, some people are not accustomed to it but are more familiar with seeing a minus sign used for negative numbers. I decided to use this format for the sake of consistency and clarity, and I am sure you will soon get used to it.

Entering Negative Values

Although negative values are displayed in parentheses, you still enter them with a leading minus sign. For example, to enter a currency value of negative 100, you would type -100 and it is displayed as $(100.00). You can enter negative values with the parentheses too, but most people find using the minus sign easier.

Individual worksheet cells are formatted depending on their role in the workbook:

- Cells you should not change are formatted with a light gray background. These worksheet cells are locked so you cannot change them by accident.
- Cells where you must enter data are formatted with a white background.
- Cells where the worksheet displays results are formatted with a light blue background.

You see in the templates that some of the white cells—those you are supposed to enter data into—already contain data. This is nothing more than sample data I have included to help show you how the template works. You have to modify this data as needed for your own situation.

About Percentages

Many financial calculations involve percentages for values such as interest rates and fees. A percentage is one-one hundredth, so when you write 2%, you really mean 0.02. In all of the templates, I have used Excel's percentage format for those cells that contain percentage values. This format handles percentages beautifully, not only displaying them with a percent sign but taking care of the conversion.

For example, if you enter the value **2** in a percentage cell, Excel assumes you mean 2%, displays the number as a percent (such as 2.00%), and uses the correct value, .02, in calculations.

However, you need to use care with values less than 1%. If you start an entry with a decimal point, Excel assumes you are entering the actual value and not a percentage. For example, if you enter .1, Excel assumes you mean 10% and not 0.1%. This problem rarely crops up because percentage values less than 1% are hardly ever used in these templates. If it does, simply enter a percent sign after the number. Thus, an entry of .1% is correctly interpreted to mean 0.1% and not 10%.

Understanding some Excel fundamentals is important for getting the most out of the workbook templates included with this book. In the next chapter I'll explain some more specialized details about how Excel works with money.

2

Using Excel to Work with Money

The Excel spreadsheet program is a general purpose tool designed for working with numbers and data of all different kinds. As you might expect, it has a lot of tools and features for working with financial information. When you are using Excel to work with the templates, it can be useful to have at least a basic familiarity with the way Excel works. That's the purpose of this chapter—to give you a fundamental understanding of how Excel works with data in general and financial data in particular.

This is by no stretch of the imagination a complete treatment of Excel! After all, books of 1,000 pages and more have been written about the program, so all I can do in a single chapter is present enough basics to help you use the book's templates effectively and perhaps make some modifications to them. If you already have a decent knowledge of Excel, you can probably skip ahead to Chapter 3, "Working with Basic Financial Calculations."

Excel Basics

In this section I cover some of the fundamentals of using Excel, such as entering data, moving around, and basic formatting.

Getting Around

At any given time Excel has an *active*, or current, cell. It is indicated by the *cell pointer*, a dark border around the cell. Actions you take in Excel affect this cell—for example, if you type in something, it is placed in this cell (replacing anything that was there originally). The *formula bar* displays information related to the active cell:

- The left section of the formula bar displays the address of the active cell.

- The right section of the formula bar displays the contents of the active cell.

These components are illustrated in Figure 2.1.

Figure 2.1

Excel displays the address and contents of the active cell in the formula bar.

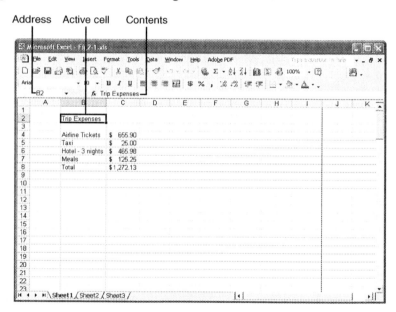

You can make any cell active by clicking it with the mouse. You can also move the active cell using the arrow, page up, and page down keys. If you try to move off the screen, the worksheet scrolls to keep the active cell in view. Excel also defines a few special keystrokes for moving the active cell:

- Press Ctrl+Home to move to cell A1.

- Press Home to move to column A in the current row.

- Press Ctrl plus an arrow key to move to the edge of the worksheet in that direction.

You can scroll different parts of the worksheet into view by using Excel's vertical and horizontal scrollbars. Be aware, however, that scrolling does not move the active cell. Be sure that the Scroll Lock on your keyboard is off; otherwise, scrolling will not work as expected.

Selecting Cells

Sometimes you want to select more than one cell in your worksheet so you can do something to all of them at once, such as apply formatting or delete data. A selected region of two or more cells, called a *range*, is displayed with a thick border and a light blue background, as shown in Figure 2.2. A range is defined by its top-left and bottom-right cells, which are B4 and C8 in the figure. In Excel shorthand this is written as B4:C8.

Selected range

Figure 2.2

A selected block of cells, the range B4:C8 in this example, is displayed with a thick border and a shaded background.

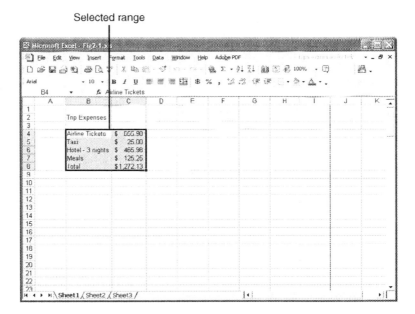

To select a range of cells using the keyboard, follow these steps:

1. Move the cell pointer to a cell at one corner of the desired range.
2. Press and hold the Shift key.
3. Use any of the methods described previously to move the pointer to the range's diagonally opposite corner.
4. Release the Shift key.

You can also define a range with the mouse:

1. Point at any corner of the desired range.
2. Press and hold the left mouse button.
3. Drag to the diagonally opposite corner of the range.
4. Release the mouse button.

To collapse a defined range back to a single active cell, press an arrow key or click any cell.

Entering and Editing Data

To enter data in the active cell, simply type it in, and then accept it by moving the cell pointer to a different cell or by pressing Enter. Before accepting the data, you can use the backspace key to make corrections. Any previous cell contents are replaced by the new data.

To edit data in a cell, move the cell pointer to the cell and press F2. A vertical editing cursor appears in the cell and you can make changes as follows:

- **Backspace and Delete keys**—Delete characters.
- **Left and right arrow keys**—Move the cursor one character at a time.
- **Home and End keys**—Move the cursor to the start or end of the data.
- **Type**—New characters are inserted at the cursor position.
- **Enter key**—Accept changes.
- **Escape key**—Reject changes.

Formatting the Worksheet

Excel offers you great flexibility in changing the appearance of your worksheets. Formatting might seem like an optional extra, but it can help to make a worksheet easier to use. In the templates, for example, I have used three different background colors to indicate worksheet cells that have different roles in the template, which helps you avoid errors and confusion. Figure 2.3 shows an example of a worksheet with some formatting applied. Let's take a quick look at Excel's formatting options.

Figure 2.3

Formatting can make a worksheet more attractive and easier to read.

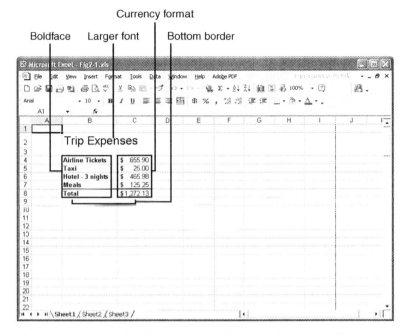

The size of cells can be controlled both vertically and horizontally. This is done most easily with the mouse, using the worksheet borders where the column letters and row numbers are displayed. Here's how:

1. To change a column width, point at the line to the right of the column letter. To change a row height, point to the line below the row number. The mouse cursor changes to a two-headed arrow.

2. Press and hold the left mouse button.

3. Drag the column or row to the desired size.

4. Release the mouse button.

Other formatting tools affect individual cells. You must first select the cell or cells you want to format, and then select Format, Cells from the menu to display the Format Cells dialog box, shown in Figure 2.4.

You can see this dialog box has several tabs, each corresponding to one aspect of formatting. The tabs are

- **Number**—Controls the display of numbers but has no effect on cells that contain text

- **Alignment**—Enables you to set the vertical and horizontal alignment of cell data and the angle at which it is displayed

Figure 2.4

You use the Format Cells dialog box to apply formatting to worksheet cells.

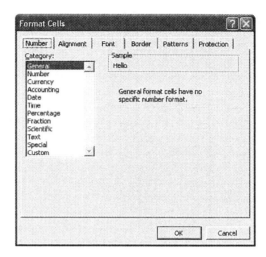

- **Font**—Enables you to select the typeface, size, color, and other aspects of the font used in a cell
- **Border**—Determines the placement and style of borders printed between cells (the default is no borders)
- **Patterns**—Selects a background color and/or pattern for cells
- **Protection**—Locks and unlocks cells

Borders and Gridlines in Excel

Excel normally displays gridlines between all cells displayed on the screen. These are different from the borders you add with the Format Cells dialog box. Gridlines display onscreen but do not print, while borders are visible onscreen and in printouts.

Tip: Displaying Multiline Text

By default, text in a cell is restricted to one line. If you want text to wrap to multiple lines in a cell, use the Alignment tab in the Format Cells dialog box and select the Wrap Text option.

Cell protection requires a bit more explanation. By default all worksheet cells are locked. This has no effect, however, unless you use the Tools, Protection, Protect Sheet (or Protect Workbook) command to protect the sheet. Then, all locked cells cannot be changed by the user, but cells that were unlocked (using the Protection tab in the Format Cells dialog box) can be modified.

I used protection and cell locking in the templates to ensure that you cannot accidentally make changes in cells that should not be changed. If you want to modify locked cells in one of the templates, turn protection off with the Tools, Protection, Unprotect Workbook command.

Formulas in Excel

Much of Excel's power comes from its ability to perform calculations on data in the worksheet. The first character of a formula is always an equal sign. This tells Excel that the cell entry is a formula and not text or a number. Then the formula is written as described here, using the standard elements:

- Numbers entered directly into the formula
- The operator symbols +, –, *, /, and ^ for addition, subtraction, multiplication, division, and exponentiation
- Cell references that tell the formulas to use data from other worksheet cells
- Parentheses, if needed, to ensure the formula works as you intend
- Excel functions (covered in the next section)

A cell that contains a formula displays the results of the formula, but the formula itself is displayed in the formula bar when the cell is active. If the data that a formula uses, such as the values in referenced cells, changes, the formula updates automatically.

A *cell reference* is simply the cell's address, such as A1 or C5. When a formula contains a cell reference, the value displayed in the cell is used in the formula. If the cell is empty, the value zero is used. If the referenced cell contains text, the formula does not work and #VALUE! is displayed in the formula cell.

When do you need to use parentheses? It depends on the operators used in the formula. Operations are, by default, performed in this order:

- Exponentiation (^) first
- Multiplication (*) and division (/) next
- Addition (+) and subtraction (–) last

For example, consider the formula

=A1+A2*A3

Because of the way operations are performed, Excel first multiplies the values in cells A2 and A3 and then adds the value in A1. Substituting values, this gives the following example:

1 + 2 * 3

or 1 + 6 evaluating to 7. But suppose you want to add the values in cells A1 and A2 first and then multiply by A3?

1 + 2 * 3

or 3 * 3 evaluating to 9 (and not 7 as before). Here's where you need parentheses. Any part of a formula inside parentheses is evaluated first. Thus, if you enter

`=(A1+A2)*A3`

you get the desired results. Note that parentheses always have to be used in pairs—if you enter a formula with an unmatched left or right parenthesis, Excel does not accept it.

Excel Functions

Excel provides a library of functions for performing commonly needed calculations. A *function* can be thought of as a prewritten formula ready for you to drop into your own formula. Each function takes the following form:

`FunctionName(ArgumentList)`

`FunctionName` identifies the function and is almost always descriptive of what it does. `ArgumentList` is a list of one or more pieces of information that the function uses to perform its calculations. Each argument can be a number for a cell reference. Some arguments are *ranges*, written as the starting and ending cell addresses separated by a colon. For example, the range A1:A5 means cells A1, A2, A3, A4, and A5.

Let's look at an example using the `Average` function, which calculates the average of a range of cells. You can enter it in a cell by itself. For example, enter this formula in cell A11 to calculate the average of the values in cells A1:A10:

`=Average(A1:A10)`

You can also use a function as part of a more complex formula. This formula, for example, displays one-half of the average of the values in cells A1:A10:

`=Average(A1:A10)/2`

Of particular interest for this book are Excel's financial functions. There are several dozen of them for performing calculations, ranging from simple loan payments to complex depreciation schedules. I have used several of these financial functions in the book's templates, and will explain the most important ones in detail in the next chapter.

Excel and Money

Excel has a number of features designed specifically for working with financial data. These are, of course, particularly relevant to this book. This section reviews these features.

Cash Flow

Excel uses a cash flow model for dealing with financial data. This is a lot simpler than it sounds, and means simply that money values are treated as positive values if the money is coming in and negative values if it is going out. For example, suppose you are using the PMT function to calculate the payment on a car loan. The amount of the loan must be entered as a positive value because this is money you receive. The result of the calculation is a negative value because this is money you pay out—your monthly payment.

This way of doing things seems counter-intuitive to some users, but there's a good reason for it because it makes things consistent when you are creating a large, complex financial worksheet. I'll remind you about cash flow as needed for using the templates.

Formatting Money and Percentage Values

I mentioned earlier that you can use the Format Cells dialog box to specify the number formatting for cells. Formats for money and percent values are most important for the topics of later chapters, so let's take a look.

The *percentage* number format multiplies the value by 100 and displays a percent sign. For example, the value 0.03 would be displayed as 3%. The only option you have with this format is the number of digits displayed to the right of the decimal point.

Currency format is ideal for most money values. It has several options (shown in Figure 2.5):

- The currency symbol used (the default is the symbol for the current locale)
- The number of decimal places displayed
- Whether negative values are displayed with a leading minus sign, in red, or in parentheses

Figure 2.5

The currency format is appropriate for most money values.

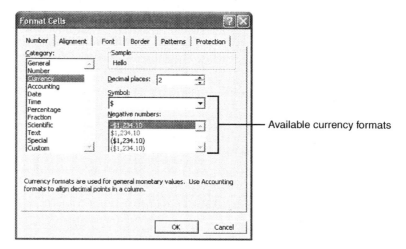

Available currency formats

The *accounting* format is the same as the currency format except for three things: Negative values are always displayed in parentheses, values in a column are lined up on the decimal point, and the currency symbol is displayed just to the left of the number rather than at the left edge of the cell.

Tip: Quick Number Formatting

Excel's Formatting toolbar has buttons that speed up certain formatting tasks:

- **$** Apply the currency format to a selected cell or range.
- **%** Apply the percentage format to a selected cell or range.
- **+.0/.00** Increase the decimal places by one digit to a selected cell or range.
- **.00/+.0** Decrease the decimal places by one digit to a selected cell or range.

Charting Your Course

One of the features that has made Excel so popular is its charting ability. You can easily create a wide variety of charts based on data in the worksheet. When the data changes, the chart updates automatically. Excel charts are very sophisticated, but, by using the Chart Wizard, you can create many great-looking charts with a few mouse clicks.

The first consideration is the data, which must be contained in a contiguous area of the chart (which is how you have your data most of the time, anyway). Figure 2.6 shows an example of worksheet data that is arranged in a way the Chart Wizard can use. Note two things about this data.

- Data is arranged in adjacent columns.
- Each row and column has an identifying label.

Figure 2.6

Worksheet data arranged for charting with the Chart Wizard.

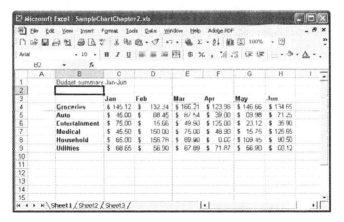

Now let's walk through the steps of using the Chart Wizard to create a chart from this data.

First, select all the data by dragging the mouse over cells B3 to H9. Then click the Chart Wizard button on the toolbar, or select Insert, Chart from the menu. Excel displays the first Chart Wizard step as shown in Figure 2.7.

In this step you select the chart type on the left side of the wizard dialog box and the subtype on the right side. For this example you should accept the default clustered column chart, but you can experiment with other types and subtypes by selecting them and clicking the Press and Hold to View Sample button. When done, click the Next button to go to step two of the wizard, shown in Figure 2.8.

Figure 2.7

The first Chart Wizard step asks you to select the chart type.

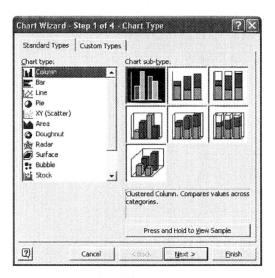

Figure 2.8

In the second step of the Chart Wizard, you verify the source data range and specify whether the data is arranged in rows or columns.

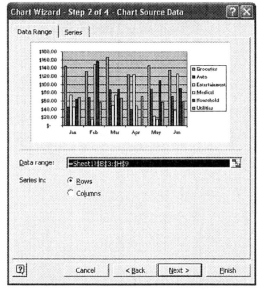

In this step you can see a sample of what the chart looks like. You can also verify the data range and select whether you want the data plotted by rows or columns. Accept the defaults for now and click the Next button to go on to step three, which is shown in Figure 2.9.

Figure 2.9

The third step of the Chart Wizard enables you to add titles and labels.

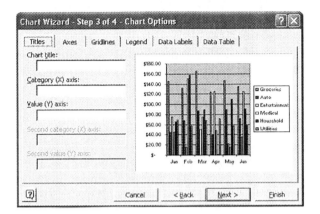

You can see the dialog box for step three has several tabs, but I'll discuss only the Titles tab. You can add text for the following items:

- **Chart title**—A title displayed above the chart

- **Category (X) axis**—A label displayed below the horizontal axis

- **Value (Y) axis**—A label displayed next to the vertical axis

For the example you should enter only a chart title. I used "Budget Jan–Jun." Then click Next to go on. The final wizard dialog box is shown in Figure 2.10.

Figure 2.10

In the last Chart Wizard step you decide how the chart is displayed.

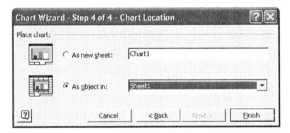

This final dialog box gives you two choices as to where the chart is placed. These choices are

- **As new sheet**—The chart is placed on a new worksheet. This is a special kind of worksheet called a chart sheet, and it can contain only this chart—it cannot contain any data or other charts. Enter the name for the new sheet in the space provided.

- **As object in**—The chart is created as a separate window on an existing worksheet (selected from the drop-down list). The worksheet can contain other data and charts, and the new chart can be moved and resized as desired.

For the example, select Sheet1 from the As Object in drop-down list and then click the Finish button. The chart is inserted into the worksheet along with the data. The chart might cover some of the data but the data is still present. Use the mouse to change the size and position of the chart as needed. The result is shown in Figure 2.11.

Figure 2.11

The worksheet displays the final chart as well as the data that the chart is based on.

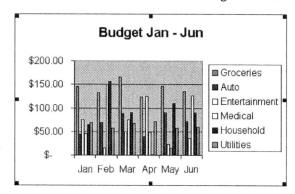

There's lots more you can do with Excel charts, and I'll let you explore these features on your own when and if you need them. Remember, Excel has excellent online documentation, and that's the first place you should turn when you want to learn more about the program.

Now that we have covered the fundamentals of using Excel, it's time to move on. In the next chapter you'll learn about some of the tools Excel provides for performing financial calculations.

IN THIS CHAPTER

3

Working with Basic Financial Calculations

As you learned in the previous chapter, Excel has a library of built-in functions for performing a wide variety of calculations. Several dozen of these functions deal with financial matters, and while most of them are highly specialized, there are several that deal with basic calculations the average Excel user might find useful. In this chapter I will explain what these functions do and how to use them. Along the way I will explain some basic financial terms and concepts.

Calculating Loan Payments

Few people can make it though life without taking out one or more loans. By extending payments over a period of time, a loan enables you to buy something now that otherwise you would have to save for over a long time. Big ticket items, such as a car or house, are perhaps the most common uses of loans.

When evaluating a loan, most people ask, "Can I afford the payments?" The overall price is not the issue, some people think, but whether the monthly payment will fit into the budget. The amount of the monthly payment depends on the three parameters of any loan:

- The *principal*, or amount you are borrowing
- The interest rate
- The *term*, or length of the loan

Larger principal, higher interest rate, and shorter term all lead to higher payments.

You should be aware that judging a purchase solely on the monthly payments is not a good idea. Lower monthly payments might seem attractive now, but all other things being equal, they mean you will pay more over the long run for whatever you are buying. Keeping this caveat in mind, you can make decisions based on Excel's loan-related calculations.

You can use Excel's PMT *function* to calculate the payment on a loan. This function is applicable only to loans where the payment amount is fixed for the length of the loan. Most mortgages and auto loans fall into this category. It is not applicable for credit card payments.

The PMT function uses the following syntax:

```
PMT(rate, nper, prin, [fv, type])
```

The first three arguments are required. They are

- rate is the interest rate for the loan.
- nper is the term of the loan expressed as the number of payment periods.
- prin is the principal, the amount you are borrowing.

When using PMT in a worksheet, it is essential that rate and nper use the same time units. What does this mean? Because most loans have monthly payments, you would have to express nper in months. For example, a five-year loan would have a term of 5 × 12 or 60 months. However, interest rate is always expressed by banks and loan companies as an annual rate. For the function to work correctly, rate must be per period, in this case the rate per month. This is easily obtained by dividing the annual interest rate by 12.

The last two arguments are optional (as indicated by the brackets in the formula):

- fv is the future value of the loan, or the amount still owed when you have completed payments. Because loans are almost always paid off in full, you will use ø for this argument or omit it, in which case Excel assumes ø.

■ type indicates when payments are made. Use a value if 1 if payments are made at the start of each period. Use a value of ø, or omit the argument, if the payment is made at the end of each period (the case for most loans).

Note on Optional Arguments

In some situations an optional argument must be included as a placeholder even if you are not planning to use that specific argument. You do this when you need to specify a later and optional argument in the argument list, such as type in the PMT function. Then any previous optional arguments must be included so Excel knows which argument you meant to use.

In most situations you omit both of these optional arguments.

Let's create a simple loan calculator using the PMT function. Start with a blank worksheet and then follow these steps:

1. Put the labels Amount of loan, Annual rate, Term in years, and Monthly payment in cells B2 through B5, in order.

2. Format cells C2 and C5 as currency with two decimal places.

3. Format cell C3 as percentage with two decimal places.

4. Enter the following formula in cell C5: =PMT(C3/12,C4*12,C2).

Note how in this formula we have done two things to make the result come out right:

■ Divided the annual interest rate (in cell C3) by 12 to get the rate per month.

■ Multiplied the yearly term (in cell C4) by 12 to get the term in months.

When you first enter the formula the cell displays #DIV/ø!, which is Excel's way of telling you an error occurred in the cell. An error occurs because the input cells are blank and the function cannot calculate. Go ahead and enter data in the three input cells and you'll see a result displayed, as shown in Figure 3.1. Note that the payment amount is a negative value. This is in keeping with the way Excel handles cash flow, as was explained in Chapter 2, "Using Excel to Work with Money."

Because a loan payment is money going out, it is expressed as a negative value.

Figure 3.1

Using the *PMT* function to calculate loan payments.

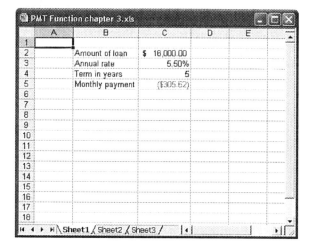

PMT **Does Not Agree with My Loan**

You might find that the actual payments on a loan offered to you by a bank or mortgage company do not agree with the payment you calculate with PMT. When this happens, usually the real payment is a bit higher. Often, this is the result of fees or insurance payments being added to the loan. You should ask your loan officer to explain the details to make sure you are not being charged something you should not be charged.

Calculating Principal Payments

When you make a payment on a loan, each payment is divided into two parts:

- Part of the payment is for that month's interest charge.
- The remainder of the payment goes toward paying down the principal.

Each month you pay down the loan balance, or principal, by some amount. This means that the next month the interest charge will be less because the charge is calculated as the interest rate multiplied by the balance. The total payment amount is fixed, which means that each succeeding month less of your payment goes toward interest and more toward the principal. To calculate the amount that goes toward principal for a specific payment, use the PPMT *function.*

To see an example of this, please refer to Figure 3.2. This worksheet presents an amortization table for a $10,000 loan at 5% for 12 months. The three columns of data are

- **Principal**—The amount of each payment that goes toward the loan balance. This is calculated with the PPMT function. You can see that this amount increases for subsequent payments.

- **Interest**—The amount of each payment that goes toward interest. This is calculated with the IPMT function (covered in the next section). You can see that this amount decreases for subsequent payments.

- **Total**—The total monthly payment, the sum of principal and interest. This amount stays constant for the entire term of the loan.

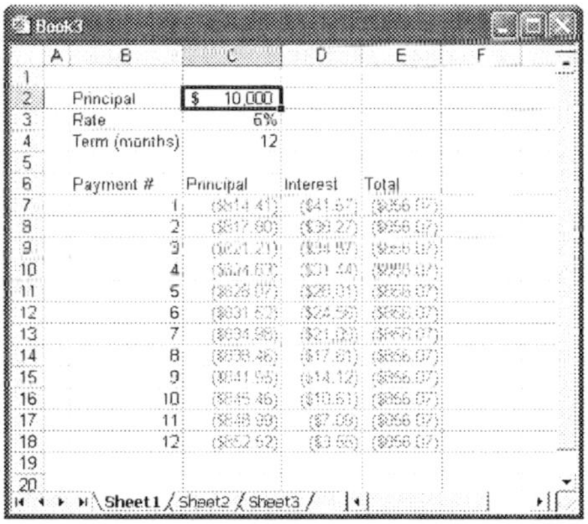

Figure 3.2

This amortization table shows how the principal payment increases while the interest payment decreases over the life of a loan.

Amortizing Loans

Like the other loan-related Excel functions in this chapter, PPMT is applicable only to the standard amortizing type of loan. These are the most common type of loan, and specify equal payments over the life of the loan. There are other specialized types of loans, such as balloon loans and zero-interest loans, and the functions covered in this do not apply to these loans.

The PPMT function uses the following syntax; you'll note that most of the arguments are the same as for the PMT function:

```
PMT(rate, per, nper, prin, [fv, type])
```

The first four arguments are required. They are

- rate is the interest rate for the loan.
- per is the period for which you want the principal payment. This argument must be in the range 1 to *nper*.
- nper is the term of the loan expressed as the number of payment periods.
- prin is the principal, the amount you are borrowing.

As explained earlier for the PMT function, both rate and nper must use the same time unit (usually months). The last two arguments are optional (as indicated by the brackets in the formula):

- fv is the future value of the loan, or the amount still owed when you have completed payments. Because loans are almost always paid off in full, you will use 0 for this argument or omit it, in which case Excel assumes 0.
- type indicates when payments are made. Use a value of 1 if payments are made at the start of each period. Use a value of 0, or omit the argument, if the payment is made at the end of each period.

In most situations you omit both of these optional arguments.

Calculating Interest Payments

Given that you can use PPMT to calculate the principal part of a specific loan payment, what about getting the interest amount? It's easily done as follows:

1. Use PMT to calculate the monthly loan payment.
2. Use PPMT to calculate the principal amount for the payment of interest.
3. Subtract step 2 from step 1 to get the interest part of the specified payment.

You can also use the IPMT function to calculate the interest part of a payment. Please refer to Excel help for more information on this function.

To try out the PPMT function, you can add to the worksheet you created earlier for the PMT function (refer to Figure 3.1). Then follow these steps:

1. Put the labels For payment #, Principal, and Interest in cells B7 through B9, in order.
2. Put the following formula in cell C8: =PPMT(C3/12,C7,C4*12,C2).

3. Put the following formula in cell C9: =c5-c8.

4. Format cells C8 and C9 as currency with two decimal places.

A sample calculation is shown in Figure 3.3. You can see that for the specified loan, the first payment consists of $232.29 going toward principal and $73.33 going toward interest. Change the payment number to 60—the last payment for the loan— and you'll see the amounts change to $304.22 and $1.39 respectively.

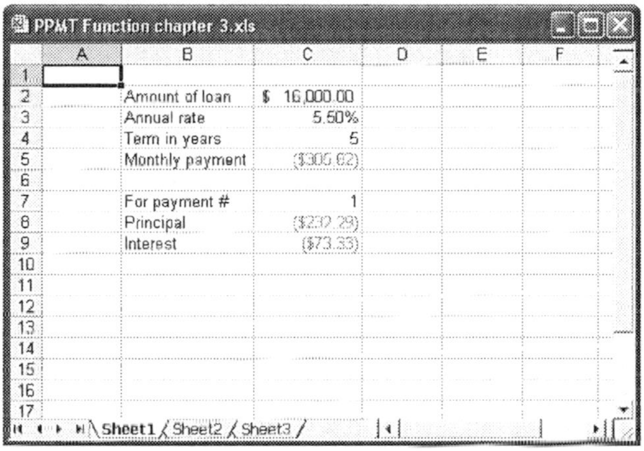

Figure 3.3

Using the *PPMT* function to calculate the principal component of loan payments.

	A	B	C	D	E	F
1						
2		Amount of loan	$ 16,000.00			
3		Annual rate	5.50%			
4		Term in years	5			
5		Monthly payment	($305.62)			
6						
7		For payment #	1			
8		Principal	($232.29)			
9		Interest	($73.33)			
10						
11						
12						
13						
14						
15						
16						
17						

PPMT Function chapter 3.xls

Sheet1 / Sheet2 / Sheet3 /

Working with Future Value

The concept of future value is quite simple and is based on the fact that a given amount of money received today will be worth more at some time in the future. It's easy to understand why this is true—money you have now can be invested and earn interest, hence its value increases.

Future value calculations are useful in a variety of situations. For example, you plan to invest $10,000 in a certificate of deposit at 4% for three years; how much will you have at the end of the three years? Another example is putting $50 a month in your daughter's college fund. How much will you have when she goes to college in 12 years, assuming the rate of return is 5%? You use the *FV function* for future value calculations.

The *FV* function has the following syntax:

```
FV(rate, nper, pmt, [pv, type])
```

The first three arguments are required:

- rate is the projected rate of return per period.
- nper is the number of periods.
- pmt is the payment per period.

The other two arguments are optional:

- pv is the present value (the amount you are starting out with). If omitted, the function assumes 0.
- type is 1 if the payments are made at the start of each period, 0 or omitted if payments are made at the end of each period.

The FV function is quite flexible. If you have a situation where you are starting with nothing and making regular payments, you will set pv to zero and enter a value for pmt. On the other hand, if you are starting with a lump sum and not making any payments, set pv to the initial value and enter 0 for pmt. You can have both an initial amount and regular payments, too, of course.

Choosing an Interest Rate

In some situations, such as when you are quoted loan terms by a bank, you will know the precise interest rate to use in your calculations. In other situations, such as most future value calculations, you must estimate a rate. This is because you are in effect asking a "what if" question—"If I invest this money at XX%, what will my result be?" When in doubt, I recommend using a rate that is readily available for safe investments, such as certificates of deposit and money market accounts. I recommend this because it is better to be conservative than to use an interest rate that might provide gratifying results but is unrealistic.

To try out the FV function, start with a new worksheet and then follow these steps:

1. Enter the labels Initial amount, Rate of return, Monthly payment, Number of months, and Future value in cells B2 through B6, in order.
2. Format cells C2, C4, and C6 as currency with two decimal places.
3. Format cell C3 as percentage with two decimal places.
4. Enter the following formula in cell C6: =FV(C3/12,C5,C4,C2).

The resulting worksheet is shown with some data entered in Figure 3.4. You can see that if you put $1,000 in an account paying 5% interest and add $40 every month, you'll have $1,542.32 at the end of the year.

Please note that in keeping with Excel's cash flow model, the initial amount and monthly payment are entered as negative values because this is money you are paying out. The future value is correctly calculated as a positive value because this is money you will receive.

Figure 3.4

Using the *FV* function to calculate the future value of an investment.

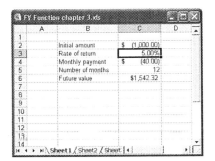

Using the Present Value Function

Present value is similar to future value in that it represents the value of an investment. However, it calculates the value of money you will receive in the future from the perspective of right now. A dollar today is always worth more than a dollar tomorrow because of the interest you can earn on today's dollar. This might not make sense right off, so let's look at a couple of examples.

For instance, suppose you know that you will need $10,000 in five years and you want to put a chunk of money away and let it earn interest to meet that goal. You know you can get a reliable 4% return. How much money do you have to put away now for it to grow to $10,000 in five years?

Here's another example. Suppose your employer gives you a choice of how to take your annual bonus—either $2,300 in a lump sum now or $200 a month for the next 12 months. You could use a present value calculation to determine the present value of that $200 per month, compare it to the lump sum payment and make your decision accordingly. Simply multiplying $200 per month for a year gives you $2,400, but you cannot say that is better than $2,300 today due to interest you might earn over the next year on today's $2,300.

As another example, you are looking to buy a new car and have decided that you can afford $290 per month payment for the next five years. Knowing the interest rate available on auto loans, you can use present value to determine the amount you will be able to borrow.

A more intuitive way to look at present value is this. Suppose you invest $X per month at Y% interest. The present value is the lump sum you would have to invest at the same rate to end up with the same total at the end of 12 months.

You use the PV function to calculate present value. The syntax is

`PV(rate, nper, pmt, [fv, type])`

The first three arguments are required:

- `rate` is the interest rate per period.
- `nper` is the number of periods.
- `pmt` is the payment per period.

The other two arguments are optional:

- `fv` is the future value, the balance at the end of the term, which is 0 in almost all situations. If omitted, the function assumes 0.
- `type` is 1 if the payments are made at the start of each period, 0 or omitted if payments are made at the end of each period.

To try out the PV function, start with a blank worksheet and follow these steps:

1. Enter the labels **Rate of return**, **Monthly payment**, **Number of months**, and **Present value** in cells B2 through B5, in order.
2. Format cell C2 as percentage with two decimal places.
3. Format cells C3 and C5 as currency with two decimal places.
4. Enter the following formula in cell C5: `=PV(C2/12,C4,C3)`.

As before, the monthly payment is entered as a negative value.

The worksheet shown in Figure 3.5 shows an example of evaluating the present value of $200 per month over 12 months assuming a 4% return. Returning to the example presented earlier, where you are offered this $200 per month or a lump sum of $2,300, you can see that the present value of these payments, assuming a 4% return, is $2,348.80. This tells you that the monthly payments are a better deal than the lump sum. If the interest rate were higher, you would see that the PV increases. Of course, if you need the money right away, that is another matter!

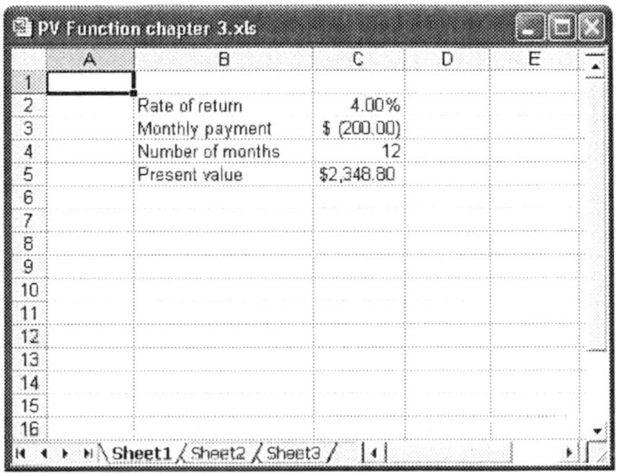

Figure 3.5

Using the *PV* function to calculate the present value of a series of payments.

Calculating Interest Rate

In the calculations that have been presented so far in this chapter, the interest rate was a variable that you either know or had to estimate. But what if you know the other parameters of a loan or other transaction but not the interest rate? Then you can calculate it using the *RATE* function.

Here's an example. Suppose you want to take out a $10,000 personal loan from a friend or family member. They agree with the condition that you repay the loan at $300 per month for three years. You'd like to determine the effective interest rate for this deal—here's where the *RATE* function comes in. Is this a good deal, or would you be better off taking a loan from the bank?

The *RATE* function has the following syntax:

```
RATE(nper, pmt, pv, fv, type, guess)
```

The first three arguments are required:

- nper is the number of payments for the loan.
- pmt is the payment amount.
- pv is the present value—the amount of the loan.

The other three arguments are optional:

- fv is the future value of the loan, the balance when the payments are completed. Usually this will be 0, which is what Excel assumes if the argument is omitted.

- type specifies when payments are made. Use 0 (the default if the argument is omitted) if the payments are made at the end of the period, 1 of they are made at the start of the period.

- guess is your guess at the answer—your estimate of the interest rate. Because of the way RATE performs its calculations using a trial-and-error iteration, it requires a guess and then works from there to calculate the actual value. If you omit this argument, the value 10% (annual) is used.

As with all Excel financial functions, the period for the rate must match the other arguments. For example, if you enter arguments that include monthly payments, the RATE function's result will be the monthly interest rate, and you must multiply this by 12 to get an annual rate.

Let's try out the RATE function. Start with a blank worksheet and then follow these steps:

1. Enter the labels **Principal**, **Monthly payments**, **Term in months**, and **Annual rate** in cells B2 though B5, in order.

2. Format cells C2 and C3 as currency with two decimal places.

3. Format cell C5 as percentage with two decimal places.

4. Enter the following formula in cell C5: =12*RATE(C4,C3,C2).

Figure 3.6 shows this worksheet using the sample data from above. You can see that the effective rate on this loan is just a hair over 5%, which is quite reasonable.

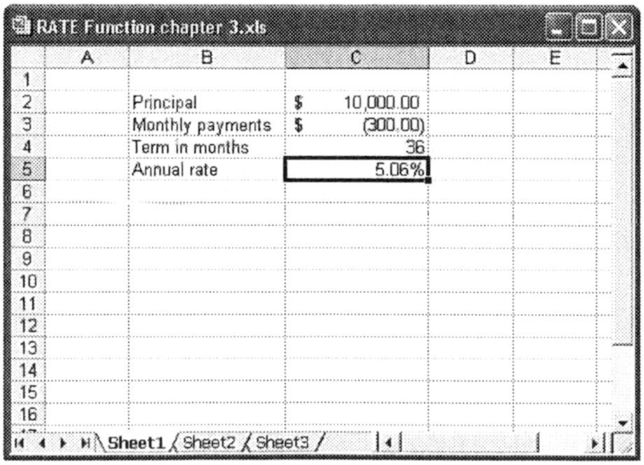

Figure 3.6

Using the RATE function to calculate the interest rate on a loan.

	A	B	C	D	E
1					
2		Principal	$ 10,000.00		
3		Monthly payments	$ (300.00)		
4		Term in months	36		
5		Annual rate	5.06%		

This chapter has shown you how you can use Excel's built-in functions to perform commonly needed financial calculations. With this information under your belt, you are ready for the next chapter that covers net worth and presents the first of the book's Excel templates.

3

4

Tracking Your Net Worth

Net worth is one of those phrases that you hear now and then, but what does it mean? Simply put, it is the sum of all your *assets* (things you own) minus the sum of all your *liabilities* (things you owe). Take what you own and subtract what you owe to get your net worth.

In this chapter we will look at how to calculate and track your net worth and why this figure might be useful in your quest to take control of your finances.

What Is Net Worth?

Net worth is a way to track your financial progress or to get a snapshot of your financial status at a given time. In a way, net worth can be thought of as a measure of your financial health. The greater your net worth, the greater your ability to achieve major financial goals and to withstand unexpected financial stresses, such as being laid off or having a serious illness.

I should emphasize, however, that net worth is not a contest. The point is not to have a higher net worth than your friends and co-workers, but rather to use net worth as a tool to evaluate your own financial situation and progress. There are no net worth yardsticks to measure yourself against.

For one thing, net worth naturally changes with age. For most people, it will increase throughout life up to the time of retirement. If, for example, you have recently graduated from college, it is very possible that your net worth will be less than zero because you owe college loans and own basically nothing, and that's perfectly okay. If you are 50 years old and have a negative net worth, however, it's a good sign of problems.

Another factor is the kind of life you have chosen to live. Some occupations are higher paying than others, and perhaps you have chosen a lower paying career based on non-financial rewards. There's no reason, for instance, that a public school teacher should expect to have the same net worth as a heart surgeon at the same age.

Assets to Include

Some assets are clearly appropriate for inclusion in your net worth calculation. These are

- Your bank and investment accounts
- Your retirement accounts
- If you own your home, the market value of the house
- Any business or investment real estate you own
- Cash value life insurance
- Money you are due, such as a tax refund or bonus

Valuing Your House and Car

How do you go about placing a value on your house and car? For a house, the value was appraised when you bought it and probably again if you took out a home equity loan. You should have received a copy of the appraisal—after all, you probably paid for the appraisal—and you can use that value. If the appraisal is more than a couple of years old or if you have made major home improvements, the value might not be accurate and you might want to consider having a new appraisal done.

Your house will also be assessed for property tax purposes. This assessment is done by the city or county and homeowners are sent a copy of the assessment soon after it is done. If your local assessments are done based on market value (not all are), you might be able to use this value in your net worth calculations. It is probably a good idea, however, to ask a local realtor if the tax assessments in your area are a good indication of a property's market value.

For cars, the best known source is the Kelly Blue Book at http://www.kbb.com. There are three values provided: The *trade-in value*, or what you might expect to get for the car if trading it in on a new one; the *private-party value*, or what you might expect to be able to sell the car for in a private transaction; and the *retail value*, or what you would expect to pay for the car if buying it from a dealer. You should use the private-party value in your net worth calculation.

As for other assets, the opinions of financial experts differ. One such category is personal possessions, such as cars, furniture, collectibles, and artwork. These possessions certainly have value, so there's a valid argument for including them. They are not readily convertible to cash, however, which is why some experts prefer to leave them out. This choice is up to you as long as you are consistent—in other words, you should consistently include or omit them in each net worth calculation. If you do include them, please remember the following tips:

- If you include a car, be sure to use a valid market value for the car. You must also include any outstanding loan on the car as a liability.

- Most furniture, the kind most of us have, is probably best omitted because second-hand furniture typically brings very little. Valuable antiques are a different matter.

- Collectibles and artwork must be valued fairly at the market value and not what you paid for them. A stamp collection that cost you $5,000 to put together might fetch only 1/10 that amount when sold, and it's this latter value you should use in a net worth calculation.

Future income generally should not be included. Examples are your next paycheck and things such as pension or social security payments. You can make an exception for one-time payments you know about but have not yet received, such as your annual bonus at work.

Liabilities to Include

Liabilities are easier than assets because you must include all of them. Any money you owe must be counted in the liability column, including personal loans from family members.

What about credit card balances? If you let them ride from month to month, they certainly must be included as a liability. If you pay the balance in full each month, you can omit it, but you also have to omit from your assets the cash you will be using to pay the card off.

The Net Worth Calculator

The Excel Net Worth Calculator template is downloaded as Net Worth.xlt. Be sure to follow the instructions in Chapter 1, "Taking Control of Your Finances," to load the template and save it as a workbook under its own name (I'll repeat these instructions below). The calculator, before any data is entered, is shown in Figure 4.1.

Figure 4.1

The Net Worth Calculator before any data is entered.

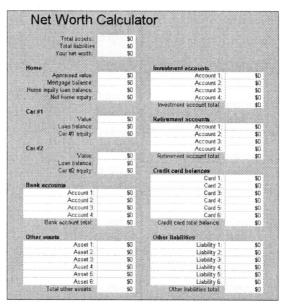

The calculator displays the final calculations at the top. There are separate totals for your liabilities and your assets and then the number you are really interested in, your net worth—which of course is just assets minus liabilities. In this template, all values are entered as positive numbers—you do not enter liabilities as negative numbers. Here are the steps to follow:

1. Assemble the information you will need to fill out the template. This includes bank and investment account statements, credit card statements, your latest mortgage statement, information about personal property, and information about loans.

2. Use the File, Open command to open Net Worth.xls in Excel.

3. Select File, Save As and specify a new name and/or location for the file.

4. Enter data for the items that are relevant to your net worth. Remember, you can enter data only in the cells with a white background, and the blue cells display the results the template calculates. Don't enter cent values—they are not relevant for these calculations. For most of the items, I have left the Name field unlocked (white background) so you can replace the default names, such as Account 1 and Card 1, with the real names of your assets and liabilities.

5. As you work, select File, Save now and then to save the new data to your hard disk.

6. At any time you can save the workbook and quit Excel. When you are ready to continue entering data, start Excel and use the File, Open command to open the workbook.

Once you have entered all your assets and liabilities, you are done. You'll see your net worth displayed in cell C5. You can print a copy of the workbook if you like by selecting File, Print.

Interpreting Your Net Worth

As I have mentioned, your net worth is important only as it relates to your situation. It is not a contest and there are no accepted benchmarks with which you can compare yourself. What seems like a small net worth to one person will appear to be a fortune to another—it all depends on your goals and expectations. Remember, the reason to get your finances in order is to help you live the kind of life *you* want, not to meet other people's expectations.

Keeping Track over Time

Many people use the Net Worth Calculator on a one-time or occasional basis to get a quick snapshot of their financial situation. You can also use it on a regular basis to track changes in your financial picture. Once a year is typical, although you might want to do it more often if there are significant changes in your financial picture. My advice is to create a new workbook based on the template each time you do it and save each one with a name that includes the date, such as Net Worth May 2005. In the future you can go back and review these workbooks to see how your net worth has changed over time. Be sure that you are consistent each time you fill out the template, including and excluding the same things each time.

Now that you have net worth under control, we can move on to the next chapter where you will learn about managing your money with a budget.

4

II

Taking Control of Your Bank and Credit Card Accounts

Managing Your Money with a Budget

A budget is one of the most important tools available to you for taking control of your finances. In this chapter you'll learn what a budget is and why it can be so useful. You'll also learn how to use the budget template to manage your own money.

What Is a Budget?

Some people say, "I'm on a budget," and mean nothing more than that they are limiting their expenditures. "I can't go to dinner at Chez Pierre's tonight because I'm on a budget." In that sense, pretty much everyone is on a budget—after all, how many of us can spend money without limitations?

In another sense, a *budget* is a way to keep precise track of your money, how much comes in and how much goes out, and to determine how much you can and cannot spend on various things. Money that comes in is divided among the various budget categories, such as mortgage or rent, groceries, and entertainment. Each expense is likewise charged against the corresponding category. There are two main advantages to a budget.

One advantage is that after a few months you will have a pretty good idea of where your money is going. Most of us know how much we spend on things such as rent and car payment, but when it comes to less defined expenses, such as clothing and dining out, we are often in the dark—or worse, under a serious misconception. A friend of mine, for example, was flabbergasted when he started a budget and soon learned he was spending almost $300 per month on restaurant meals and take-out food. That was more than twice what he thought he was spending and he soon took corrective measures. He learned some basic cooking skills and now eats at home much more often. The end result is that he now has an extra $150–$200 per month he can put toward more important things, such as saving for a vacation.

Another advantage of a budget is that it takes the guesswork out of some purchase decisions. Without a budget, the question, "Can I afford it?," is often answered based on guesswork and wishful thinking. With a budget, you'll know right away. For instance, suppose your sofa is getting rather threadbare and you see a really nice one on sale. A quick look at your budget balance will tell if you have the required amount in your household account. If so, you know that you can go ahead and buy it without any worries. If not, you know you'll have to wait.

You should not think that a budget is a straightjacket that leaves you with no options or flexibility. We all know that unexpected expenses come up and can't be avoided, such as car repairs or a dentist's bill. Or perhaps there's a sale that's just too good to pass up. You should expect your budget to change over time as your income and expenses vary. I'll show you how a budget can be flexible enough to let you deal with such unexpected events.

Budget Fundamentals

The basis of a budget is a set of categories for your expenses, such as entertainment, insurance, and groceries, and your income, such as salary and interest. When money comes in, such as your paycheck, it is divided up among the various categories. Likewise, each and every expense is charged against the appropriate category. Sounds like a lot of work—and it can be. This is why the Excel template that is part of this chapter is such a valuable tool. By taking most of the drudgery out of keeping a budget, the template lets you have the advantages of budgeting without the hassle—or with a lot less hassle, at any rate!

Let's take a look at the Home Budget Calculator. Then I'll explain some ways you can use it to help take control of your finances.

The Home Budget Calculator

The Home Budget Calculator template, in the file `Home Budget.xls`, provides you with a convenient way to keep a budget. It automates some of the tasks, such as entering your paychecks and performing calculations of the totals. Let's look at the parts of this template.

Macros and Excel Security

This is the first of several templates in this book that use macros. A *macro* is nothing more than some instructions, or code, that is a part of a workbook and helps it to perform its functions. Macros are powerful but have the potential for misuse. A malicious person could distribute a workbook containing a macro that would delete critical files or do other mischief on your system.

For this reason, Excel has a macro security feature that detects macros in workbooks you are opening and responds according to the security level you have set. To set your security level, select Tools, Macros, Security to display the Security dialog box. You're offered three choices:

- **High**   Only macros that are digitally signed by trusted sources will be enabled; all others will be disabled without warning. This setting is not recommended because the macros in this book's templates are not signed and would be automatically disabled, causing some of the templates to function incorrectly.

- **Medium**—Excel asks you to enable or disable macros each time you open a workbook that contains macros. This is the setting that I recommend. You can enable macros in the workbooks that come with this book as well as those from other known, safe sources, while disabling macros in workbooks from any questionable sources.

- **Low**—Excel enables all macros without warning. This setting is not recommended, certainly not if you're not running an up-to-date virus scan program.

The Overview

One worksheet in the Home Budget workbook is called Overview. On this worksheet the template displays the current balances in all your budget categories. You will not be entering or changing anything on this worksheet—it is all done automatically. This is where you will look to see how you are doing on your budget and whether a particular category has enough money in it for an expense you are considering. At the bottom is an Overall Total field that calculates the sum of all budget categories. The Overview worksheet is shown in Figure 5.1. This figure shows the worksheet after some data has been entered. When you first start, all values are 0.

Before moving on, please note that a new menu, Budget, has been added to the right end of the Excel menu bar. You use commands on this menu to carry out most of the template's actions, as I'll explain in the next sections. The Budget menu appears only when you have the Home Budget worksheet loaded and vanishes when you close the worksheet.

About the Categories

The Home Budget template provides a set of categories for you to use. I have tried to include enough categories to cover all eventualities. You do not have to use all categories, of course. Any unused categories will simply show a balance of zero on the Overview worksheet. I have also included three general categories called Special 1, Special 2, and Special 3 you can use if the predefined categories do not meet all your needs. If you need a Travel category, for example, you could use one of the Special categories for this purpose.

Figure 5.1

Use the Home Budget Calculator's Overview worksheet to display current balances in your budget categories.

Home Budget Calculator

Category	Balance
Auto payment	$235.50
Auto fuel	$30.05
Auto service	$50.00
Charity	$40.00
Clothing	$90.00
Education	$0.00
Entertainment	$67.00
Groceries	$106.13
Household	($22.00)
Insurance	$110.00
Medical	$100.00
Miscellaneous	$88.00
Petty cash	$50.00
Rent/mortgage	$1,175.00
Savings	$890.00
Special 1	$80.00
Special 2	$0.00
Special 3	$0.00
Tax	$145.00
Telephone	$12.55
Utilities	$30.00
Current total:	**$3,337.23**

5

Transactions

The Transactions worksheet is where all the individual transactions are stored. A *transaction* is whenever you add money to or take money out of a budget category. Each transaction consists of four items of information:

- The date of the transaction
- The category of the transaction
- The amount of the transaction, with deposits and withdrawals entered as positive and negative values respectively
- An optional Note field that lets you enter more information about the transaction if desired

The Transactions worksheet is not locked, which means you could enter transactions directly. Do not do this! As I'll show you soon, the template has automated ways of entering transactions that are much less likely to cause an error.

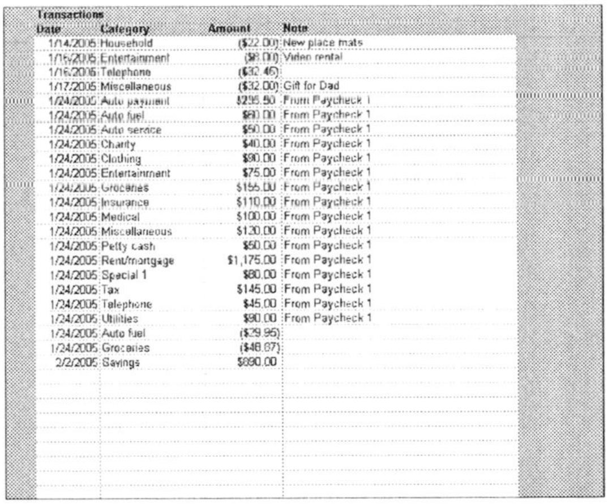

Transactions

Date	Category	Amount	Note
1/14/2005	Household	($22.00)	New place mats
1/15/2005	Entertainment	($8.00)	Video rental
1/16/2005	Telephone	($32.46)	
1/17/2005	Miscellaneous	($32.00)	Gift for Dad
1/24/2005	Auto payment	$295.50	From Paycheck 1
1/24/2005	Auto fuel	$80.00	From Paycheck 1
1/24/2005	Auto service	$50.00	From Paycheck 1
1/24/2005	Charity	$40.00	From Paycheck 1
1/24/2005	Clothing	$90.00	From Paycheck 1
1/24/2005	Entertainment	$75.00	From Paycheck 1
1/24/2005	Groceries	$155.00	From Paycheck 1
1/24/2005	Insurance	$110.00	From Paycheck 1
1/24/2005	Medical	$100.00	From Paycheck 1
1/24/2005	Miscellaneous	$120.00	From Paycheck 1
1/24/2005	Petty cash	$50.00	From Paycheck 1
1/24/2005	Rent/mortgage	$1,175.00	From Paycheck 1
1/24/2005	Special 1	$80.00	From Paycheck 1
1/24/2005	Tax	$145.00	From Paycheck 1
1/24/2005	Telephone	$45.00	From Paycheck 1
1/24/2005	Utilities	$90.00	From Paycheck 1
1/24/2005	Auto fuel	($29.95)	
1/24/2005	Groceries	($48.67)	
2/2/2005	Savings	$890.00	

Figure 5.2

Individual budget transactions are stored on the Transactions worksheet.

It is okay, however, to edit existing transactions. After all, everyone makes mistakes and you need a way to correct them. If you are editing an existing transaction, please keep these rules in mind:

- Always enter deposits as positive values and withdrawals as negative values. This is essential if the Overview worksheet totals are to calculate correctly.

5

- Be sure to use only the predefined category names and be careful with spelling. Only those transactions where the category name matches the predefined list in both spelling and case will be included in the Overview worksheet calculations.

Paychecks

One of the more tedious aspects of maintaining a budget is the entering of regular deposits. Each time you receive a paycheck, the take-home pay has to be divided among the various budget categories. The Home Budget Calculator automates this process and also provides for two separate paychecks if needed. This is found on the Paycheck 1 and Paycheck 2 worksheets, which are identical. Figure 5.3 shows how the income from Paycheck 1 is allocated among the budget's expense categories.

Only One Paycheck?

If you have only one paycheck, enter it on Paycheck 1 and leave Paycheck 2 as all zeros. The unused paycheck worksheet will be ignored.

Figure 5.3

Use the Paycheck worksheet to specify how your paycheck is allocated among the budget categories.

Paycheck 1 total	$2,770.50
Category	Amount
Auto payment	$235.50
Auto fuel	$60.00
Auto service	$50.00
Charity	$40.00
Clothing	$90.00
Education	$0.00
Entertainment	$75.00
Groceries	$155.00
Household	$0.00
Insurance	$110.00
Medical	$100.00
Miscellaneous	$120.00
Petty cash	$50.00
Rent/mortgage	$1,175.00
Savings	$150.00
Special 1	$80.00
Special 2	$0.00
Special 3	$0.00
Tax	$145.00
Telephone	$45.00
Utilities	$90.00

You can see that the Paycheck worksheet lists the budget categories in column B. You enter the amount from each paycheck that is to go to each category in the adjacent cell in column C. These must all be positive amounts. At the top, in cell C3, the total is calculated. This should, of course, match the total take-home amount of your paycheck.

Each time you receive a paycheck, add it to the budget by selecting Budget, Paycheck 1 (or Paycheck 2, depending on which paycheck you are doing). The process adds the required transactions to the budget. Each transaction includes a Note field indicating that it is from Paycheck 1 or 2.

Expense Predictions

The Budget calculator has no place to explicitly enter the expense predictions for your budget—in other words, the amount you think you'll spend for each category. Actually, the two Paycheck worksheets serve this exact function. When you divide your take-home pay between the various budget categories, you are actually estimating how much you will spend in those categories. A negative or positive balance on the Overview worksheet tells you whether you are overspending or underspending in that category.

It's important to understand when you are supposed to use the paycheck feature of the budget workbook and when you should use a transaction. The *paycheck feature* is only for regular income from your (and perhaps your spouse's) paychecks. You enter a paycheck by selecting Paycheck 1 or Paycheck 2 from the Budget menu, only when you receive your pay and only after making sure that the allocations on the Paycheck 1 or Paycheck 2 worksheets are correct.

Transactions, on the other hand, are for any and all expenses. Each expense should be entered once and only once by selecting Transactions from the Budget menu. You also use a transaction for any income aside from your paycheck, such as a gift or a bonus.

What if your paycheck changes? Maybe you got a raise (nice!) or your benefits or tax deductions changed. Then simply edit the Paycheck worksheet, adding or subtracting from each category's amount until the total matches your new take-home pay. Changes you make here do not affect entries already made in the budget, just future paycheck entries.

Entering Transactions

Of course, there are many other transactions to enter in a budget besides your paycheck. This includes all your expenditures as well as one-time income items, such as a bonus from work. Here's where the Enter Transaction dialog box comes in, as shown in Figure 5.4. To display this dialog box, select Budget, Transactions. Each entry made in

5

this dialog box is entered into the Budget Calculator workbook on the Transactions worksheet and is included in the category totals displayed on the Overview worksheet.

Figure 5.4

Use the Enter Transaction dialog box to enter individual expenses and deposits.

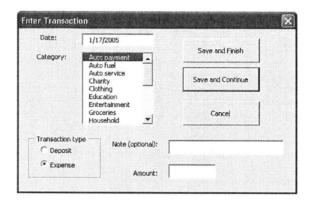

Here's how to use this dialog box to enter a transaction:

1. Enter the transaction date in the Date field. By default, this displays today's date so you can usually leave this as-is.

2. Select the transaction category from the Category list.

3. Select the transaction type, deposit or expense.

4. Enter an optional note to be saved with the transaction.

5. Enter the transaction amount in the Amount field. You should enter a positive amount for both expenses and deposits.

6. Click Save and Finish to save the transaction and close the dialog box. Click Save and Continue to save the transaction and keep the dialog box open to enter another transaction. Click Cancel to discard the transaction and close the dialog box.

What About Transfers?

When using a budget, it is not that unusual to need to transfer money from one category to another. For example, maybe you have built up a few hundred dollar balance in Utilities and want to move some of that to Entertainment because it's spring and you now use less heat than predicted. All you need to do is enter an expense transaction for the category you are taking the money from and a deposit transaction for the category you are moving the money to. These are two separate transactions and they should, of course, be for the same amount. I advise also using the Note field to indicate that it is a transfer.

Getting Started with Your Budget

Once you get your budget started and you are in the swing of entering paychecks and expenses, the Budget calculator is pretty easy to use. But what about when you are first getting started? There are a few steps you need to take to get started.

First, gather your bank statements and figure out how much money you have right now. Include the cash in your wallet or purse. This should be the cash you have on hand for day-to-day expenses. Do not include savings accounts unless you plan to use the budget category for savings—which, as I have already mentioned, is an excellent idea.

Next, decide how you want to allocate this cash among the budget categories. This can be done with paper and pencil, and will be, at best, informed guesswork. Don't worry about being 100% accurate or even 50% accurate—you can always correct misjudgments later by transferring funds between categories as explained earlier in this chapter.

Now, open the Budget Calculator worksheet and use the Budget, Transactions command to enter these amounts into the budget. You'll use one deposit transaction for each category you are putting money into. As I have already mentioned, you should use only the categories you need.

The final step is to decide how your paycheck(s) will be allocated. Display the Paycheck 1 worksheet and divvy up your take-home pay among the various categories according to your predicted expenses. Again, this will be partly guesswork at this point—that's okay, you will almost surely need to change paycheck allocation in a month or so. Repeat for Paycheck 2 if needed.

That's it. You are ready to go.

Living with a Budget

Once you have decided that a budget is something you want to do and you have learned how to use the Home Budget template, then what? I won't kid you, living on a budget is not the easiest thing to do. The potential benefits are huge, however, so it's really worth your best shot. Let's take a look at how the budget can help you and some of the difficulties people experience.

5

Analyze Your Spending

People usually have a pretty good idea of where their money comes from. It's the spending that's the big mystery! This is perhaps the most important area where a budget can help—enabling you to figure out exactly where your money is going.

Of course, you need some data before you can analyze your spending patterns. In most cases, there is no choice but to keep the budget for two or three months and then look at the information you collected. If you have been careful about keeping receipts, it might be possible to enter your spending information from the past few months, but few people are so organized! So you might have to start fresh on the first of next month.

One place many people find it easiest to start is to list the first month's income and expenses. That can be your starting-point budget. Most expenses and income are similar each month for most categories. The second month, make adjustments as necessary. By the third month, you should have a budget that will work well for the following month.

The Jar System

It can be a bother to keep track of all your receipts, but you'll need them for entering expenses into the budget calculator. This is particularly true when a single payment, such as a check you wrote at Wal-Mart or Target, includes expenses in more than one category. Here's where the jar system comes in handy. Put a large jar in a handy place and put all your receipts in it. Then at the end of the month (or whenever) when you are working on the budget, you'll have them together in one place.

Another idea is to keep a small pad and pen with you at all times to record small expenses as they occur. Or you can use your PDA for this if you have one. Remember, you have to capture your cash transactions as well as checks and charges!

Once you have a few months' data, how does it look? How do the actual expenses in each category fit with your general perception of how you are—and should be—spending your hard-earned money? Are there categories where the expenditures are a lot more than you expected? These might be areas to cut back. Some expenses, such as rent and car payments, are fixed and cannot easily be reduced. Other categories are discretionary, such as entertainment and clothing, and deserve close examination.

Pay Yourself!

Financial advisors generally agree that a budget should always include a savings category—in other words, a pay yourself category. No matter how small the amount, a saving category is a good idea because of the many benefits of building up some financial reserves. Furthermore, it is a lot easier to stick to a budget if you know you are putting something away for the future.

Live Within Your Means

Perhaps the most important question is how your expenses compare with your income. In other words, are you spending more or less than you earn? If you are spending more than you earn, you might already be aware of it from the mounting credit card bills. This is perhaps the most serious sign of financial trouble and calls for immediate action on your part. You will never be able to take control of your finances if there's more going out than coming in.

This is perhaps the most important reason why a budget is such a valuable tool. Only after you know what your budget is can you hope to stay within its boundaries. A budget is not an end in itself, but rather is a tool to help you achieve your goal of taking charge of your finances.

Live Beneath Your Means

The phrase "live beneath your means" sums up what is perhaps the best financial philosophy. In today's consumer-oriented society, it is not always easy to do, but it's the best—perhaps the only—route to taking control of your finances for most of us. If you spend less than you earn, you have money to save, and it's savings that are at the basis of eventually achieving financial independence.

5

Balancing Your Budget

Believe me, it's a rare event for someone to analyze her expenses and find she is spending less than she should be! Like 99% of people, you are likely to be faced with the prospect of balancing your budget by adjusting things so expenses are equal to, or preferably less than, income.

Some ways of reducing expenses, such as reducing or avoiding credit card and bank fees, are covered in later chapters. In this section I present a few additional tips and suggestions for successfully balancing your budget by reducing expenses.

Increase Your Income

Wouldn't the easiest way to balance your budget be to bring in more money? Sure, that sounds great—but actually doing so is not that easy. You could ask for a raise or hope for a promotion, and good luck to you, but don't count on it. How about a new, better paying job? That's a great idea if you can manage it, but few people can. A second part-time job might be a temporary expedient to help pay down some debts, but it's not something many people want to do for the long term. The unavoidable fact is that budgets are almost always balanced by cutting expenses.

Watch Impulse Buying

The shops and catalogs are filled with great products of all kinds, and it's easy to just pull out your credit card or checkbook to buy that latest new item that caught your fancy. Danger!! It's just this kind of impulse buying that gets a lot of people in trouble. When the urge hits you, think.

First think, "Do I really need this?" In most cases the answer is definitely no—your life will go on just fine without it.

But of course life is not just about needs. Buying things for pleasure and enjoyment is perfectly valid, too. Then you need to think about how much enjoyment you will really get from the item you are considering. When you really think about it, a lot of our purchases do not bring that much lasting pleasure to our lives. Will this $50 item just bring you a short-lived distraction and then be forgotten? Or will it really enhance your life and make a difference over the months and years? Perhaps the item might be less expensive if you wait, as is the case with most electronic equipment?

You also need to recognize and resist the psychological justifications many people use for purchases. Perhaps most common is the "I deserve this" approach. Perhaps you do, but that's hardly justification for buying something you cannot really afford! I figure that I deserve a new red Ferrari, but I still don't have one! What you *really* deserve is financial comfort and security and making unnecessary purchases for psychological reasons is not the way to get it!

Look for Sales

Some people love looking for sales, others hate it. Either way, there's no doubt that sales can be a great way to trim your expenses. It takes some patience because you might need to wait for a sale rather than buying something right away.

Here's a good example. I recently needed some clothes and instead of rushing right out to the department store, I kept my eyes peeled for a sale. A few weeks later I found just what I was looking for at an outlet store. For less than $150 I got pants and shirts that would have cost at least $700 at regular prices.

Of course, not all sales let you save so big, but they're still worth looking for. Food, clothes, electronics, books—most everything you shop for is on sale at one time or another. For nonperishable staples, such as soap, canned food, and napkins, buying in bulk from a warehouse store can produce big savings (but make sure that any membership fees do not cancel those savings!).

Learn to Cook

There sure is something nice about going to a restaurant. A nice selection of food, no cooking, no cleanup—no wonder Americans eat out so often! But let's face it, restaurants are expensive. Even the moderately priced places will add up if you eat there regularly. Let's run some numbers for John Doe's restaurant bill:

- Lunch at work twice per week @ $8.00 = $64.00 per month
- Dinner out three times per week @ $15.00 = $180.00 per month
- Pizza delivery once per week @ $12.00 = $48.00 per month

That's $292.00 per month or over $3,500 per year. Yikes, sure seems like a place you could cut back.

Of course, eating at restaurants is sometimes about more than just eating. It might be a chance to socialize with your colleagues at work or to relax with friends at the end of a busy week. Think about your restaurant habits and decide which restaurant visits are important for work or social reasons and which are for convenience only. Then you can start cutting back.

5

But wait, you still have to eat. Yep, and that means fixing more meals yourself, including "brown bag" lunches. Basic cooking is not at all difficult and there are plenty of sources of information, including your family, friends, books, and classes. A modest investment in kitchen equipment can lead to big savings.

A budget is a very important part of taking control of your finances. With that under your belt, we can move on to a financial tool that almost everyone uses—and some people misuse—your checking account.

5

6

Being Smart with Your Checking Accounts

If there's any one kind of bank account that almost everyone has, it's a checking account. As useful as they are, checking accounts still provide several ways for you to get into financial trouble. In this chapter I'll show you how to get the most out of your checking account without the usual downsides.

How Checking Accounts Work

Wait—doesn't everyone know how a checking account works? Make deposits, write checks, and hope that you don't have an overdraft. Yes, that's certainly true, but there are more details you should know about.

Types of Checking Accounts

The most basic kind of checking account is sometimes called a *fee account* because you pay fees for the services the bank provides. There is usually a monthly fee as well as a per-check fee, but there are no minimum balance requirements.

Banks also offer a variety of *fee-free accounts*. In most cases this kind of account requires that you always keep a certain minimum balance—perhaps $800—in the account. As long as you maintain this minimum balance, there are no monthly or per-check fees. If, however, the balance dips below the minimum, even if just for a day and for one dollar, you are hit with the regular monthly service fee.

How can banks offer a fee-free checking account? The answer lies in the minimum balance. This is money they, in effect, have on permanent deposit and is part of the capital they have available to lend out to other customers. In other words, they earn interest on the money in your account and this lets them offer the account without fees. Also, by offering fee-free accounts, they attract customers who will probably use (and pay for) other bank services, such as loans and safety deposit boxes.

Many checking accounts are touted as paying interest. Hey, sounds great—earn interest on your money while it sits in the account! But take a look at the rates being paid. The last time I did, I was receiving a paltry 0.1%—that's right, one-tenth of a percent—on my checking account. If my average balance for the year is, say, $1,000, I will earn—drum roll, please—exactly one dollar in interest for the year. Sure, every dollar counts, but the point is that the interest on your checking account is not going to make any real difference one way or the other. In addition, with rates far below inflation (even though inflation is historically low now), you are in theory losing money while it sits idle in your account.

What About Money Market Accounts?

You might have heard about money market checking accounts that offer much better interest rates. This is correct—such accounts are currently paying in the range of 1.5%–2.5% per year, a lot better than a standard checking account. The downside is that these accounts almost always have restrictions, such as the minimum check amount (typically $250 or $500) or the number of checks you can write per month. This means that money market checking accounts are not suitable for your everyday expenses. They can be a good place to park cash you want to have available when needed but do not foresee needing in the short term.

Suppose, for instance, that you write about $2,500 a month in checks for things such as rent or mortgage, car loan payment, groceries, and credit card bills. Put the cash in your money market account to take advantage of the better interest rate. The few large items, such as rent/mortgage and a car payment, you can probably pay directly from the money market account. Then write one check from the money market account and deposit it in your regular checking account to be used for the more numerous, smaller expenses, such as groceries.

Other Checking Account Fees

Aside from any regular service fees your checking account might accrue, several other fees are imposed if you misuse the account. The most common fee is the *overdraft fee*, imposed if there's not enough money in your account to cover a check you wrote. In common parlance this is *bouncing* a check, and in banker-talk it is an *overdraft*. The overdraft fee can be hefty, $25 or more, and to make things worse, you are often charged a bounced check fee by the merchant you wrote the check to. Bouncing a $15 check can cost you $50 in fees—clearly a horrendous waste of your money and something to avoid.

The best way to avoid overdrafts is to take charge of your checking account and always be aware of how much money you have in it. The Excel template presented later in this chapter is a great tool for doing this. If you never write a check for more than is in the account, you will never pay an overdraft fee.

Another way to avoid overdrafts is to get *overdraft protection* for your checking account. This service goes by different names at different banks, but the idea is the same. It is a line of credit that is attached to your checking account. If you do write an overdraft, the bank automatically advances enough money from the line of credit to cover the check. Usually this is done in multiples of $100. Then you repay this loan in monthly installments that are usually deducted automatically from the checking account. Of course you pay interest.

Overdraft protection is a good idea as long as you never or at best rarely use it. Why? The interest rates that banks charge for overdraft advances are usually pretty high, making this a bad way to borrow money. Unfortunately, some people get in the habit of using their overdraft protection on a regular basis as a source of extra cash. This is not a good idea!

I recommend getting overdraft protection but never using it. It is there to protect you from overdraft fees in case of an error. The only time I have ever used mine is when I wrote a check for $1,495.00 and then mistakenly entered $14.95 in my register! I thought my balance was fine, but without that overdraft protection, I would have bounced at least a couple of checks. Sure, I paid a few dollars in interest but I saved $50 or more in overdraft fees.

The third technique that can help you to avoid overdrafts is to use a debit card. They are covered in the next section.

6

Don't Count on the Float

People used to sometimes use the *float* to help when finances were tight. Suppose you were going to receive and deposit your paycheck on Friday but needed groceries on Wednesday. You could write a check to the grocer, safe in the knowledge that by the time the grocer took the check to his bank, his bank processed it and sent it to your bank, and your bank processed it, your paycheck would be in the account to cover it. The advance of modern technology has doomed the float. In particular, with the advent of the Check 21 program as of October 28, 2004, electronic check processing and communication have essentially abolished the float, and you cannot count on any real delay in a check you write getting to the bank.

Understanding Debit Cards

Most checking accounts give the option of a debit card. These cards look like a credit card and, from the shopper's perspective, work virtually the same way. When you are shopping, hand the card to the cashier to pay for your purchases. Behind the scenes, however, a debit card is very different from a credit card.

When you make a purchase with a credit card, the company that issues the card pays the merchant and adds the amount to your balance. Each month you receive a statement and must pay off all or part of what you owe. In other words, when you use a credit card, you borrow the money.

In contrast, a debit card is connected directly to your bank account, either checking or savings. When the cashier swipes the card, the amount of the purchase is deducted immediately from your account. If there's not enough money in the account to cover the purchase, the transaction is rejected. You can think of using a debit card as writing an "instant" check.

Debit cards have a couple of advantages over credit cards. One is that you cannot overdraw your account because you cannot spend money you don't have when using a debit card. Some people who find it difficult to restrain their spending use a debit card in preference to a credit card for just this reason. Another advantage is that anyone can get a debit card while individuals with bad credit might find it impossible to get a credit card. Since there's no borrowing of money involved, a debit card is risk-free to the institution that provides it to customers.

There are also some disadvantages to debit cards when compared to credit cards. An important one is that with a debit card you are always

6

using your own money, while a credit card gives you free, temporary use of the bank's money. Many credit cards offer premiums, such as airline miles or cash back, and debit cards do not. I'll cover these features in more detail when I explain how to use your credit cards wisely in Chapter 7, "Getting the Most from Your Credit Cards."

Be Smart with ATM Cards

ATMs, or automated teller machines, are a great convenience. They are located just about everywhere, or so it seems. All you do is insert your ATM card (which might be the same card as your debit card), enter your personal identification number, and out pops some cash. The withdrawal is deducted from your bank account—and of course, if your balance is not enough, you won't get the cash!

As convenient as ATMs are, they can be dangerous to your financial health. Whenever you use an ATM that does not belong to the bank where you have your account, you are changed a fee. Actually, you are usually charged two fees—one by the owner of the ATM for using their machine, and another by your bank for using an out-of-network ATM. These can add up to $3–$4 for a single withdrawal—ouch! If you make an average of one out-of-network withdrawal per week, you are easily looking at $100–$200 in fees a year.

Sure, when you really need cash and cannot find a bank machine, the convenience might be worth the fee—once in a while. But generally you should avoid making out-of-network ATM transactions. Here are some tips that can help:

- Find out where your bank's ATMs are located. Keep the list in your car or wallet.
- Ask if your bank has a cooperative relationship with any other banks, permitting fee-free ATM transactions at the other bank's machines.
- Think ahead and get enough cash so you won't be caught short-handed when you cannot get to an in-network ATM.

Cheap Checks

With most checking accounts, you have to pay for new checks. Most people just go ahead and order from their bank without realizing that

6

they do not have to. There are numerous independent check printing companies that can make your new checks. Not only are they usually a lot cheaper than the bank, but you will generally have a much wider choice of styles and designs.

Next time you need to replenish your supply of checks, look into these companies. I usually find their advertisements in the newspaper supplements.

Checking Account Dos and Don'ts

Do keep accurate track of your balance.

Do get overdraft protection for your account.

Don't use overdraft protection as a source of quick cash.

Don't use your ATM card at machines where you'll pay a fee.

Do consider accounts that are free with a minimum balance or other bank services.

Do look into buying new checks from a third party rather than from the bank. They are usually less expensive.

Other Account Services

When evaluating checking accounts, people understandably look first at the most important features of the account, such as fees and required minimum balance. Some other factors might make a difference depending on your needs and situation. Here are some you might want to ask about:

- How extensive is the "home" ATM network (where withdrawing cash is free if your bank is a member of the network)?
- Does the account provide free or discounted services, such as money orders, cashier's checks, foreign currency exchange, wire transfers, travelers' checks, or notary service?
- Do account holders get a discount on safety deposit boxes?
- Are replacement checks and checkbook covers free?

Banks are always competing for customers, and you might be surprised at the extras that come along with some checking accounts.

Watch Out for Teller Fees

An unfortunate development at some banks is the imposition of teller fees. You will be allowed a certain number of in-person transactions, such as making a deposit at a teller window. Beyond that number, there is a fee for each in-person transaction. The idea of course is to encourage customers to use automated services, such as online account information and ATM machines, that reduce the bank's expenses. Maybe you almost never use a teller and these fees will not bother you, but you need to ask.

How to Get a Free Checking Account

We all like things that are free, and sometimes it's possible to get a full-featured checking account that is totally free. Banks want to encourage customers to do all of their business with them, and will often offer a package that gives you free checking if you have some other kind of account at the bank. For example, I receive completely free checking because I have a home equity loan at the same bank. You might get a similar deal with a home mortgage or an investment account. Ask at the bank—they will be happy to tell you about their offerings.

The Checkbook Register Application

However you decide to arrange and manage your checking account, there's one thing you'll need to do and that's to keep track of your balance. The most important reason to do this, of course, is to avoid bouncing checks and the attendant fees. It's also useful if you are in the pleasant situation of building up a large balance. If you know you have excess money in your checking account, you can transfer it to another account that pays more interest.

It's perfectly possible to keep track of your checking balance using the paper register that comes with your checkbook. But let's face it, this is not much fun and it's easy to make mistakes. Why not use the power of Excel?

6

How the Checkbook Register Workbook Works

My goal is to encourage as many people as possible to keep accurate track of their checking accounts. To this end I made the Checkbook Register workbook as simple as possible, so it is easy to use. The application is shown in Figure 6.1 with some of its features marked.

Cleared and current balances

Figure 6.1

The Checkbook Register workbook makes it easy to keep track of your checking account balance.

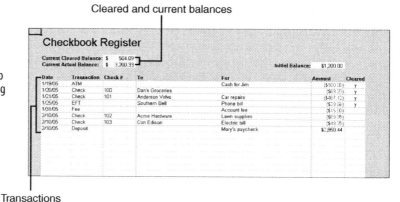

Transactions

At the heart of the application is a list of all the transactions for your checking account. This includes checks, debit and ATM card withdrawals, deposits, fees, and interest payments. Your current balance is, of course, the sum of all these additions to and subtractions from the account. Do you have to drag out all your old statements and enter every transaction since you opened the account? No—that would be asking too much. I'll show you how to deal with past transactions soon.

Getting Started with the Register

The steps that are required to get started using the Checkbook Register application are easy. They start with the same steps as you use for all the Excel templates:

1. Open the Check Register.xls workbook.
2. Use the File, Save As command to save the workbook under a new name, such as "Jane's Checkbook."

The next steps will depend on your situation. If you are just now opening a new checking account, enter **0** in the Initial Balance cell (cell G5) and then start entering transactions, including your initial deposit, as described below.

6

If you have an existing checking account, there are a few more things you must do. It's essential that the initial balance you enter in the Register application is accurate. Here's what to do:

1. Locate your checkbook and make sure it's up–to-date, with every transaction recorded in the written register.

2. Locate your two most recent bank statements.

3. Find the Ending Balance (sometimes called Closing Balance) on the most recent bank statement and enter it in the Initial Balance cell in the workbook (cell G5).

4. Compare the bank statements with the written checkbook register. In the register, make a mark next to every transaction that has cleared (is listed on one of the bank statements).

5. Go through the written register and find the uncleared (unmarked) transactions over the past two months (transactions before that are assumed to have cleared). These uncleared transactions are not reflected in the statement's closing balance, and so must be entered in the workbook.

6. Enter each of the uncleared transactions into the Checkbook Register workbook, as described in the next section.

Help! My Register Is Not Accurate.

What if you are one of the many people who do not keep accurate track of transactions in your written checkbook register? Then you won't be able to follow these steps—after all, for the Checkbook Register workbook to function properly, it needs accurate information.

Here's what you can do. Start immediately to keep full and accurate records of each and every transaction in your written register. Do this for at least 3–4 weeks, and when a new bank statement comes, you can follow these steps to get started with the Checkbook Register workbook.

Entering Transactions

You won't type checkbook transactions directly into the workbook's Checkbook Register. The Checkbook Register workbook has a form that you use to enter transactions. Display the Transactions form by selecting Transactions from the Register menu. This form, shown in Figure 6.2, has fields for you to enter or select all the transaction details. They are

- **Date**—This defaults to today's date, but you can change it if needed (for example, if entering checks you wrote last week).

- **Transaction**—Select the type of transaction, such as check or ATM withdrawal. The available types are described below.

- **Check #**—Enter the check number. Leave this field blank for noncheck transactions, such as ATM withdrawals and deposits.

- **To**—For payments, enter the payee name here. For deposits, it can be left blank.

- **For**—This is an optional field and you can use it for any related information you desire.

- **Amount**—The amount of the transaction. Enter a positive amount for payments and deposits—the program automatically converts payments to negative values before recording them.

Figure 6.2

The Transaction form simplifies the task of entering transactions into the register.

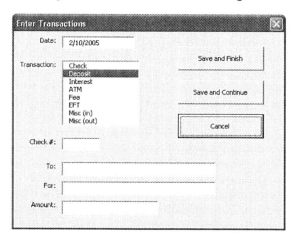

The Checkbook Register application has provision for several kinds of transactions. You can select these from the Transaction list. They are

- **Deposit**—Use for all deposits into the account.

- **Interest**—Use for interest earned on the account.

- **Check**—Use for checks you have written.

- **ATM**—Use for ATM withdrawals.

- **Fee**—Use for bank fees.

- **EFT (electronic fund transfer)**—Use for electronic payments (for example, if you have instructed your phone company to draft your bill from your account).
- **Misc (in)**—Use for any transaction that puts money into the account but does not fit one of the other categories.
- **Misc (out)**—Use for any transaction that takes money out of the account but does not fit one of the other categories.

Can I Enter Transactions Directly?

There's nothing to prevent you from entering your transactions directly in the Checkbook Register workbook without using the Transactions form. Even so, I strongly recommend against this because the Transactions form has some error prevention tools built in. If you enter transactions directly, you are more likely to make an error, so my advice is to always use the Transactions form.

Sorting Transactions

When your register has more than a couple of dozen entries, it can be useful to sort the transactions in various ways to help you find the information you are looking for. You can sort by date, by check number, or by the To field. Simply select the desired sorting from the Register menu to perform the sort.

Editing Transactions

Even the most careful person makes mistakes, and to get the best value out of the Check Register workbook, you need to make sure it is accurate. If you make an error entering a transaction, you can edit the transaction and correct it. Remember, Excel gives you two ways to change the data in a cell:

- To replace the data, move the pointer to the cell, type in the new data, and press Enter.
- To edit the existing data, move the pointer to the cell and press F2 to enter editing mode. When you are done editing, press Enter.

6

You must keep the following warnings in mind when editing data:

- The amount value must be negative whenever money goes out of the account (checks, fees, and so forth) and positive when money comes into the account.
- The only fields that can be left blank are check number (when the transaction is not a check) and the For field.

Keeping Headings in View

If you have more transactions than will fit on one screen, scrolling down the list can make the top part of the Checkbook Register workbook scroll out of view. It can be handy to have the balances and column headings in view at all times. You can do so as follows:

1. Point at the splitter bar at the top of the vertical scroll bar (see Figure 6.3).

2. Push and hold the left mouse button. A horizontal line will display across the worksheet window.

3. Drag the bar down until it is just below the row of headings (row 7).

4. Release the mouse button.

Figure 6.3

Use the splitter bar to keep the worksheet's headings in view at all times.

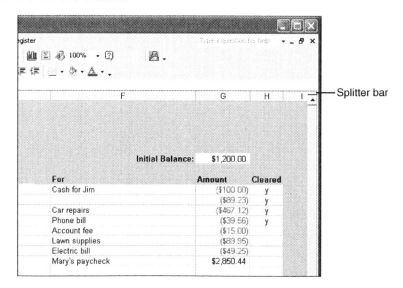

Now you can scroll the transactions in the lower part of the screen while the balances and headings remain visible at the top. When you save your worksheet, Excel remembers the locked heading section the next time you use the worksheet so you don't have to repeat these steps to keep headings in view.

Reconciling Your Register

No matter how careful you are, there's no guarantee that an error or two won't creep into your register. Such errors can have serious consequences down the road, so it's highly advisable to validate the data in the register every so often. This is done by comparing the transactions in the register with the transactions on the checking account statement your bank sends you, a process called *reconciling*. If the transactions in your register accurately mirror the transactions on your statement, you know the register is accurate.

When you look at your monthly bank statement, you will see an Ending Balance listed. This is the account balance at the time the statement was prepared and includes all transactions up to that date. It does not include checks, deposits, or other transactions that occurred after the statement date.

You might think that the statement ending balance is not that useful because it is not the up-to-date balance that, after all, is what you want to know. It can be very useful, however, in that it provides a way to verify, or reconcile, the data in your check register. You should reconcile your register every month, preferably shortly after you receive your bank statement. You'll need to have your check register open in Excel.

For each transaction on the bank statement, locate the corresponding entry in the register and put an *X* (or any other character) in the Cleared field. At the same time, place a checkmark next to the transaction on your bank statement. When you have finished, one of three things has happened.

Ideally, you have marked all the transactions on the statement and the ending balance on the statement matches the Current Cleared Balance on the register (cell D4). Congratulations! You know that the cleared transactions have been entered into the register accurately. Assuming that the uncleared transactions are also accurate and complete, your Current Actual Balance is accurate, too.

6

Another possibility is that there are one or more transactions remaining unmarked on the bank statement. This means that you forgot to enter them into the register. Now's the time to do so. After you have entered them, finish the reconciling by marking the transactions on the statement and putting an *X* in the Cleared column of the register.

The third possibility is that all the transactions on the bank statement have been marked as cleared, but the ending balance does not match the register's Current Cleared Balance. There are several ways this can come about:

- You made an error entering the amount of one or more transactions.
- You entered the wrong transaction type for a transaction, such as entering an electronic fund transfer as a deposit.
- You mistakenly marked a register transaction as cleared when it was not listed on the bank statement.
- You mistakenly checked off a transaction on the bank statement without marking it as cleared in the register.

If you find yourself in this situation, you'll have to carefully review your bank statement and register to find the error. After everything has been fixed, your ending balance and current cleared balance will match.

Reconciling might sound like a huge hassle, but it is essential if you are going to take charge of your checking account. Trust me, it gets easy pretty quickly! As you gain experience, it will become a 5 or 10 minute task each month you can just breeze through.

Now that you have your checking account under control, it's time to move on to credit cards. That's the topic of the next chapter.

7

Getting the Most From Your Credit Cards

It's hard to believe that there was a time—and not all that long ago, either—when there were no credit cards. People paid by cash, check, or money order. In today's connected, online world, it would be unthinkable for most people to get by without a credit card or two (or five or six!). Credit cards can indeed be a great convenience and can, if used properly, even save you money. But, as all too many people have discovered, these little pieces of plastic have a lot of potential for misuse and misery. In this chapter we will take a look at what to look for and what to avoid in your credit cards and how to use them so they work for you and not the other way around. Remember, credit card companies are not your friend—they are out to make money any legal way they can.

How Credit Cards Work

Credit cards are not all the same, of course, but there are enough similarities in how they work that it is worthwhile understanding this. I am talking here about the so-called major credit cards, such as Visa, MasterCard, and Discover, and not about more specialized cards such as those issued by department stores and oil companies.

When you make a credit card purchase, the merchant contacts the credit card company to verify that the card is valid and the amount of the purchase will be validated. This is almost always done automatically and very quickly by the electronic credit card readers, or swipers, that are in common use. If the charge is accepted, the amount of the purchase, less a transaction service fee, is credited to the merchant's account and the full amount is debited from your card account. These merchant service fees, which can range from less than 1% to 5%, are one of the ways the credit card companies make their money.

This merchant fee is why some businesses resisted accepting credit cards. They preferred offering lower prices to the convenience of letting their customers use the cards. The popularity of credit cards has made this practice rare these days, and almost all merchants accept the major credit cards—even in some unlikely places, such as fast food restaurants, parking garages, and vending machines. It's also true that competition among the credit card processing firms has resulted in much lower fees for the merchants.

Credit Card Fees = Higher Prices?

As you might have guessed, those credit card transaction fees are really paid by you, the customer, as higher prices. Like any cost of business, they are figured into the price of whatever goods or services are being offered. Yes, you pay the higher price even when you pay by cash or check and there is no fee. The agreement that merchants have with the credit card company almost always prohibits them from offering a discount for cash sales.

At the end of your billing cycle (which is almost always a month long but does not necessarily coincide with the calendar months) the credit card company generates your statement. They add to your balance all purchases, cash advances, interest charges, and fees for that month. They subtract from your balance any payments made and other credits, such as credits for returned merchandise. In addition to the details of each transaction, your statement includes three important pieces of information:

- The new total balance
- The minimum payment due
- The payment due date

Usually you have between one and a half and two weeks from the time you receive your statement to the payment due date.

Cash Advances

The "Using a Credit Card for Cash Advances" section later in this chapter explains how to calculate the cost of using your card for this purpose.

Credit Card Interest Rates

Every credit card has an interest rate, and, in fact, most have more than one. A typical account might have the following:

- One interest rate, relatively low, for balance transfers and the account checks that are sometimes sent to you
- A higher rate for your purchases
- A third, still higher, rate for cash advances you take when you use your credit card at a bank or ATM

Interest rates are quoted as annual rates because that's what people are accustomed to dealing with. For calculations, they are converted to a daily rate. For example, an annual rate of 14.99% is a daily rate of 0.041068% (14.99 divided by 365). Each and every day, the relevant interest rate is used to calculate the daily interest charge on your account and that amount is added to your balance. And guess what— the next day's interest calculations are performed on this new balance, which is the original balance plus the previous day's interest charges.

This is one of the ways credit card companies squeeze every possible cent out of their customers. A more traditional way of calculating interest, used by most mortgages and consumer loans, is to calculate the interest and add it to the balance on a monthly basis. By calculating interest daily, the credit card companies increase the effective interest rate you are paying. For example, 10% annual interest becomes a real rate of approximately 10.25%. This is all perfectly legal because the fine print in your credit card agreement spells out exactly how interest charges are calculated. Even so, it's another reminder that credit card companies do not have your best interests at heart.

Yet Another Interest Rate Gotcha

Credit card companies have another trick up their sleeves to maximize the amount of interest you pay. In almost every instance, payments you make are always applied first toward the lowest interest rate part of your balance. Suppose your balance consists of a $600 balance transfer on which you are paying 4.99%, and a $300 cash advance on which you are paying 18.99%. All of your payments are applied to the $600 balance transfer amount until it is paid off, and only then are they applied toward the cash advance amount. The result? You pay the maximum possible amount in interest.

Another way the card companies gouge their customers is by including a clause in the card agreement so that your seemingly reasonable interest rate shoots up to a much higher level if you have even a single infraction, such as a late or missed payment. You might also find that if you miss the grace period, the interest is charged retroactively to the date of the actual purchase.

Carrying a Credit Card Balance

Lots of people carry a balance on their credit cards. The average balance is somewhere between $5,000 and $7,000, depending on which information source you believe. This is one of the worst things you can do because it costs so much. If you carry a $5,000 balance on a card with a 20% interest rate, you are paying approximately $1,000 a year in interest! What are you getting in return? Nothing. Can you afford to waste $1,000 a year? I know I can't! See the section "Paying Off Your Balance" later in this chapter for more information on credit card balances and what you can do about them.

Credit Card Fees

Although it's less common these days, some credit cards charge an annual fee. This might be the only kind of card that's available to you if you have a bad credit rating or there's some other factor that makes the card issuer cautious. With all the competition for customers between the card companies, however, most people should never have to pay an annual fee.

Other fees are present on all or most cards but by using your credit card properly you can always avoid them. These include

- A late payment fee that is assessed if your monthly payment is even the slightest bit late
- An overlimit fee if the account balance goes over your credit limit
- An inactivity fee that is charged if your account is idle for too long

Credit Card Advantages

There's no doubt that credit cards are convenient. You can just pull your card out and buy almost anything, from clothes and hardware to groceries and a haircut. There are other advantages as well, advantages that some people might not be aware of. Let's take a look:

- **Online shopping**—It's essentially impossible to shop online without a credit card. Yes, debit cards work, too, but as I explain elsewhere in this chapter, there are several reasons to prefer a credit card.

- **Fraud protection**—If someone gets hold of your credit card number or steals your card, they might run up thousands of dollars in charges. By law you are generally liable only for the first $50 of such charges for credit card fraud. With a debit card, a smart thief can empty your account and you are out the entire sum.

- **Transaction protection**—Suppose you order something online or buy it on eBay and you receive the wrong or a defective item. If the merchant will not fix the problem, you can turn to your credit card company and contest the charge. Such protection is not available with debit cards.

- **Free insurance**—Some credit cards, particularly the higher-end gold and platinum cards, offer free, automatic insurance on certain items, such as rental cars.

Some Fraud Protection for Debit Cards

While it's not required by law, some banks are offering a degree of fraud protection on their debit cards, limiting your liability if the card is stolen. This is a desirable account feature, so be sure to ask if it is available.

The bottom line is that credit cards offer significant advantages if—and this is a big if—they are used correctly.

7

What About Debit Cards?

From the perspective of the user, debit cards work much like credit cards. Behind the scenes, however, they are quite different. A purchase made on a debit card is deducted immediately from your bank account. Debit cards have their uses, particularly for people who find it hard to restrain their spending when they have credit cards burning holes in their pockets. When you have taken charge of your finances, however, you'll find debit cards have several disadvantages when compared with a credit card:

- You do not get the use of the bank's money, free, for the time between making the purchase and paying the credit card statement.
- There are no rewards available.
- You do not have the purchase and fraud protection provided by a credit card.
- You cannot take advantage of special services, such as free auto rental insurance, some credit cards offer.

Debit cards do have one advantage—most merchants will give you cash back with no fee when making a purchase.

Hooray for the Grace Period

The *grace period* is a very important feature of credit cards and makes them a valuable tool for the savvy spender. If you pay your balance in full, on time, you incur no interest charges or other fees. This means you have the use of the bank's money, free, for the period between when you make the purchase and when you pay your balance. This period can range from a couple of weeks to well over a month, depending on how the purchase date relates to the closing and payment due dates.

Let's look at a real example. One of my cards has its closing date on the 12th of each month and the payment due date on the 5th of the following month. Suppose I used the card to buy a $1,000 television on January 15. That charge would not show up on my statement until the next closing date, February 12, and I would not have to actually pay the balance until March 5. I would have, in effect, borrowed $1,000 from the bank for 7 weeks without paying a cent! And—this is the important part—the $1,000 I had set aside to buy the TV spent those 7 weeks in my account earning interest for me. Although the interest earned during the float for a single purchase might seem like small potatoes, getting in the habit of doing this for all purchases can make a small but meaningful difference in your finances. When you combine this with the premiums a credit card might pay, it's hard to see how you can go wrong.

Grace Period for Purchases Only

Be aware that the grace period applies only to purchases and not to cash advances or balance transfers. The interest charges start accumulating instantly, the moment you take the cash advance.

One strategy for making the most of your credit cards is to use the grace period to your advantage with two cards. If you have two cards with staggered closing dates, say the first and the fifteenth of each month, you can use one card or the other for purchases depending on which closing date is furthest away. You can use this timing feature to give you more freedom when you make a large purchase.

Reward Cards

Many credit card companies are offering reward cards that give you something back based on how much you use the card. Some examples of the rewards you can get are

- Airline frequent flier miles
- Credit toward purchases at a particular store
- Cash rebates, perhaps 0.5% to 1% or more of purchases

Reward cards can be a good deal and should definitely be part of your credit card strategy. There are some things you need to be aware of, however.

For one thing, the initial offer on the card rarely lasts very long. It's common to get a credit card offer in the mail that promises great-sounding rewards. Six months later, however, there will be a notice included with your bill—in tiny print of course—notifying you that the terms of the offer have been changed, always for the worse.

Another thing to consider is that the terms of some reward cards make the reward contingent on your good behavior. A single late payment or one instance of going over your credit limit might be enough to wipe out a lot of the rewards you have earned.

Reward cards are most effective if you charge a lot on your card. But don't charge a lot trying to pile up the rewards unless you can pay your balance in full each month. The interest you pay on a balance carried over will cancel out any rewards you get, many times over.

Using Your Credit Cards Wisely

I have emphasized throughout the preceding sections that credit cards have both good and bad sides. Used wisely, they can be an important part of your healthy financial situation. Used unwisely, they are a sure road to debt and lost control of your finances. The following sections contain my prescriptions for credit card wisdom.

Never Charge Anything You Cannot Pay Off

This is the most important piece of advice I can give you. The evil side of credit cards comes out when you start carrying a balance from month to month and paying those nasty interest charges. If you always pay your balance in full each month, you will never have this problem. And of course, this means that you should not charge anything you cannot pay for when the bill comes. When you look at some desirable item in a store, you should ask yourself, "Can I afford this?" What you are really asking is, "Do I have enough cash to pay for this when the credit card bill comes?" If not, don't buy it, period, end of discussion.

But what about emergencies? There are some expenses that simply cannot be put off, such as car repairs, a visit to the dentist, or replacing a worn-out refrigerator. If you do not have the cash, your only alternative might be to charge it even though you know that you will not be able to pay the balance off in full when the credit card bill comes. In this situation you can still minimize the financial consequences:

- If you have more than one credit card, use the one with the lower interest rate on purchases.
- Attempt to time the purchase to coincide with as much float as possible (see the section "Hooray for the Grace Period" earlier in this chapter).

■ Make sure that the card's available credit limit is sufficient for the charge you will be making.

Then, you should make paying off that balance a top priority. This might mean cutting back in other areas, such as new clothing or restaurant meals, but getting that balance off your card account is essential if you are to retain control of your finances.

Use the Grace Period

Take advantage of the grace period to use the bank's money for free for a few weeks. If you have two cards, try to stagger their closing dates and use the one with the furthest off closing date for purchases. If you are planning a large purchase, check your closing date and if it's coming up in a few days, consider postponing the purchase. Waiting a few days on a purchase might give you a whole extra month before the payment is due.

Get a Rewards Card

Find a rewards card that suits you and take advantage of it. One of my cards gives a 1% cash rebate on all purchases. That might not sound like much but over the course of a year it can add up. A few years ago my wife and I flew business class to Japan, free, thanks to frequent flier miles piled up on a rewards card. Make rewards work for you!

Be Careful to Make Payments on Time

To me, there's nothing more annoying than having to pay a late fee and interest because my credit card payment was a day or two late. This money might as well be flushed down the toilet. I know it's easy to lose track of payment due dates, but it is important! I enter the payment date as a reminder in my PDA so even if I forget, the PDA will remind me.

Also, make sure to allow for time in the mail. The credit card company must receive the payment by the due date, which means you must mail it a few days before. Check a couple of past statements and compare the date they received your payments with the dates you mailed them— this will give you an idea of the typical transit time. Always leave at least a couple of days extra just to play it safe.

Online Account Access

Many banks now offer online access to your account information. Log on to your bank's website and you can see an up-to-date summary of your account. This can be a good way to check your current balance and see if it is getting too close to the credit limit. Some also offer online payment of your bill. You enter information about your checking account and the amount to pay, and the money is transferred to your credit card account electronically. This is a great way to pay your bill just before it is due without worry about delays in the mail—plus you save a stamp!

Another Sneaky Tactic

I was reviewing the fine print on one of my credit card agreements—boring, yes, but not a bad idea—and I found yet another way the company was trying to take advantage of its customers. Payments, the fine print said, had to be received by 8 a.m. on the due date to be considered on time. Since the mail is never delivered that early, this has the effect of making the real due date one day before the stated due date. Here's yet another illustration of how credit card companies do not have the customers' best interests at heart.

Mind Your Credit Limit

You should be mindful of the credit limit on your card and be sure never to exceed it to avoid the resulting fees. Even if you pay your balance in full each month, your charges since the last payment might be pushing up against that limit. Then it's time to put your card away and not use it until the balance has been paid off, or at least brought down.

How Much Will It Really Cost?

When you see that snazzy new digital camera, gorgeous widescreen TV, or stylish jacket, it's easy to just whip out your credit card and buy it. But if you do not have the discipline and ability to pay off your credit card bill in full each month—in other words, if you carry a balance—that item is going to cost you more than what it says on the price tag. Sometimes it will cost a lot more, and knowing what the true cost of a credit card purchase is might give you second thoughts about the purchase.

The Real Cost Calculator

The Real Cost Calculator lets you quickly determine the actual cost of an item charged to your credit card and paid off over time. It also tells you how long it will take to pay off. Take a look at the calculator in Figure 7.1.

In this example, an item costing $1,999.95 is charged to a credit card that has a 16.99% interest rate. You plan to pay $75 per month on the balance. Wow! It will take you almost 3 years to it pay off and the real cost is $2,550,00! Would you have bought that item if the price tag had said $2,550 and not $1,999? Probably not.

You should be aware that the real cost as calculated by this workbook is not accurate to the penny. The workbook calculates the real cost by multiplying the monthly payment by the number of months to pay off the balance. In reality, however, your last month's payment will almost always be less than the amount you have been paying regularly—$75 in the example. Even with this minor discrepancy, the data provided by the workbook is certainly accurate enough to let you evaluate whether paying off a purchase over time is really worthwhile.

Item's price sticker

Figure 7.1

The Real Cost Calculator tells you how much it really costs to charge a purchase on your credit card.

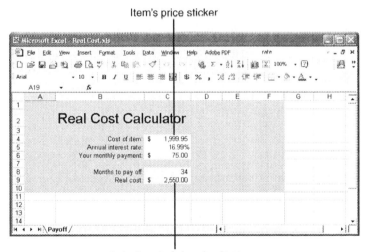

Actual cost of charging item

Credit cards can be very useful financial tools, but the only way to make the card work for you rather than the other way around is to avoid carrying a month-to-month balance. In the next few sections we'll take a closer look at the consequences of paying off your credit card balances.

Why Carrying a Balance Is to Be Avoided

As discussed earlier in the chapter, the most common way people get into trouble with credit cards is by carrying a balance from statement to statement—in effect using the credit card as a source of a long-term loan. If you are one of these people carrying a balance regularly on your cards, perhaps the most important thing you can do on your road to taking charge of your finances is to pay off that balance. That's the topic of this section.

There's no mystery as to why carrying a balance on a credit card is a bad idea. It's the interest you pay, plain and simple. Credit card interest rates range from the high to the extremely high, and throwing your hard-earned money away on interest charges is completely at odds with taking charge of your finances.

Suppose you carry a $5,000 balance on your cards. You charge new items each month and also make a payment, but on average your balance is this amount. If you are paying 10% interest—relatively low by credit card standards—you are wasting $500 a year on interest. At 20% interest it grows to $1,000 a year. I bet you have things you could do with that $1,000 that are a lot more important and more enjoyable than making the credit card company rich!

Paying Off Your Balance

Suppose someone offered you an investment opportunity with the following features:

- An annual return of 12%, 16%, 20%, or more
- Absolutely guaranteed, no way you can lose so much as a cent
- Free of all taxes
- Perfectly legal

Would you be a little bit suspicious? I wouldn't blame you, it sounds too good to be true, but this one's for real. By investing in paying off your credit card balances, you'll get all these benefits—and be making a huge step toward taking charge of your finances.

But wait—if you had the cash to pay off your credit cards you wouldn't have run up the balance in the first place, right? This is true for most people, but there are still approaches to paying off, or at least paying down, your card balance.

If you do have some money socked away, you really should consider using it to pay off your credit cards. No matter where you have this money and what return you are getting on it, paying off your cards will give you a much better return. If the money is your emergency fund, you might wisely hesitate to touch it. But consider, after the card balances are paid off, you can always use a cash advance in the event of an emergency and you'll still save money.

What about your investment account? Saving and investing are good things, so you shouldn't touch that money to pay off your card, right? Wrong! As I mentioned above, paying off your card balances is a much better investment. It's really silly to have $5,000 in a mutual fund earning maybe 8% (if you are lucky) while at the same time paying 20% interest on a $5,000 credit card balance.

If you do not have any spare cash you can use to pay off your cards, consider borrowing it. If you can borrow the money at a lower rate than you are paying on the cards, you will still come out ahead.

If you own your home, you might consider a home equity loan as a source of funds to pay off your cards. Home equity rates are always lower, usually much lower, than credit card rates—plus, interest you pay might be tax deductible.

Another option is to look for another credit card with lower rates. Many cards offer particularly attractive rates on balance transfers, although you need to watch out for one-time fees on such transactions.

Pay It Off—And Keep It That Way

Some people go to a lot of trouble to pay off their credit cards and then just charge them up to the limit again. This is not a good idea because it defeats the whole purpose of paying the cards off. If you pay off your balances, consider it the first step on your way to taking charge of your finances. You should vow to do whatever it takes to never build up a balance again. If you have borrowed the money to pay off your balance, your vow should include paying off that debt as soon as possible.

After evaluating your situation, the next step is to use the Payoff Calculator to determine just how much you will save.

7

The Payoff Calculator

If you are considering paying off your credit card balances, there's nothing more motivating or surprising than seeing how much you will actually save. The Payoff Calculator is designed for just this purpose.

The Payoff Calculator workbook assumes you would not be making new charges on the card, but would be making regular monthly payments until the debt is paid off. It also assumes you would not incur late or any other fees. The interest you would pay over this period is the money you will save by paying the balance in full now. The calculator uses the following information to perform its calculations:

- The amount you owe on the credit card
- The interest rate being charged on the balance
- The monthly payment you make

The output of the calculator is the number of months it will take to pay off the balance and the amount of interest you will pay during this period. It's this interest that represents the savings you will realize by paying off the balance in full now.

Be aware that the calculator provides approximate results. It's not possible to give precise-to-the-penny results because different credit card companies have slightly different ways of calculating interest.

Figure 7.2 shows the calculator with some numbers entered. These are not atypical—a balance of $2,250 and an interest rate of 19.99%. Are you surprised to see that, even with no additional charges, it will take you 42 months to pay the balance off and you will pay approximately $900 in interest in this period? Pretty chilling if you ask me—and a darn good motivation to get that balance paid off now!

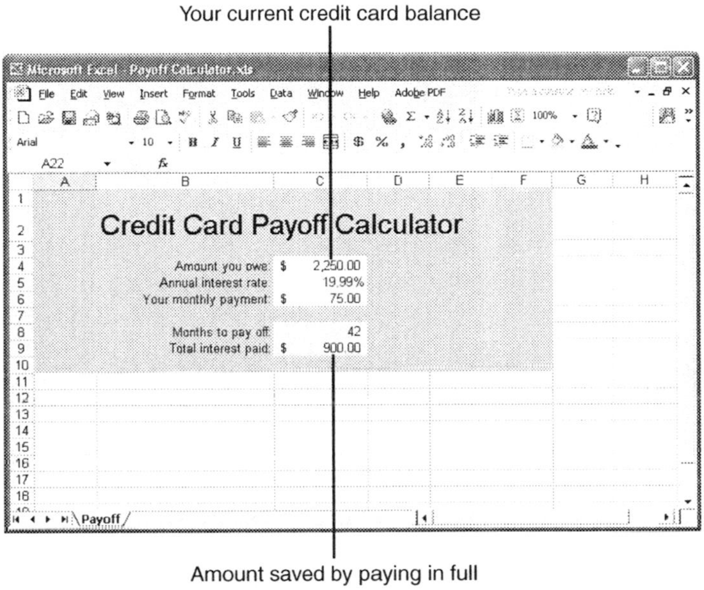

Your current credit card balance

Figure 7.2

This calculator tells you how much money you'll save by paying off your credit card balance.

Amount saved by paying in full

Using a Credit Card for Cash Advances

As mentioned earlier in the chapter, one of the things you might want to do with a credit card is get a cash advance. This can be a useful feature sometimes, but—as always—you need to understand the details in order to use cash advances wisely.

Understanding Cash Advances

Credit cards give you the option of getting cash that is, in effect, a loan against your account. There are several ways you can do this—at a bank teller, using an ATM, or with the blank checks the credit card company often sends to account holders. Be aware that the interest rate charged on cash advances is sometimes different depending on which method you use to get the cash.

There's no doubt that the ability to quickly get some cash can be very useful. Maybe you are shopping at a flea market or some other place where credit cards are not accepted. Maybe you just need some "walking around" money for incidentals such as coffee, the newspaper, and chewing gum. You can take your credit card to essentially any bank or ATM and get the cash you need right then and there. When travelling overseas, cash advances are a real convenience because you can get local currency when you need it and avoid carrying large sums of cash with you.

Cash advances can be expensive, however! First of all, there's no grace period as there is with purchases—the interest charges start accumulating the moment you take the advance. In addition, there is almost always a flat fee that is typically 3% of the amount of the advance. If you are getting your advance at an ATM, there might be additional ATM fees as well. For overseas use, a currency conversion fee is sometimes tacked on. Even if the interest rate on cash advances sounds appealing, the fees usually change the picture.

Let's look at an example. Card companies often have special promotions for cash advances, offering very low interest rates for some period, such as six months. But figure in the fee and it is not such a good deal.

For example, I received an offer of a cash advance at 0.5% for six months. I though I could take the cash and invest it in a money market account at 2%, resulting in a net gain of 1.5% for me. But wait—the 3% fee I would pay to have that money for 6 months is equivalent to a 6% annual interest rate, so my real cost would be 6.5%, not 0.5%. Not such a good idea after all! But suppose you were going to use the cash advance to pay off the balance on a second credit card that is charging 24.99%. Then that 6.5% effective rate looks pretty attractive! By knowing the effective rate on a cash advance, you can intelligently evaluate whether it is a wise move.

The Cash Advance Cost Calculator

Cash advances have their uses, but you need to be aware of the real costs in order to use them wisely. The Cash Advance Cost Calculator lets you do this. Based on the amount of the advance, the interest rate being charged, the fixed fee that is assessed, and the number of months you plan to take to pay back the advance, the calculator tells you the amount the advance will cost you. This amount is above and beyond the payback of the advance itself, of course.

The calculator is shown in Figure 7.3. In this example, a $1,000 advance incurs a 3% flat fee and 19.99% interest. Paid back over 24 months, you will make monthly payments of $52.42 and pay approximately $258 for the advance—in other words, you will pay back the $1,000 advance itself plus $258 in fees and interest. Are you sure you really need that cash advance?

Some people prefer to think of payback in terms of a monthly payment amount rather than a number of months—for example, I can afford $40 a month. To use the calculator this way, adjust the Months to Pay Back figure until the Monthly Payment is at or near your desired level.

Cost of advance over the full payback period

Figure 7.3

The Cash Advance Cost Calculator tells you the true cost of a cash advance.

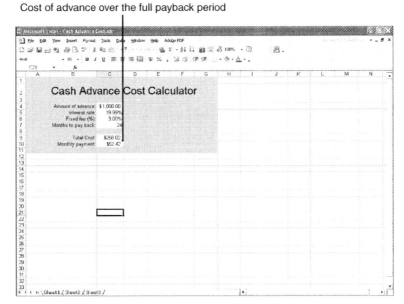

This chapter has shown you how avoid credit card pitfalls and to use your cards to your best advantage. The next chapter takes on a topic of interest to many people—mortgages.

Financing Your Home and Car

8

Understanding Mortgages—And Getting the One That's Best for You

Home ownership is a dream for many people. It's a major step, but one with many rewards. Buying a home means getting a mortgage. Choosing the best mortgage for you and your situation is an essential part of the home buying process.

In this chapter you will learn about the various kinds of mortgages, expenses related to buying a home, and how to compare different mortgage offerings with each other.

The Many Benefits of Home Ownership

There's a good reason why so many people are attracted to owning their own home—there are so many benefits to be had! Some benefits are intangible, such as pride of ownership and freedom from landlord hassles.

Other benefits translate directly into dollars and cents. The possibility of appreciation in value is a factor for many home buyers. There's undoubtedly something very satisfying about buying a home and seeing it go up in value over the years. There's no guarantee this will happen, of course, but the potential for appreciation is surely an important factor for many home buyers.

When you buy a home, your monthly payments are going toward something of lasting value. After five years of renting, you have nothing to show for all the rent you paid. After five years of paying your mortgage, you will have built up some equity in the house.

What Is Equity?

The term *equity* refers to the difference between a home's value and the amount still owed on it. For example, if your home is appraised at $250,000 and you owe $190,000 on the mortgage, you have $60,000 of equity in the house.

There are also numerous tax benefits to owning a house. These tax benefits can make the real cost of home ownership significantly lower than it seems. I'll cover this topic in more detail later in the chapter.

Types of Mortgages

When you are shopping for a mortgage, the different types that are available can make one's head spin! Let's take a look at the most common types of home mortgages available.

Traditional Fixed Rate Mortgages

The *fixed rate mortgage* was the only kind available for many years, and is still preferred by many home buyers. The mortgage is issued at a certain interest rate and that rate remains fixed for the length, or term, of the mortgage. Fixed rate mortgages are usually issued for 30 years, although 15-year mortgages are becoming more common.

The advantage of a fixed rate mortgage is that your payment remains constant. You do not have to worry about the payment increasing sometime down the road (at least the mortgage payment won't increase—escrow is another matter, as I'll explain soon). The disadvantage is that the interest rate tends to be higher than some other kinds of mortgages.

Adjustable Rate Mortgages

An *adjustable rate mortgage*, also known as an ARM, is issued for a fixed term, again typically 30 but sometimes 15 years. The interest rate is pegged to some measure of general interest rates across the economy as a whole, most often the prime rate (set indirectly by the Federal Reserve Board). The terms of the mortgage will specify the way the rate is calculated, such as "prime rate plus 1/2%." These terms will also specify how often the rate is adjusted, perhaps every year or every three years.

The advantage of adjustable rate mortgages over fixed rate mortgages is that the initial rate is always lower, often a lot lower, and this can make a huge difference in the payment amount. The disadvantage, of course, is that this rate might rise in the future, with a corresponding bump in your monthly mortgage payments. More adjustable rate mortgages have a lifetime cap, specifying, for example, that the rate cannot rise by more than 6% during the life of the loan. There is usually also an annual cap that limits how much the rate can increase at one time.

Adjustable rate mortgages are a gamble in a way. You are betting that rates do not go up, or at least not too much. They are particularly attractive in certain situations:

- If you know you will not be keeping the house for long. If, for example, you know you will be selling in three years, a three-year adjustable rate mortgage (one whose rate is adjusted every three years) would be a good idea.

- For young families just getting started, the lower rates of an adjustable rate mortgage will let you get into more house than you could afford otherwise. Down the road, as your income rises, you will be able to afford any payment increases that happen.

While ARMs are often attractive and are in fact a good choice in some situations, they do carry real risks. Many people do not realize the practical impact that a small rate increase will have. A 1% increase sounds small, but on a $200,000 mortgage, it amounts to $2,000 more per year or $167 a month. Could you really afford that? Also, life always seems to throw curveballs and the plans you have now might change. Your plans to sell in three years might have to be abandoned, or your prediction of a promotion and hefty raise might not come to pass. These are all factors to bear in mind when selecting a mortgage.

Balloon Mortgages

A *balloon mortgage* is the same as a traditional fixed rate mortgage with one difference—the remaining balance is due in full after a certain number of years. This is the balloon payment and is where this kind of mortgage gets its name.

For example, with a 7-year balloon payment, your monthly payments would be the same as for a 30-year fixed mortgage, but at the end of the 7th year, you will have to pay off the balance in full. Balloon mortgages offer slightly lower interest rates than fixed mortgages.

If you know you will be selling your house before the time of the balloon payment, this kind of mortgage is a great choice. Even without this knowledge, a balloon mortgage might be worth considering. When the balloon payment is due, assuming you have not won the lottery and can just pay it off, you have two options:

- Refinance the mortgage with another company (or even the same company).
- Continue the mortgage for a fee. Most balloon mortgages include the option to convert the mortgage to a conventional fixed rate mortgage at a slightly higher rate than what is prevailing at the time.

Like ARMs, balloon mortgages face the risk of increased future interest rates, and the same cautions apply.

Hybrid Mortgages

A *hybrid mortgage* can be viewed as a cross between a fixed rate mortgage and an adjustable rate mortgage. The interest rate is fixed for an initial period, typically five or seven years. Then it is adjusted, up or down, based on the rates prevailing at the time. There's only the one adjustment—after it is made, the new rate remains in place for the life of the loan.

Your Mortgage Payment

For most people who are house-shopping, the question "what can we afford" does not refer directly to the price of the house but to the monthly payment that will be required. After all, that's the money you will be paying out each month. Trying to decide whether you can afford a $150,000 or a $200,000 house is next to impossible, but deciding whether you can afford $600, $800, or $1,200 a month is a lot easier.

It might be helpful to start by getting some idea of what the mortgage payment is for specific mortgage rates and amounts. Table 8.1 lists the monthly payment for fixed rate 30-year mortgages at various amounts and rates.

Table 8.1   Monthly Mortgage Payment Amounts

	Mortgage Amount				
Interest rate	$100,000	$150,000	$200,000	$250,000	$300,000
4.00%	$477	$716	$955	$1,194	$1,432
4.50%	$507	$760	$1,013	$1,267	$1,520
5.00%	$537	$805	$1,074	$1,342	$1,610
5.50%	$568	$852	$1,136	$1,419	$1,703
6.00%	$600	$899	$1,199	$1,499	$1,799
6.50%	$632	$948	$1,264	$1,580	$1,896
7.00%	$665	$998	$1,331	$1,663	$1,996

You can use the Mortgage Payment Calculator to perform simple calculations related to mortgage payments. This calculator is shown in Figure 8.1. You can see that it has two independent parts.

In the upper part, you enter the price of the house you want to buy, the amount of down payment you will be able to pay, and the mortgage interest rate you expect to get. The result is the monthly mortgage payment that will result, based on a 30-year fixed rate loan.

In the lower part, you start with the amount of monthly mortgage payment you can afford. Then enter the down payment amount and mortgage interest rate and the calculator displays the price of house you can afford.

In both cases, the calculator assumes a 30-year fixed rate mortgage because that is the most popular kind.

It's essential to realize, however, that your actual monthly payment will be quite a bit more than this, sometimes by as much as 20%–30%. This is because of *escrow*. With few exceptions, mortgage lenders require that you pay into an escrow account for your homeowners insurance and property taxes. Each month you pay approximately 1/12 of the annual cost of insurance and taxes into your escrow account, and the mortgage company pays these bills for you from the escrow account. Your total monthly payment is sometimes called the *PITI payment*, which stands for principal, interest, taxes, and insurance.

It's difficult to precisely account for escrow in calculations because it depends on your local taxes, which can vary a great deal, as well as your insurance costs. You can, however, get an estimate of escrow as a percentage of the mortgage payment by talking with real estate agents and home owners in the area where you want to buy a house. Entering this estimate percentage in the calculator will provide much more realistic answers.

The calculator also enables you to enter a dollar amount for yearly escrow in cell E5. If you enter an amount here, it will be used in the calculations, and the percentage value in cell E4 will be ignored. If you enter 0 in cell E5, the percentage value in cell E4 will be used in the calculations.

Getting Accurate Figures for Tax and Insurance

Property tax figures are public information and can be obtained for a specific house from the county or city tax office. Sometimes this information is part of the real estate listing for a house. As for homeowners' insurance, your insurance agent might be able to give you an estimate.

Calculate payment for a specific house

The house you can buy with that payment

Figure 8.1

The Mortgage Payment Calculator can calculate the payment for a specific house purchase and can also calculate the house price you can afford based on a monthly payment.

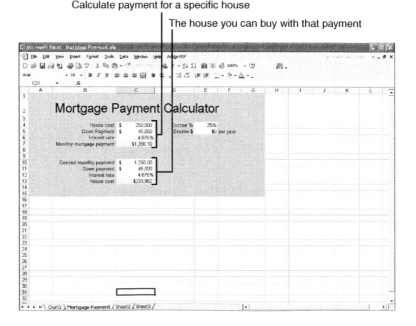

Escrow accounts are covered in more detail in Chapter 11, "Understand Escrow Accounts." For now, it's important to know that your monthly payment will be more than what's required on just the mortgage itself.

Other Mortgage Costs

Unfortunately, a mortgage is never a simple matter of borrowing a certain amount of money for a specified term and rate. There are various other costs involved, and it's these costs that often separate a good mortgage deal from a bad one. Some of these costs cannot be avoided; others can be avoided or at least reduced. The more you know about them, the better you will be prepared to find the best mortgage deal for you.

Other Home Buying Costs

There are some costs that are part of buying a home that are not part of the mortgage costs *per se*, although they are sometimes rolled into the amount financed. These fees include appraisal, surveyor, attorney, electrical/mechanical/plumbing inspection (called *EMP inspection*), deed registration, and title search. These topics are beyond the scope of this book, but you do need to be aware of them.

Origination Fee

Every mortgage I have ever heard of includes a 1% *origination fee*. This is a one-time flat fee, 1% of the borrowed amount, that you pay up front when you take the mortgage out. The fee is usually rolled into the mortgage amount.

Points

Points are an additional one-time fee that is paid at the time you get the mortgage. They are expressed as percentages—one point equals one percent of the mortgage amount. Technically speaking, points are considered to be prepaid interest and, as such, might be tax deductible. Mortgages differ widely on the points charged, ranging from none to as high as four points. Generally speaking, higher points means the mortgage is better in some other way, usually a lower interest rate. Points are usually rolled into the mortgage.

8

Evaluating different mortgages based on their points can be tricky because there are so many factors involved, including how long you plan to stay in the house. At a simpler level, however, it's easy to compare the monthly payments of two mortgages that have different points and interest rates.

The Mortgage Points Comparator workbook does just this. It lets you enter information on two mortgages: the amount of the mortgage (assumed to be the same for both) and the points and interest rate for each. It then displays the amount financed and the monthly payment for each (again, based on a 30-year fixed rate mortgage).

This calculator is shown in Figure 8.2. For this sample data, you can see that with a $200,000 mortgage, a 4.5% mortgage with 2 points results in a monthly payment that is about $10 lower than a 4.75% mortgage with no points. Be sure to remember that the payments calculated by this workbook do not include escrow.

It's important to realize that the balance between points and interest rate depends on the length of time you will own the house. Lower points save you a significant amount of money upfront, while a lower interest rate saves you a little each month. It also depends on whether the points are rolled into the mortgage amount or, as is sometimes required, paid upfront in cash. An unofficial rule of thumb says that the breakeven point is when 1 point reduces the interest rate by 1/8%.

Figure 8.2

The Mortgage Points Comparator enables you to compare monthly payments for mortgages with different interest rates and points.

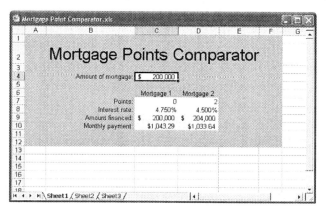

Private Mortgage Insurance

Private mortgage insurance (PMI) is one of those nasty little "gotchas" that many home buyers are surprised to find hiking up their payments. It comes into play when the amount of your mortgage is more than 80% of the assessed value of the house you are buying.

To understand this, think about how a mortgage works. It is a secured loan, meaning that if you default on payments, the mortgage lender can foreclose on the house, taking it over and selling it to recoup the money loaned to you. But what if the real estate market has tanked, or if the condition of the house has deteriorated so it is not worth as much as when you first bought it? Then the lender might not be able to sell it for the same price you paid for it. If, however, the mortgage is limited to 80% of the house value, the lender has a 20% cushion and can be pretty sure of getting the money back in the event of foreclosure.

Here's where PMI comes in. For mortgages of more that 80% of the house value, the insurance protects the mortgage lender in the event of foreclosure. If the lender cannot sell the house for the amount still owed on the mortgage, the insurance makes up the difference. And guess who pays for the insurance—you, of course!

PMI serves a useful purpose. It can be difficult or impossible for some people, particularly first-time home buyers, to come up with a 20% down payment. Without PMI, they would be shut out of the mortgage market. Note that PMI is even more expensive when the mortgage is more than 95% of the appraised value. Even if you cannot get down to the magic 80% level, it is worthwhile to make every effort to get below 95%.

The Tax Benefits of Home Ownership

Home ownership is a cornerstone of the American economy. In order to encourage home ownership, the government has instituted tax policies that help home owners. These tax benefits are an important part of the overall financial picture when it comes to buying and owning a home.

The most important is the tax deduction for mortgage interest. You can deduct this interest from your income, and this can mean a large tax savings.

Let's look at an example. Suppose you have just taken out a $250,000, 30-year mortgage at 5%. During the first year, you will pay approximately $12,400 in interest. If you are in the 28% marginal tax bracket, your tax savings will be 28% × 12,400 = $3,472 or almost $300 per month. If you live in a state with a state income tax, your savings will be even greater.

What Is the Marginal Tax Rate?

The *marginal tax rate* is the rate you pay on the last few dollars of your income. It is not the rate you pay on all of your income. For example, in the year 2004, if you were a single person with $48,000 in taxable income, your federal rates were

- 10% on the first $7,125
- 15% on everything between $7,126 and $29,050
- 25% on everything between $29,051 and your total income of $48,000

It's this last figure—25%—that is your marginal tax bracket. If you had earned $49,000 instead of $48,000, you would pay 25% tax on that extra $1,000.

The second major tax benefit for homeowners is the deduction for property tax. This is not as large an item as interest, but the tax savings can still be substantial.

Deducting the points you pay when you get a mortgage is another possible, albeit one-time, tax benefit. There are some restrictions, however, so you should get the advice of a tax professional on this matter.

Of course, these tax benefits are available only if you itemize deductions on your tax return. For some people, having mortgage interest to deduct raises them to the point where it is better to itemize than to take the standard deduction. This can bring an unexpected benefit when you can suddenly deduct things you did not deduct before because you did not use the itemized deduction. There's no guarantee that mortgage interest will automatically make itemized deductions better than the standard deduction for your specific situation, but this is the case for most people.

The tax savings that come with a mortgage might let you afford more house than you thought. The tax savings can offset part of the mortgage payment, in effect. Of course, a potential problem is that you must come up with the full mortgage payment each month, but your tax savings might not be realized until you file your return.

If you want to get some idea of how tax savings can affect the real cost of a mortgage, use the Mortgage Tax Saving Calculator. This workbook is shown in Figure 8.3 with some sample data entered.

Figure 8.3

You can use the Mortgage Tax Savings Calculator to determine how your tax savings will affect your real mortgage cost.

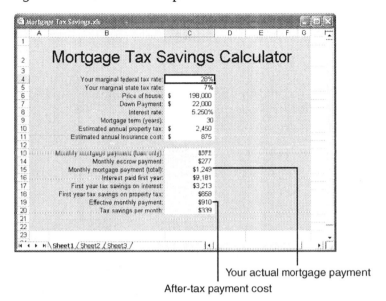

Your actual mortgage payment

After-tax payment cost

Most of the input items in this calculator are self explanatory. Those that might not be are

- Marginal federal tax rate is your federal tax bracket.
- Marginal state tax rate is your state tax bracket. If your state does not have an income tax, enter **0** here.

On the output side, you have the following:

- **Monthly mortgage payment (loan only)**—The monthly payment on the loan itself.
- **Monthly escrow payment**—The estimated monthly escrow payment. This is the estimated annual tax plus estimated annual insurance cost divided by 12.
- **Monthly mortgage payment (total)**—The total payment (loan + escrow)
- **Interest paid first year**—The amount of interest you'll pay during the first year of the mortgage.
- **First year tax savings on interest**—The tax savings you'll realize by deducting the interest on your tax returns.

- **First year tax savings on property tax**—The tax savings you'll realize by deducting the property tax on your tax returns.

- **Effective monthly payment**—The effective monthly mortgage payment when tax savings are figured in.

- **Tax savings per month**—The amount you save per month due to the mortgage-related tax deductions.

Looking at the example in the figure, you can see that tax savings can be substantial. For this scenario, the tax savings reduce a $1,249 monthly payment to an effective $910.

Be aware that this calculator's results are valid only for the first year of a mortgage. In subsequent years, your interest payments and hence the tax deduction will be less (please refer to the next section about amortization for details).

Understanding Mortgage Amortization

The term *amortization* refers simply to paying off a loan by making regular payments. An amortization schedule lists all of those payments and breaks each one down into principal and interest components.

Let's see how this works. When you make your first payment on a mortgage, part of the payment is for that month's interest charge on the loan. The remainder of the payment goes toward the principal and reduces the balance you owe.

The next month's payment works the same. But since the first payment reduced the principal, even if only by a small amount, the second month's interest charge will be slightly less and the amount of the payment that goes toward the principal will be correspondingly greater.

Over the life of the loan, therefore, the amount of each payment going for interest gradually decreases, and the amount going for principal gradually increases. To illustrate, Table 8.2 shows the principal and interest amounts for the first 10 and last 10 payments on a $250,000, 30 year, 5% mortgage.

Table 8.2   Interest and Principal Changes in a Mortgage Payment

Payment #	Interest	Principal
1	$1,041.67	$300.39
2	$1,040.42	$301.64
3	$1,039.16	$302.90
4	$1,037.90	$304.16
5	$1,036.63	$305.43
6	$1,035.36	$306.70
7	$1,034.08	$307.98
8	$1,032.80	$309.26
9	$1,031.51	$310.55
10	$1,030.21	$311.84
351	$54.66	$1,287.40
352	$49.29	$1,292.76
353	$43.91	$1,298.15
354	$38.50	$1,303.56
355	$33.07	$1,308.99
356	$27.61	$1,314.44
357	$22.14	$1,319.92
358	$16.64	$1,325.42
359	$11.11	$1,330.94
360	$5.57	$1,336.49

There are two reasons to be aware of how amortization works. The first is to realize that the balance will decrease slowly during the first years of the mortgage. You should not be surprised when you see your still-high balance after two or three years! The second reason is to understand that the tax benefits of deducting the mortgage interest will slowly decrease over the life of the mortgage as the amount of interest paid decreases.

8

How Much Can I Borrow?

A common question among mortgage seekers is, "How much can I borrow?" You won't know for sure until you actually apply for a mortgage and are (hopefully) approved, but there are still some guidelines followed by mortgage lenders. Perhaps the most common way mortgage lenders determine this amount is to perform two calculations:

1. 28% of your (and your spouse's, if applicable) gross monthly income.

2. 36% of your gross monthly income, less other monthly obligations (credit card and auto loan payments, for example).

The lower of these two figures is considered the largest PITI (principal, interest, taxes, and insurance) payment you can handle. Let's look at an example using actual figures:

- Your gross annual income = $45,000 = $3,750/month
- Your spouse's gross annual income = $32,000 = $2,667/month
- Total monthly income = $6,417/month
- Other obligations = $645/month
- 1) 28% of $6,417 = $1,797/month
- 2) 36% of $6,417 = $2,310 minus $645 = $1,665/month

The lower of these figures, $1,665 per month, is the maximum PITI payment permitted in most cases. The amount of the mortgage itself, of course, depends on the interest rate, taxes, and insurance.

The Maximum Mortgage Calculator

Using the guidelines given in the previous section, it is possible to calculate the approximate maximum mortgage amount you could expect to get based on your income and other obligations. That's exactly what the Maximum Mortgage Calculator does. You enter information about yourself and the calculator determines and displays the maximum mortgage amount at each of several interest rates. The Maximum Mortgage Calculator is shown in Figure 8.4.

Figure 8.4

The Maximum Mortgage Calculator determines the maximum mortgage you can expect to get.

Your mortgage information

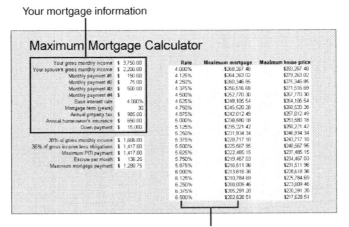

Maximum mortgage at various interest rates

In the input section of the worksheet, you enter information about your monthly income and obligations. The latter includes things such as credit card payments and auto loans. Do not include current rent or mortgage payments. If you have more than four obligations, add two or more of them together and enter in one of these cells. You can also enter the amount of the down payment you propose to make.

The base interest rate tells the calculator where to start. It will compute maximum mortgages at this rate and for 2.5% above, at 0.125% intervals. Enter a value for base interest rate that is at or slightly lower than the lowest rates available in your area.

When you have entered the input information, the calculator displays some basic results in cells C15:C19. The most important results are in the table to the right, which lists the maximum mortgage you can expect to get at each interest rate level. In the next column, the maximum house price is simply the maximum mortgage amount plus the down payment.

The results are also displayed graphically on the worksheet named Chart. Click the tab to display the chart, as shown in Figure 8.5.

It's important to understand that although the Maximum Mortgage Calculator provides useful results, they are just ballpark figures. Not every mortgage lender follows exactly the same guidelines as used by the calculator. Also, your success at getting a mortgage for a certain amount depends on other factors as well, such as your credit history. But, by adding the result provided by this calculator to the amount of down payment you can pay, you'll get at least a rough idea of how much house you can afford.

Figure 8.5

The Maximum Mortgage Calculator can also display its results graphically.

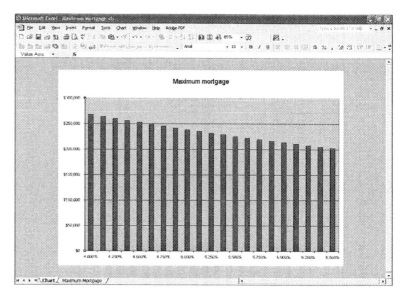

The Mortgage Detail Calculator

I will end this chapter with the most detailed mortgage-related calculator yet, the Mortgage Detail Calculator. Shown in Figure 8.6, this calculator takes essentially all the details about a potential home purchase and mortgage and calculates all the information you need to make an informed decision.

Most of the input and output fields in this calculator are self-explanatory, but here are a few details.

The Federal and State marginal tax rate fields are for your marginal tax rates, as explained earlier in this chapter. If there is no income tax in your state, enter o here. If you do not itemize your deductions, enter o in both fields. Note, however, that it is almost always advantageous to itemize deductions if you have a mortgage.

The Amount Financed is the principal amount of the mortgage. It is calculated by adding the house price to the origination fee, points, and other fees and then subtracting the down payment.

You can use this calculator to compare different mortgage offerings or to see the effect of a larger or smaller down payment. All you need to do is open two or more copies of the template, save each under its own name, and enter the relevant information for each scenario.

Figure 8.6

The Mortgage Detail Calculator provides complete information on a potential house purchase and mortgage.

Information about you

House information   Results of your payments and tax savings

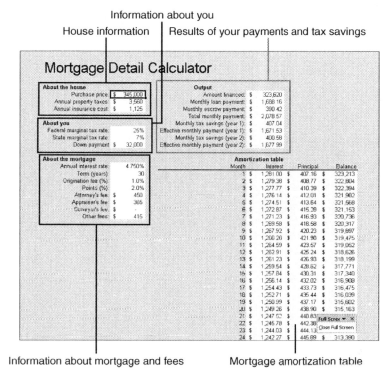

Information about mortgage and fees   Mortgage amortization table

In the next chapter we will consider another kind of mortgage, one that can be very useful—the home equity loan.

9

Considering Home Equity Loans

Home equity loans—borrowing against the value of your home—have become an important financial strategy for many home owners. This chapter explains what home equity loans are and what's involved, and helps you to decide if a home equity loan is right for you.

What Is a Home Equity Loan?

Before you can understand what a home equity loan is, you need to understand the concept of equity. It's a simple concept, really, and refers to the extent to which you actually own something. In the case of your home, *equity* is the value of the home minus the amount you owe on your mortgage.

This equity can be looked at as untapped value. If you sold your home, the equity would be cash in your pocket. Suppose your home is worth $195,000 and you owe $140,000 on your mortgage. If you sell the home for $195,000 and pay off the mortgage, you'll be left with $55,000—that's your equity.

What About Negative Equity?

Negative equity is an unfortunate situation that arises when the amount you owe on your mortgage (or mortgages) is more than the value of the home. The most common cause is when the value of the home goes down suddenly because of external factors, such as a freeway being built right next door.

A *home equity loan*, then, is a loan that is backed by the equity in your home. In other words, the lender can take your home if you default on paying back the loan. The home equity lender is actually second in line in this situation, behind the primary mortgage holder. But the fact that the loan is backed by the property gives home equity loans two major advantages:

- The interest you pay is tax-deductible in almost all cases (but check with a tax advisor to be sure).
- Because the loan is secured and the lender is taking essentially no risk, the interest rates are generally quite low.

The tax deductibility of home equity loan interest makes the low interest rates even lower. For example, suppose you are in the 25% federal and 6% state marginal tax brackets, for a total of 31%. In this situation, the effective interest rate on a home equity loan is 31% less than the actual rate. For example, for a 5% home equity loan:

Effective rate = 5% − (5% × 31%) = 3.45%

Like regular mortgages, home equity loans can be fixed rate or adjustable rate. If the loan is adjustable, each adjustment is typically made on a monthly basis. As with regular mortgages, it is a trade-off. An adjustable rate means a lower rate now but possibly higher rates in the future.

How They Work

Most home equity loans these days are arranged as a line of credit. Based on the appraised value of your home and the remaining balance on your primary mortgage, the lender issues you a line of credit for a certain amount. You are given a checkbook you use to draw on the credit, sometimes with a restriction on the minimum amount you can write a check for (for example, $250) or the maximum number of checks you can write per month. The monthly payment you must make on a line of credit varies with the amount you owe and the current interest rate. A typical minimum monthly payment would be 1.5% of the outstanding balance. There is usually a dollar minimum payment that comes into play at low balances.

Look for Additional Value

Some banks offer additional value if you take out a home equity loan with them. Perhaps the most common enticement is a free or reduced cost checking account. For instance, I have my checking and home equity credit line at the same bank. As long as my home equity balance remains about $5,000, the checking account is free. This is a premium account with online banking and lots of other extras, and the normal cost is $25/month. That's a significant savings!

Less common is a home equity loan that is configured like a fixed-rate mortgage. You receive a single lump sum and then pay it off with fixed payments over a specified term, such as 10 or 15 years.

What About Second Mortgages?

Second mortgage is just another term for a home equity loan.

Which type of home equity loan is best for you? If you are borrowing for a single fixed, one-time expense such as remodeling your kitchen or buying a car, the fixed rate with a fixed term loan is probably the better choice. If, however, you will need to borrow unspecified amounts several times over some time period—Junior's college expenses, for example—the line of credit is preferable.

How Much Can I Borrow?

The amount you can get on a home equity line of credit depends on several factors in addition to the amount of equity you have in the house. These include the policies of the lender, your credit rating, your income, and sometimes the age and location of your house. The amount of the credit line is sometimes expressed as a percentage of the home value. For example, if a lender advertises "Borrow up to 95% of your home value," here's what it means.

1. Take 95% of the house's appraised value.
2. Subtract the amount owed on the primary mortgage.
3. The result is the amount of the equity line.

Some lenders offer home equity lines of more than 100% of the appraised value. They might come with a higher interest rate, however. Also, interest on the amount of the loan that exceeds your home's value is not tax deductible.

Home Equity Loan Cautions

Taking out a home equity loan can be an excellent financial strategy in some situations, and can help you to take charge of your finances. Let's look at some examples:

- Using a home equity line of credit to pay off your credit card balances can mean big savings in interest payments.
- Making major home improvements with a home equity line of credit can improve your quality of life and pay off down the road in a higher resale value.
- Financing a new car with a home equity loan rather than a regular auto loan can mean both interest and tax savings.

The fact is, however, that home equity loans can be misused. They can be a step backwards, providing some quick cash but worsening your financial situation in the long run.

I have mentioned that using a home equity loan to pay off high-interest credit card balances is a good idea. But if you just run up those credit card balances again, you have defeated the whole purpose, and you end up worse off than before. Now you have the credit card balance again plus the home equity balance! This is a real bad idea.

In recent years, some areas of the country have experienced a long-term real estate boom. People see the value of their homes go up year after year, and this can be a dangerous trap. As their equity increases, they repeatedly borrow against it. Somehow this seems like "free money" that can be spent without consequence. But that's not true. Borrowing is borrowing, and it all has to be paid back eventually. If you continually borrow against your home's increasing equity, you'll find

- More and more of your monthly income is going to pay back your home equity loans.
- Because your monthly income is being squeezed, you'll need to borrow more and more to maintain your lifestyle.
- You are not building up any equity in the house because you are always borrowing against it.

Like any form of borrowing, home equity loans need to be used with caution and with full awareness of the trade-offs involved.

Home Equity Calculations

Home equity loan calculations depend on the type of loan. For a fixed loan, you can treat it like a regular mortgage and use the calculators that were presented in Chapter 8, "Understanding Mortgages—And Getting the One That's Best for You."

For a line of credit home equity loan, however, things are a bit more complex because the payment is not fixed. As the balance changes and the interest rate is adjusted, your payment can go up or down each month. As a result of these uncertainties, it is impossible to predict exactly what your payment will be.

This does not mean, however, that you cannot calculate some interesting and useful figures for a home equity line of credit. The Home Equity Line of Credit Calculator lets you

- Determine how long it will take to pay off a home equity line of credit
- Calculate how much interest you will pay over the life of the loan
- Determine what each month's payment and balance will be

The calculator has to make some assumptions, namely

- That you will have an initial balance and will not add to it
- That you will make the minimum required payment each month
- That the initial interest rate will not change

You need several pieces of information in order to use this calculator. The initial balance and interest rate are required, of course. You also need the minimum payment, both as a percentage of the balance and as a dollar amount. You can ask your bank for this information.

How exactly does the minimum payment work? For most loans, it is determined as the lower of a percentage of the balance or a fixed amount. Suppose your loan has a minimum payment of 2% or $15. If your balance is $4,500, 2% of that amount is $90 and because that is more than $15, your minimum payment will be $90. But suppose your balance is only $500. The 2% value is $10, and because that is less than $15, your minimum payment will be $15.

After you have entered the required information in the calculator, it displays results, as shown in Figure 9.1.

Figure 9.1

The Home Equity Line of Credit Calculator shows total interest and monthly payments.

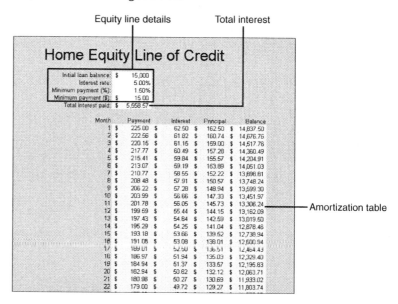

One thing that surprises many people is how long it will take to pay off a home equity line of credit with minimum payments. To see this for the loan information you have entered, scroll the worksheet down until there are no more payments listed and the balance is zero. This is shown for the example in Figure 9.2. The last payment is not until month 327, more than 27 years!

Home equity loans are one way to use your home to improve your financial situation. Another way is by refinancing your mortgage, covered in the next chapter.

Figure 9.2

Determining how long it will take to pay off a home equity loan.

311	$	15.00	$	1.02	$	13.98	$ 230.02
312	$	15.00	$	0.96	$	14.04	$ 215.98
313	$	15.00	$	0.90	$	14.10	$ 201.88
314	$	15.00	$	0.84	$	14.16	$ 187.72
315	$	15.00	$	0.78	$	14.22	$ 173.50
316	$	15.00	$	0.72	$	14.28	$ 159.23
317	$	15.00	$	0.66	$	14.34	$ 144.89
318	$	15.00	$	0.60	$	14.40	$ 130.49
319	$	15.00	$	0.54	$	14.46	$ 116.04
320	$	15.00	$	0.48	$	14.52	$ 101.52
321	$	15.00	$	0.42	$	14.58	$ 86.94
322	$	15.00	$	0.36	$	14.64	$ 72.31
323	$	15.00	$	0.30	$	14.70	$ 57.61
324	$	15.00	$	0.24	$	14.76	$ 42.85
325	$	15.00	$	0.18	$	14.82	$ 28.03
326	$	15.00	$	0.12	$	14.88	$ 13.14
327	$	15.00	$	0.05	$	14.95	$ (1.80)
328	$	-	$	-	$	-	$ -
329	$	-	$	-	$	-	$ -
330	$	-	$	-	$	-	$ -
331	$	-	$	-	$	-	$ -
332	$	-	$	-	$	-	$ -

Last payment at month 327

10

Refinancing Your Mortgage

Although the traditional mortgage is for 30 years, very few last that long. Of course, mortgages are paid off when people sell their houses, but another reason for mortgages ending early is refinancing. This can be an important tool for a home owner. In this chapter you will learn about refinancing and how to evaluate whether it is right for you.

Why Refinance?

Refinancing a mortgage is simple in concept. You take out a new mortgage and use the proceeds to pay off the old one. Why would you want to do this?

Perhaps the most common motivation for mortgage refinancing is to get a better interest rate. If rates have fallen since you took out the original mortgage, a refinance can result in significant savings in interest payments and a correspondingly lower monthly payment.

Another reason for refinancing is to take some cash out of the equity you have built up in your house. You can build up equity by paying down the balance on your original mortgage or by having the value of your house go up. In either case, you can take out a new mortgage for more than you owe on the old one and pocket the difference, using it for whatever purpose you desire.

These two reasons are not mutually exclusive, of course. It's possible, under the right circumstances, to get a lower interest rate, lower monthly payments, and take cash out of a refinance all at the same time.

Refinance Tax Cautions

There are some unusual situations where a refinance with cash out might not qualify for a full interest deduction. Although it is unlikely that you will find this applying to you, it is always advisable to check with a tax advisor to be sure.

Does this sound too good to be true? Often it is—for the simple fact that refinancing is not free. Taking out a new mortgage is essentially the same process as taking out your original mortgage, and there are significant expenses involved. Deciding on whether refinancing is right for you is basically a process of comparing the costs with the benefits and deciding if it is worth it.

The remainder of this chapter deals with situations where you are refinancing solely to take advantage of better mortgage terms and not trying to take cash out.

Costs of Refinancing

The costs of taking out a mortgage were covered in Chapter 9, "Considering Home Equity Loans," but it will be a good idea to revisit them here.

- **Origination fee**—Essentially every mortgage charges an upfront origination fee equal to 1% of the mortgage amount.
- **Points**—Most mortgages charge points, with each point equal to 1% of the mortgage amount. Higher points correlate with lower interest rates.
- **Appraisal**—Most mortgage companies require a new appraisal of the house. They might accept an existing appraisal if it is not more than a year or two old.
- **Attorney's fees**—You'll probably want an experienced real estate lawyer to take care of the complex paperwork.

These and other miscellaneous costs can add up to several thousand dollars. This cost of refinancing can be paid in cash or can be rolled into the new mortgage (in other words, you are borrowing the money for the fees) or some combination of the two. It's these costs that you must balance against the advantages of the new mortgage.

It might be helpful to look at an example. Suppose you currently owe $145,000 on your original mortgage. Interest rates have gone down, and you are considering refinancing. What will the costs be? The following are typical, but could be higher or lower depending on your precise situation.

1% origination fee	$1,450
Two points	$2,900
Appraisal	$550
Attorney	$750
Miscellaneous fees	$600
Total	**$6,250**

The result is that you will have to either borrow enough for the fees, making the new mortgage equal to $151,250 ($145,000 to pay off the old mortgage plus $6,250 for the fees), or you will have to come up with $6,250 in cash at closing.

Making a Decision

At first glance, evaluating a refinance seems simple. Compare the fees you will pay with the amount your monthly payment will go down each month. Then you can calculate the *payback period*, the number of months before you come out ahead. For example:

> Old monthly payment: $1,165.00
>
> New monthly payment: $998.00
>
> Savings: $167/month
>
> Fees: $3,600
>
> Payback = $3,600 / 167 = 22 months (approximately)

Then you can go a step further and calculate your total savings. Suppose you expect to stay in your house for at least five years. Then you have

> Payment savings = 5 years × $167 / month = $10,020
>
> Fees: $3,600
>
> Net savings: $10,020 − $3,600 = $6,420

Unfortunately, things are not quite so simple. To accurately evaluate a potential refinancing, there are several other factors to take into account.

- If you are paying the fees in cash, what would you have earned on that money if it had remained invested instead of being used for the refinancing fees?

- If you are rolling the fees into the mortgage, how will this affect your monthly payments and mortgage balance?

- If you will be paying a lower interest rate, how does this affect your tax return?

The Mortgage Refinance Breakeven Calculator takes these factors into consideration.

The Mortgage Refinance Breakeven Calculator

To refinance or not to refinance, that is the question. The Mortgage Refinance Breakeven Calculator is designed to perform the calculations to help you answer that question, and to compare different refinancing options. The calculator is shown in Figure 10.1.

This calculator is a little more complicated than some of the other ones you have seen, so let's take a detailed look at the input and output information.

In the Current Mortgage section, enter the following information:

- **Original amount**—The original principal amount of the mortgage.

- **Current balance**—The amount currently owed on the mortgage.

- **Interest rate**—The annual interest rate. If you have a variable rate mortgage, use the current rate.

New mortgage information

Current mortgage information

Figure 10.1

The Mortgage Refinance Breakeven Calculator enables you to determine if refinancing your mortgage makes financial sense.

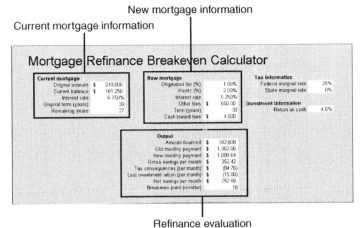

Refinance evaluation

- **Original term**—The original length of the mortgage.
- **Remaining years**—The remaining time on the mortgage, to the nearest year.

In the New Mortgage section, most of the entries are self-explanatory. Under Cash for Fees, enter the amount of cash you will be using toward the refinance fees. If the fees exceed this amount, the extra will be included in the mortgage amount. Leave this field at zero if you will not be putting any cash toward fees. If you enter an amount that is greater than the fee total, the cell displays a red background. In this case you should reduce the amount to be equal to or less than the fee total.

The Tax Information section should not need explanation. If your state does not have an income tax, enter **0** here. If you do not itemize deductions, enter **0** for both federal and state marginal rates.

The Investment Information section is relevant only if you will be putting cash toward the refinance fees rather than including these fees in the amount financed. Enter the annual percent return you would expect to get on your cash if you left it invested rather than putting it toward the refinance fees. This figure comes into play only if you enter a non-zero amount in the Cash Toward Fees field.

Now let's look at the output created by the calculator. The Amount Financed field is calculated as

(Current balance of current mortgage) + (Sum of all fees) – (Cash toward fees)

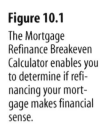

The two monthly payment fields are simply the old and new monthly mortgage payment. This is the mortgage payment alone and does not include *escrow* (insurance and taxes, which in any case should be essentially the same before and after refinancing).

The *gross savings* is simply the difference between the old and the new monthly payment.

Tax consequences are the monthly tax effects of the refinance. A negative value here means that you will be paying less interest after refinancing and will have less to deduct, resulting in a higher tax bill. A positive value means the opposite. These values are calculated based on interest that will be paid during the first year of the refinance.

Lost investment return is applicable only if you will be putting cash toward the refinance fees. It is the amount, prorated per month, you would have earned on the cash had you left it invested rather than putting it toward the refinance.

Breakeven point is the number of months it will take to recoup the cash that was put toward the refinance. It is calculated as the Cash Toward Fees amount divided by the Net Savings per Month amount. If you are not putting cash toward the fees, this field is not relevant and will display *NA*.

The Hidden Worksheet

The Mortgage Refinance Breakeven Calculator contains a hidden worksheet that is used for some background calculations. If you want to investigate how this calculator works and perhaps modify it, you can display this worksheet by selecting Format, Worksheet, Unhide.

Deducting Your Points

Technically, mortgage points are prepaid interest and are therefore deductible. If the points are rolled into the new mortgage amount, they can be amortized as a tax deduction over the life of the loan. The calculator does not take this factor into account because it is minor and will have no practical impact on your decision to refinance or not. If, however, you pay the points out-of-pocket at the time of the refinance rather than rolling them into the loan, you might be able to deduct the full amount that year. Please consult with a tax advisor for details on your specific situation.

How to Use the Calculator

There are two scenarios for using this calculator. The first one is when you are putting cash toward the refinance, as in the example shown in Figure 10.1. In this case, the breakeven point is 18 months—the mortgage payment savings will have balanced the cash you put in for fees as well as the tax and investment income consequences. After the breakeven point, the savings are money in your pocket. Be aware, however, that the savings calculated will be approximate for two reasons:

- As the mortgage is amortized, the interest portion of your payments, and hence the tax benefits, will go down.

- If you have used your monthly savings to replenish the cash used for fees, your investment loss will not be a factor anymore.

Even so, an approximate savings figure can give you a good idea of the long-term benefits of a refinancing.

If you will not be putting cash toward the fees, but rather financing them as part of the new mortgage, you use the calculator in a slightly different way. Such a scenario is shown in Figure 10.2.

Figure 10.2

When you are not putting cash toward the refinancing fees, you use the Net Savings per Month figure to evaluate the refinancing.

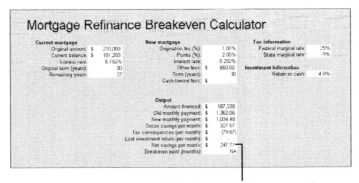

Net refinance savings per month

In this case the breakeven point is meaningless. Rather, you use the Net Savings per Month figure to evaluate the refinance. You have to balance the amount of your monthly savings against the higher principal on the new mortgage and determine if it is worthwhile for you.

What exactly do I mean by this? Lower monthly mortgage payments are great, of course, but they might be obtained at the cost of some negatives. Specifically

- You might have a higher balance on the new mortgage than you did on the old one. This means that you will have a higher amount to pay off if you sell the house, and also that you will not be able to take out as much of a home equity loan.

- Your new mortgage will be for a term of 30 years (most likely) and you might have had a much shorter period left on the old one.

The bottom line, so to speak, is that refinancing a mortgage involves many factors, some of which cannot be reduced to figures in a workbook. While the calculator presented here can help, it cannot provide all the answers.

In the next chapter we will look at another aspect of mortgages where there is the potential for the savvy homeowner to save some money—escrow accounts.

10

11

Understanding Escrow Accounts

Almost every mortgage comes with an escrow account for payment of taxes and insurance. Although an escrow account can be a convenience, it is not without its costs. This chapter explains what escrow accounts are, how they work, and how you might be able to save money by doing without one.

Escrow Is for Taxes and Insurance

An unavoidable downside of owning property is the associated *real estate taxes*. These taxes are usually assessed by the city or county, and go toward things such as public schools, police, and other municipal services. Property tax is based on the value of the property in question, and is usually expressed as the annual tax per $100 of assessed valuation. This works out the same as a straight percentage. Thus, if your assessed value is $165,000 and the tax rate is 1.05, your annual property tax will be

$165,000 \times 1.05\% = \$1,732.50$

Another unavoidable homeownership cost is *homeowner's insurance* (sometimes called *hazard insurance*). This type of insurance policy protects you against damage to your property from fire, storms, and similar dangers. Mortgage lenders require you to have homeowner's insurance because, after all, the house is collateral for the mortgage.

Your escrow account is maintained by your mortgage lender. Each month, you are required to pay into the account an amount equal approximately to 1/12 of the annual cost for taxes and insurance. This escrow payment is part of your regular monthly payment. When the tax and insurance bills come due, they are paid for you out of the escrow account.

So far this sounds pretty good. You do not have to make an effort to set the cash aside for these bills because the monthly payment is automatic. Plus, having the mortgage company pay the bills is one—or actually two—fewer things for you to remember.

Check Your Escrow Analysis

Once a year, your mortgage company will perform an escrow analysis and send you a statement with the results. This analysis looks at the balance in the account, the anticipated payments for insurance and taxes that will be made over the next year, and then adjusts your monthly escrow payment up or (rarely) down accordingly. It's worthwhile to spend a few moments looking this statement over. Mortgage companies have been known to make errors and—guess what—they are never in the customer's favor!

But there's a cost for this convenience. You do not receive any interest on the balance in your escrow account, and this can add up to an escrow balance of a couple of thousand dollars or more over the course of a year. Wouldn't you rather be earning interest on that money rather than letting the bank do so? If you have the discipline to set aside money each month in a savings or other interest-paying account for your taxes and insurance, why have an escrow account at all?

How much can you save? To be honest, we are not talking about big bucks here, but part of the discipline of taking charge of your finances is to plug all the little leaks of money, as well as the big ones. Suppose your house is assessed at $350,000 and that the property tax rate is 1.5%. That means you pay $5,250 in taxes each year. Suppose your homeowner's insurance is an additional $1,500 per year. This makes a total of $6,750 that you will put into escrow each year. If you can earn a 2.5% annual rate on this, assuming you put 1/12 aside each month, it will amount to about $85 a year in interest. No, not a fortune, but enough for dinner for two at a pretty nice restaurant!

Escrow Does Not Calculate?

In theory, your monthly escrow payment should be 1/12 of the combined total for taxes and insurance. Some people are surprised to find that it is significantly more. This is because some mortgage contracts require that you maintain a surplus in your escrow account. This is just another one of the nasty ways that mortgage companies put the squeeze on their customers. This makes the appeal of canceling your escrow account even greater.

Canceling Your Escrow Account

In theory, you should be able to cancel your escrow account at any time. The money in it will be returned to you, your monthly payment will decrease by the amount of the escrow payment, and you'll have to pay the tax and insurance bills when they come due. In the meanwhile, your money will be earning interest for you.

Unfortunately, it is not always that easy. Banks are well aware that escrow accounts are a source of profit for them. After all, your money and the money of thousands of other mortgage holders, on which they are paying no interest, can be lent out to earn interest for the banks. As a result, many mortgage contracts specify that you cannot cancel your escrow account without paying a fee, and sometimes the fee is quite hefty. You need to check with your mortgage lender to determine the relevant terms for your mortgage. If your mortgage is through a bank with which you have other dealings, you might have more leverage for convincing it to let you cancel the escrow account.

The Escrow Cancellation Calculator

If you are considering canceling your escrow account, you can use the Escrow Cancellation Calculator to determine exactly what the financial benefits will be. If your bank charges a fee for cancellation, you can take that into account as well and determine how long the financial benefits of managing your own insurance and tax payments will take to balance the payment.

The calculator is shown in Figure 11.1.

11

Figure 11.1

The Escrow Cancellation Calculator lets you determine the benefits of closing your escrow account.

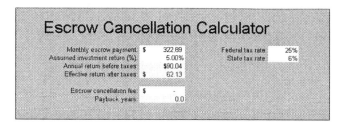

The calculator assumes that you will take your monthly escrow payment and, each and every month, put it in a savings or other account that earns the specified return (assumed investment return). Because you usually have to pay income tax on investment returns, enter your marginal tax brackets in cells E4 and E5. If, however, you plan to put the money in a nontaxable account or investment, such as one that invests in municipal bonds, enter **0** for both tax rates.

The Effective Return After Taxes figure is the annual net benefit you will gain from canceling your escrow account and investing it as described here. If you have to pay a fee for cancellation, enter it in cell C9 and see how many years it will take for payback in cell C10.

You might be underwhelmed by the results of using this calculator. That is to say, the dollar benefits of canceling your escrow account are usually rather modest. You might decide that it is not worth the bother, particularly if there is a fee involved. But if you can do it without paying a stiff fee, it's worth considering. Looking at the example in Figure 11.1, I consider $62 dollars to be a pretty good return for writing a couple of checks each year!

In the next chapter we will examine a question that many people face—whether to continue renting your home or whether to take the plunge and buy a house.

11

12

Renting Versus Buying Your Home—Making the Right Choice

Many people follow a similar course in life—they start out renting an apartment or house and then at some point take the plunge and purchase their own place. This is a major decision and there are many factors involved, not all of them financial. But for those considerations that do involve dollars and cents, you should be well-informed and have the tools at hand to help you make a decision. That's the goal of this chapter.

Why Buy a Home?

There are many factors to consider when deciding to buy a home. Some of these factors are psychological. There's no doubt that it can be very satisfying to have your own place to decorate as you see fit without the hassles of landlords and leases. As long as you keep up on your payments, no one can make you leave. Pride of ownership definitely plays a role!

More relevant to this chapter, however, are the practical aspects of home ownership versus renting. There are many financial factors to consider. For many people considering their first home purchase, money is most definitely an issue. You are likely to be at an early stage in your career and not making a great salary. You might be just starting a family, with all the expenses that entails. What it boils down to for many people is the simple question, "Can I afford to buy a house?"

All About Mortgages

Buying a house almost always involves a mortgage. You'll find more information about mortgages and choosing the best one in Chapter 8, "Understanding Mortgages—And Getting the One That's Best for You."

When you are renting, you pay your monthly rent and basically that's it—although you might buy renter's insurance for your belongings. There are no maintenance costs to worry about because the landlord takes care of it. But after you pay the rent, it is gone forever. You are not building up equity in something you own.

When you own your home, part of each monthly payment goes to build up equity in the house (by reducing the balance owed on the mortgage). There's also the possibility that the home itself will increase in value due to real estate trends in your area. After a few years you will likely have built up a nice bit of equity in your house. This equity will be profit in your pocket when you sell the house, and can also be used to get a home equity line of credit for major expenses such as home improvements (see Chapter 9, "Considering Home Equity Loans," for more information on home equity loans).

Financial Factors of Home Ownership

There are a lot of financial details involved in buying and owning a home. They are all relevant when you are trying to decide whether buying is right for you at a particular time.

At Least Three Years

Real estate professionals generally advise that you consider home ownership only if you plan to stay in the house for at least three years. This is because it usually takes about three years to establish enough equity in the house to offset the extra costs of buying the house and getting a mortgage.

First of all, there are the expenses of the purchase itself. You need a down payment to buy a home, and that's a significant chunk of cash. Then there are the expenses of ownership itself. Your monthly payment is highly unlikely to be less than your rent, and there are other expenses that renters usually do not have to pay, such as repairs, maintenance, landscaping, and so on. Let's look at these factors.

The Down Payment

Ideally, you should place a down payment of at least 20% of the purchase price when buying a house. There are two reasons for this:

- You are likely to get more favorable mortgage terms.
- You can avoid paying for private mortgage insurance, or PMI, which is required when the mortgage amount is more than 80% of the house value.

If you cannot come up with a 20% down payment, it does not mean you are shut out of the market. Many lenders will give mortgages with down payments of 10% and even less, but it will cost more. It still might be well worth it, however, to become a home owner.

Sources for Down Payment Funds

If you cannot come up with the down payment yourself, perhaps you can get a loan from a family member. You should avoid the temptation to take cash advances on your credit cards. Given the high interest rates charged, this is all too likely to lead to serious financial binds down the road. If you have trouble with the down payment, you might want to set your sights on a less-costly house or perhaps wait for another year to allow yourself to put more savings away. Be aware, however, that many lenders require you to sign an affirmation that you have not borrowed any of the down payment funds, including loans from family members.

Closing Costs

The term *closing* refers to the legal transaction that actually transfers ownership of the house to you. There are numerous one-time costs involved. They include

- Attorney's fees
- Appraisal fee

12

- House inspection fee
- Deed registration fee
- Prorated property taxes

This list is not exhaustive. Depending on your locality, various other costs might apply, such as a termite inspection and state or local transfer taxes. All applicable fees should be disclosed in the good-faith estimate of closing costs provided by your mortgage broker.

Depending on your specific situation, some of these costs might be rolled into the mortgage amount and others might be paid by the seller. When evaluating a home purchase, you need to find out how much these fees will be and which ones you are responsible for.

Ownership Costs

After you have made the purchase, gotten a mortgage, and moved in, there are costs of home ownership that you did not face as a renter. The two major ones are property taxes and hazard insurance. As I have explained elsewhere (see Chapter 11, "Understanding Escrow Accounts"), the payments for these are rolled into your monthly payment and go into your escrow account. In other words, your monthly payment goes partly for paying back the mortgage and partly for escrow. Escrow can make up 20%–30% of your monthly payment, so it is a significant part of the expense of buying a home.

Other expenses are more difficult to predict. If you are moving from an apartment to a house, your utility bills will probably be higher. You can ask the sellers to give you some idea of what the utilities run each month, or the utility company might provide you with average costs for homes of a particular size. Even though your usage will be different, at least you will not be completely in the dark.

What about appliances? Will the house come with a stove, refrigerator, dishwasher, and the other appliances you want? If not, there are those expenses to consider.

Upkeep is something that comes as a nasty surprise to many first-time homeowners. If you bought a brand new house, it will be less of a concern, of course, but eventually any house will need a new roof, painting, a replacement furnace, and so on.

Although it is impossible to predict all the costs of home ownership, there are some you can judge accurately. With this information, you can perform a comparison between the financial consequences of continuing to rent versus buying a house.

The Rent Versus Buy Calculator

The Rent versus Buy Calculator is designed to help you with the financial aspects of deciding whether to buy a house or continue renting. As I have mentioned earlier in this chapter, you cannot predict all the costs of home ownership, but the calculator takes into account those that are predictable. The input worksheet of the calculator is shown in Figure 12.1.

Figure 12.1

The Rent versus Buy Calculator enables you to evaluate the financial considerations when deciding to buy a house or continue renting.

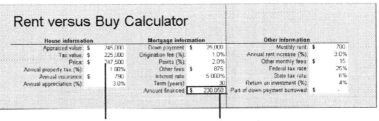

Purchase price of house   Amount financed

This workbook has three worksheets. The first one, shown in Figure 12.1, is for input. You must enter information for three sections.

In the House Information section, you need to enter the following:

- **Appraised value**—The appraised market value of the house.
- **Tax value**—The assessed tax value of the house. This might be the same as the appraised value, but in many localities it is not (it is usually lower).
- **Price**—The selling price of the house.
- **Annual property tax**—The property tax rate as a percentage of the tax value.
- **Annual insurance**—The amount that hazard insurance will cost per year.
- **Annual appreciation**—The estimate of how much the house's appraised value will increase per year. Your real estate agent can give you some idea of the recent appreciation for houses in your area. This percentage is applied to both the appraised value and the tax value.

12

Appreciation—Be Realistic

Many areas of the country have experienced short- or long-term bursts in real estate appreciation, with values going up at a rapid rate for years on end. This has been a bonus for property owners and a negative for would-be buyers. But are such rates sustainable? Only the future will tell—but for now, you should be careful about using unrealistically high appreciation rates in your calculations. Just because those rates occurred in the past is no guarantee they will continue.

The Mortgage Information section is self-explanatory. The Amount Financed figure is calculated as (house price) + (origination fee) + (points) + (other fees) – (down payment).

Most of the items in the Other Information section are also self-explanatory, except for these:

- **Annual rent increase**—The amount you estimate your rent will increase each year.

- **Other monthly fees**—Amounts you pay monthly for renter's insurance, clubhouse membership, and the like.

- **Return on investment**—The amount you would earn if the down payment cash remained invested instead of being used for a house purchase.

- **Part of down payment borrowed**—If any of the down payment is borrowed, enter the amount here.

The second worksheet, named Output, is where the results are displayed. This worksheet is shown in Figure 12.2. Let's take a look at the results that are displayed here and how the calculator comes up with its results.

The output consists of data on a month-by-month basis for 10 years. Most of the output information is in the Buying section. Some of these numbers are not, strictly speaking, relevant to the rent versus buy question, but they might be of interest to you anyway. They are

- **PITI payment**—This is your total monthly payment for principal, interest, taxes, and insurance. It increases every 12 months because the tax value of the house, and hence the taxes you owe, go up each year.

- **PI payment**—This is the portion of the payment that is for the principal and interest; in other words, the mortgage payment proper. It remains constant.

12

Figure 12.2

The Output worksheet of the Rent versus Buy Calculator displays detailed information on the two scenarios.

Equity if buying   Equity if renting

	Buying							Renting	
Month	PITI Payment	PI Payment	Principal	Interest	Effective PITI Payment	Balance	Equity	Rent Payment	Equity
1	$1,488.29	$1,234.96	$276.42	$958.54	$ 1,191.14	$229,774	[illegible]	$ 715.00	$ 25,000
2	$1,488.29	$1,234.96	$277.57	$957.39	$ 1,191.50	$229,496	[illegible]	$ 715.00	$ 25,560
3	$1,488.29	$1,234.96	$278.72	$956.23	$ 1,191.86	$229,217	[illegible]	$ 715.00	$ 26,122
4	$1,488.29	$1,234.96	$279.89	$955.07	$ 1,192.22	$228,937	[illegible]	$ 715.00	$ 26,686
5	$1,488.29	$1,234.96	$281.05	$953.91	$ 1,192.58	$228,656	[illegible]	$ 715.00	$ 27,253
6	$1,488.29	$1,234.96	$282.22	$952.73	$ 1,192.94	$228,374	[illegible]	$ 715.00	$ 27,822
7	$1,488.29	$1,234.96	$283.40	$951.56	$ 1,193.31	$228,091	[illegible]	$ 715.00	$ 28,393
8	$1,488.29	$1,234.96	$284.58	$950.38	$ 1,193.67	$227,806	$21,514	$ 715.00	$ 28,966
9	$1,488.29	$1,234.96	$285.77	$949.19	$ 1,194.04	$227,520	[illegible]	$ 715.00	$ 29,541
10	$1,488.29	$1,234.96	$286.96	$948.00	$ 1,194.41	$227,233	[illegible]	$ 715.00	$ 30,119
11	$1,488.29	$1,234.96	$288.15	$946.81	$ 1,194.78	$226,945	[illegible]	$ 715.00	$ 30,700
12	$1,488.29	$1,234.96	$289.35	$945.61	$ 1,195.15	$226,656	[illegible]	$ 715.00	$ 31,282
13	$1,493.92	$1,234.96	$290.56	$944.40	$ 1,201.15	$226,365	[illegible]	$ 736.00	$ 31,851
14	$1,493.92	$1,234.96	$291.77	$943.19	$ 1,201.53	$226,074	[illegible]	$ 736.00	$ 32,423
15	$1,493.92	$1,234.96	$292.98	$941.97	$ 1,201.90	$225,781	[illegible]	$ 736.00	$ 32,997
16	$1,493.92	$1,234.96	$294.21	$940.75	$ 1,202.38	$225,486	[illegible]	$ 736.00	$ 33,573
17	$1,493.92	$1,234.96	$295.43	$939.53	$ 1,202.66	$225,191	[illegible]	$ 736.00	$ 34,152
18	$1,493.92	$1,234.96	$296.66	$938.30	$ 1,203.04	$224,894	[illegible]	$ 736.00	$ 34,733
19	$1,493.92	$1,234.96	$297.90	$937.06	$ 1,203.43	$224,596	[illegible]	$ 736.00	$ 35,316
20	$1,493.92	$1,234.96	$299.14	$935.82	$ 1,203.81	$224,297	[illegible]	$ 736.00	$ 35,902
21	$1,493.92	$1,234.96	$300.39	$934.57	$ 1,204.20	$223,997	[illegible]	$ 736.00	$ 36,489
22	$1,493.92	$1,234.96	$301.64	$933.32	$ 1,204.59	$223,695	$34,484	$ 736.00	$ 37,080
23	$1,493.92	$1,234.96	$302.89	$932.06	$ 1,204.98	$223,392	[illegible]	$ 736.00	$ 37,672
24	$1,493.92	$1,234.96	$304.16	$930.80	$ 1,205.37	$223,088	[illegible]	$ 736.00	$ 38,267
25	$1,499.71	$1,234.96	$305.42	$929.53	$ 1,211.55	$222,783	[illegible]	$ 757.63	$ 38,849
26	$1,499.71	$1,234.96	$306.70	$928.26	$ 1,211.95	$222,476	[illegible]	$ 767.63	$ 39,432
27	$1,499.71	$1,234.96	$307.97	$926.98	$ 1,212.35	$222,168	[illegible]	$ 757.63	$ 40,019
28	$1,499.71	$1,234.96	$309.26	$926.70	$ 1,212.74	$221,859	[illegible]	$ 757.63	$ 40,607
29	$1,499.71	$1,234.96	$310.55	$924.41	$ 1,213.14	$221,548	[illegible]	$ 757.63	$ 41,198

- **Principal**—The amount of the PI payment that goes toward the principal.
- **Interest**—The amount of the PI payment that is interest.
- **Effective PITI Payment**—The PITI payment reduced by the amount of tax savings you realize from deducting your interest payments.
- **Balance**—The amount owed on the mortgage after that month's payment. It is the previous month's balance minus the current principal payment.
- **Equity**—The appraised value of the house minus the mortgage balance.

The Renting section has only two columns of output:

- **Rent Payment**—The rent payment for that month, including any fees such as renter's insurance.
- **Equity**—The value of your investment. This assumes that you invest the cash that would have gone for the house down payment (the unborrowed portion) and then add, each month, the difference between your rent payment and the effective PITI payment you would be paying if you had bought a house.

You might note that the Output worksheet has five hidden columns, O through S. These are used for the results of intermediate calculations and for creating the chart, but are of no interest themselves.

Finally, the third worksheet, named Chart, presents a graph of the equity values from the Output worksheet. This chart is shown in Figure 12.3. When you enter new information on the Rent versus Buy worksheet, you must switch to the Chart worksheet to see the new graphical results.

Figure 12.3

The Chart worksheet displays a graphical representation of the renting and buying equity values.

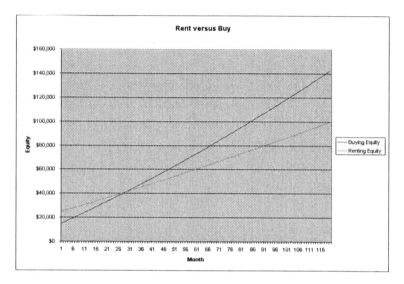

Now let's look at the logic behind the calculations. For continuing to rent, it is assumed that the money you would have used for a down payment (the part that was not borrowed) remains invested, and that the difference between the mortgage payment (with tax benefits taken into consideration) and the rent payment, assuming the former is larger, is also invested. This amount grows over time, of course.

For buying, your equity is simply the difference between the appraised value of the house and the balance owed on the mortgage.

Tax Value Versus Appraised Value

The Rent versus Buy Calculator handles tax value and appraised value slightly differently. Both are assumed to go up annually by the amount you enter in the Annual Appreciation cell. However, the calculations apply this increase to the appraised value on a monthly basis (1/12 of the annual appreciation, of course) and to the tax value on a yearly basis. This is because reevaluations of tax value and a corresponding increase in your property tax are done on at most a yearly basis, and often less frequently than that.

12

The breakeven point is the month at which the buying equity exceeds the renting equity. In other words, this is how long it will take you come out ahead financially if you buy a house. The Output worksheet uses conditional formatting so that the Buying Equity value is displayed in red if it is less than the Renting equity, and in black if it is more. This is not visible in the figure, but when you are using the workbook, all you need to do is look down the Buying Equity column to find the first value that is not red. That month marks your breakeven point.

Remember, given all the uncertainty about expenses when buying a house, this calculator can at best give you a ballpark answer. You also have to take the emotional factors into consideration when making your decision. In addition, the calculator does not take private mortgage insurance (PMI) into account, and this will increase your mortgage payments if your down payment is less than 20% of the purchase price.

This is the final chapter dealing with home buying. The next chapter looks at what is often a person's second largest purchase after a home— a car.

12

13

Your New Car— Lease or Buy?

For most people, a car is a necessity. And let's face it, there's something quite satisfying about having a shiny, brand-new car. But when it comes time to finally trade in the old clunker, getting the best deal on your new wheels is an important consideration. The most important question is whether you should lease your new car or buy it outright. This chapter will help you find the answer.

Do You Really Need a New Car?

In your quest to take charge of your finances, this is the first question you should ask yourself. A new car is a major purchase and will put you into debt for several years, at least. It's easy to get excited about a new car, and people can come up with all sorts of justifications for the purchase:

- I deserve it.
- My old car isn't reliable.
- I should buy now before prices or interest rates go up.
- My friends all have new cars.
- New cars are safer than old cars.
- It will help my image at work.
- New cars sure smell good!

But if you are struggling to pay down your credit card debt or trying to save the down payment for a house, buying a new car might not be a wise move. Maybe keeping your current car for a few more years is possible—maintenance costs are very unlikely to come anywhere near the payments on a new car. Or perhaps a used car makes more sense. Remember, cars depreciate fastest in the first couple of years, so you can get a used car with 75% of its life left for a lot less than 75% of the new price.

Understanding Auto Leases

Leases are appealing to many people because the monthly payment and down payment are almost always less than if you were buying the same car. But remember, there's no free lunch, and you need to understand how a lease differs from the purchase of a car.

In the simplest terms, here's how a lease works:

1. The dealer sells the car to a leasing company. This occurs behind the scenes and you might not even be aware that this is being done as part of your transaction.

2. You make monthly lease payments to the leasing company for the duration of the lease.

3. At the end of the lease period, the car is returned to the leasing company that then sells it on the used car market. The value of the car at the end of the lease is called the *residual value*.

You can see that the payments you make plus the sales price for the used car must equal the price of the new car plus the leasing company's profit. This leads to the seemingly paradoxical situation where more desirable cars—those with higher resale value—are usually cheaper to lease than less desirable cars. Let's see how this might work.

Consider first car A, a popular model in high demand. Suppose it sells new for $22,000 and when 3 years old has a value of $14,500. It will depreciate by $7,500 over 3 years, resulting in a monthly lease payment of about $210.

A Lease Is a Kind of Loan

It might be easier to get a handle on auto leases if you realize they are nothing more than a special kind of loan. The leasing company is loaning you the car. You pay back the loan in two ways, with the monthly lease payments and by returning the car at the end of the lease period. During the term of the loan—the term of the lease—you pay a finance fee, or interest, on the loan.

13

Car B, however, is not so popular. While it too sells new for $22,000, after 3 years it has depreciated to a value of $10,000. The depreciation of $12,000 means a monthly payment of about $330.

These examples are highly simplified, but they get the point across that the cost of a lease depends on more than the new price of the car alone.

Advantages and Disadvantages of Leasing

There's no doubt that leases offer some advantages. Otherwise, they would not be as popular as they are. Let's take a look at them:

- **Lower payments**—Because lease payments cover only part of the car's value, they are almost always lower—sometimes a lot lower—than the loan payments you would have for buying the same car. This means you can get a nicer car for the same payments, or have lower payments on the same car.

- **Lower upfront costs**—Leases almost always have lower upfront costs than an outright purchase. If you are short of ready cash, this can be a plus.

- **Easy disposition**—At the end of the lease, you can simply walk away. There are no worries about selling the car.

- **Sales tax**—In most states, sales tax is charged on the down payment you make and on each monthly lease payment. This can be a lot less than paying tax on the entire purchase price when buying a car.

Lease Payments—Not Always Lower?

Lease payments are always lower than purchase payments if you finance the car over the same period as the lease. But car dealers are offering longer and longer terms on car loans, as long as five or six years in some cases. If you buy a car on these terms, you might be able to get payments as low as leasing—over a longer period, of course.

There's another side to the coin, of course. Leases have disadvantages as well.

Perhaps the most serious one is when early termination is required. This happens if the car is stolen or you have an accident and the car is totaled. You will find there is a significant gap between what you will receive from insurance and what you have to pay to the leasing company.

Why does this gap exist? Figure 13.1 shows what happens for a hypothetical example where the capital cost of the car is $22,000 and the residual after 3 years is $14,000. As you make your regular lease payments, the amount owed on the car—the amount you are responsible for in event of theft or accident—decreases in a straight line. However, the actual value of the car—the amount the insurance company will pay you—does not depreciate in a straight line but is fastest at the beginning.

Figure 13.1

Early lease termination often results in your being stuck with the value gap.

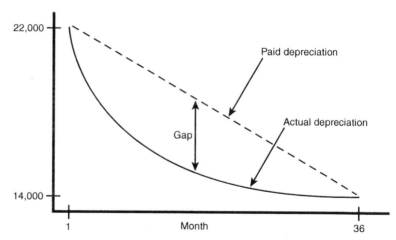

Consider what might occur if thieves steal the car about halfway through the lease payment. The car is worth $16,500 at that point (shown by the curved line in Figure 13.1) but you've paid the depreciation down only to $18,000 (shown by the broken line in Figure 13.1). A gap remains of $1,500 between what the car is worth and what you've paid for the car.

Some lease companies offer special gap insurance for an extra fee, so you won't have to worry about covering the gap if anything occurs. That gap insurance, however, adds more cost to your lease.

Leases can make early termination even more unpleasant. Some require full payment of all remaining payments. Others impose hefty fees if you want to end the lease before the original termination date.

Insurance is another area to consider. Because the car is actually owned by the leasing company, they want you to insure the car well. The leasing company might require higher insurance levels than you would take out on a car you purchased and you must factor this extra insurance cost into your overall lease cost.

Types of Leases

Auto leases fall into two broad categories, depending on how the residual car value is handled.

The most common type of lease is the closed-end lease. In a *closed-end lease*, the residual value of the car is determined at the start of the lease. At the end of the lease, you can buy the car for this amount or you can just return the car to the dealer and walk away.

An *open-end lease* is less common, and is used mostly for commercial rather than consumer leases. At the start of the lease, the residual value of the car is estimated. At the end of the lease, this estimate is compared with the actual market value of the car and, if the actual value is lower than the estimate value, you must pay the difference.

Lease Conditions

Auto leases always come with conditions. The most important one is a mileage limitation. If you drive the car more than a certain number of miles, such as 15,000 per year, you will be charged an excess mileage fee at the end of the lease. This fee might be 15 cents a mile. It's important to understand the mileage limitations on a lease and how they relate to your driving habits. Having to pay a hefty excess mileage fee at the end of the lease can negate any financial advantages.

The other thing that leases always spell out is the condition of the car when the lease is over. Obviously the dealer does not want to take back a car that is scratched and dented with torn upholstery at the end of the lease! You are expected to keep the car in good condition (including regular maintenance) and you must pay for any problems that are found at the end of the lease. Check the fine print in the lease to make sure it does not include an unreasonable definition of good condition.

Lease Payment Calculator

Calculating the payments on a lease is not too difficult after you know what is involved. The ability to calculate your expected lease payment can be a valuable tool for verifying the dealer's quoted payment. If your quoted payment is greater than your calculated payment, you need to ask why. There might be extra fees involved that you were not told about. It is also not unheard of for dealers to make "mistakes," always in their favor, of course.

First you need to understand some terminology used in leasing.

- **Capital cost**—The price of the vehicle. You can negotiate this with the dealer just as if you were making a purchase.

- **Capital cost reduction**—Extra cash you pay at lease signing to reduce the capital cost of the car. This works as a down payment and is not required for most leases. Capital cost reduction can come from your old vehicle's trade-in value also.

- **Net capital cost**—The price at which the dealer sells the vehicle to the leasing company. This cost equals the capital cost less capital cost reduction.

- **Residual**—The value of the car at the end of the lease.

- **Finance fee**—The interest rate of the lease.

- **Money factor**—The way the finance fee is usually expressed in lease agreements. The money factor equals 1/24 of the interest rate. Therefore, a money factor of 0.00375 is equal to an interest rate of 9% ($0.00375 \times 24 = 0.09$ or 9%).

Your monthly lease payment consists of two parts: depreciation and finance charge. Depreciation is calculated as follows:

(Net capital cost – residual) / term in months

The finance charge is the sum of the net capital cost and residual multiplied by the money factor. I know this seems counterintuitive—wouldn't you subtract the residual rather than adding it? No, this is correct because of the way the money factor operates to adjust the finance fee.

The third and final component of your lease payment is sales tax that, of course, varies from place to place.

The Lease Payment Calculator is shown in Figure 13.2. To use the calculator, you will have to get certain information from the dealer, such as the capital cost for the car you are interested in, the value of your trade-in (if any), and the money factor. Then you can use the result of the calculator to verify that the lease payment quoted by the dealer is accurate.

Figure 13.2
Calculating the monthly payment on an auto lease.

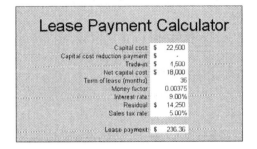

Remember that the payment quoted to you by your dealer might include other fees. You must compare the result provided by the calculator to the lease payment itself, which might be less than the actual monthly payment.

The Lease or Buy Calculator

Knowing the payment on a lease is important, but it might not be enough to decide whether you should lease or buy your next car. As with any major financial decision, there will be emotional factors involved, and Excel cannot help with that! Even restricting consideration to financial matters, it's not always clear which factors are important.

For example, if you lease a car, you will almost surely have lower monthly payments than if you bought the same car outright. The money you save each month can be saved toward a house purchase, invested, or just used for day-to-day expenses. But at the end of the lease, you are suddenly without a car and are faced with the same decision again: Do you lease or purchase?

In terms of the long-term financial picture, it is always best to buy a car and drive it for its entire useful life. Few people do that, however. Because there is no definitive answer to the "lease or buy" question, all you can do is to examine the relevant financial details and make a decision based on your specific situation. If you're likely to stay with the same car for many years, you'll almost always be better off purchasing the car than leasing it. Still, you must compare the financial specifics of each situation. That's what the Lease or Buy Calculator helps you to do.

The calculator lets you enter information for either buying or leasing a car. It's the same car in both cases with the same purchase price. Then the calculator evaluates the situation you'll be in, lease or buy, at the end of the lease period. Your purchase loan is assumed to be the same term as the lease. The calculator is shown in Figure 13.3.

Figure 13.3

Comparing leasing a car to buying.

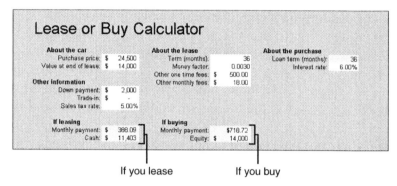

Now let's look at the input information required. In the About the Car section, you enter the price of the car (purchase price if buying or capital cost if leasing, which should be the same) and the residual value, or the value of the car at the end of the lease period.

In the About the Lease section, you enter the term and money factor. Use the Other One Time Fees field for things such as a security deposit you must pay at the lease signing. The Other Monthly Fees field is for additions to the monthly fee, such as gap insurance.

In the About the Purchase section, you enter the interest rate you would get on a car loan. The term is assumed to be the same as the lease and is automatically copied from that section.

The Other Information section enables you to enter a down payment and trade-in value (which would be applied as capital cost reduction in the case of a lease). You also enter the local sales tax rate that is applied to the lease payments and to the purchase price.

The Output section calculates your monthly payment, both for a purchase and for a lease. For leasing, the Cash field is the sum of the cash you would have at the end of the lease period if you saved the difference between the purchasing monthly payment and the leasing monthly payment for the entire lease duration (less the One Time Fees amount). For buying, the Equity field is simply the residual value of the car at the end of the lease or purchase loan period. Of course, the actual value of the car at this time might be more or less than the residual, depending on its condition and other factors.

How do you evaluate the results this calculator displays? Looking at the figures in Figure 13.3:

- If you lease, your monthly payment is approximately $330 less than if you buy (Cell E14 minus cell C14). If you put this savings aside each month, you will have accumulated about $11,400 by the end of the lease period. However, you will have no car.
- If you buy, you have a much higher monthly payment. However, at the end of 36 months you will own, free and clear, a car that is worth $14,000.

Based on the numbers alone, it appears the purchase is better in this situation. How you interpret the results, however, depends on your specific situation. In the long term, buying is clearly better here because you will come out more than $3,000 ahead after 36 months. But if you cannot afford the higher monthly payments required for purchasing, leasing might be the better short-term option for you.

In the next chapter we tackle an increasingly important topic—investments. More and more people are investing these days rather than just saving. You need to know the fundamentals if you are going to plan your investments intelligently.

PART

IV

Managing Your Investments

14

Learning the Fundamentals of Investing

Investing is a topic that more and more of us need to know about. Fewer people are satisfied with savings accounts and their low interest rates, and a greater proportion are getting into mutual fund and stock investing. This chapter provides some background information about the world of investing.

Investment Vehicles

No, I am inot talking about cars and trucks! An *investment vehicle* is simply something you invest your money in. It helps to understand what's available before starting to think about how you will invest your money. This section provides information on the most common investment vehicles. There are certainly other ways to invest your money, such as real estate, but they are beyond the scope of this chapter.

Stocks

Stocks are bought and sold on the stock market, and everyone has heard of that! A share of stock represents an ownership stake in a company. As the value of the company goes up or down, the price of the stock shares goes up or down as well. The value of a company in this context is not a literal calculated value but a perceived value. For example:

- A small company might have an idea for a great new product or service. The stock market—meaning the collective opinion of all the people who are invested in stocks—thinks that this product will lead to huge increases in sales and profits in a few years. The perceived value of the company goes up and the stock price increases along with it.

- An old established company might have been doing business the same way for decades. The market feels that it will soon be overtaken by competitors who have new and better ideas. The perceived value goes down, along with the stock price.

Stocks are a very popular investment for one very good reason. Historically, stocks have provided the best return on investment. This does not mean that every stock is a winner, of course. But averaged over many years, the market as a whole has consistently beaten all other forms of investment.

The Importance of Diversification

Financial experts are essentially unanimous in agreeing that diversification is an important principal of stock investing. This is just another way of saying "don't put all your eggs in one basket." You should not concentrate your investments in a single stock or even in a single sector (for example, oil stocks or automotive stocks). Of course, it is difficult to achieve much diversification when you are just getting started in stocks and can purchase stocks in, at most, one or two different companies. For this reason, many people start out investing in mutual funds, with their built-in diversification, and then start moving into stocks when their portfolio has grown a bit.

Some stocks pay *dividends*, a cash payment of a certain amount per share. Dividends might be paid quarterly, biannually, or annually. Dividends are a way for the management to return part of the company's profits to the shareholders—who, after all, are the owners of the company. Dividends can change from year to year and tend to be in the range of 1%–5% of the share value. Generally speaking, older, established companies and companies in certain areas, such as banking, pharmaceuticals, and oil, tend to pay dividends while smaller and newer companies do not. Companies that do not pay dividends are retaining all their profits to help with future growth.

Buying and Selling Stock

To invest in stocks, you usually need an account at a brokerage. When you buy or sell a stock, you pay a commission. This can range from $10 or lower at discount brokerages to more than $100 per transaction at full-service brokerages. Please see the section "Choosing a Brokerage Account" later in this chapter for more information.

You must remember, however, that stocks can and often do lose value. This is why they are generally considered best for long-term investments. See the section "Your Investment Timeframe" later in this chapter for more information.

Bonds

When you invest in a bond, you are in effect loaning money to a company or government agency. When a bond is issued, it has two important characteristics:

- A maturity date, the date at which the loan will be paid back to the bond holder.
- An interest rate, sometimes called the *coupon*, which is the amount of interest paid to the bond holder. Most bonds have a fixed interest rate and others have variable rates.

When you own a bond, you receive regular interest payments, usually quarterly or semi-annually. If the bond matures while you own it, you receive a payment equal to the bond's face value, ending the loan.

Bonds are usually issued in increments of $1,000. If you buy a bond when it is first issued, you'll pay face value. After a bond has been issued, however, it trades on the bond market and the price can go up or down.

It's important to realize that there is an indirect correlation between a bond's price and its effective interest rate. To illustrate, consider a $1,000 bond issued with a 6% coupon. This means that the bond pays 6% of $1,000 or $60 interest per year.

Suppose the bond price drops to $800. It still pays $60/year, so the effective interest rate is now 60 / 800 = 7.5%. If, on the other hand, the price rises to $1,100, the effective rate drops to 5.45%.

Municipal Versus Corporate Bonds

Some bonds are issued by corporations and are called *corporate bonds*. Corporations will issue bonds to finance expansion, product research, and the like. Other bonds are issued by governmental bodies, such as cities and states, and are used to fund public works, such as highways and schools. These municipal bonds tend to pay a lower interest rate than corporate bonds, but the interest you earn can be tax-exempt in most cases.

A different kind of bond than what I have been describing is the *zero coupon bond*. As the name suggests, this kind of bond does not pay interest on a regular basis. Rather, it is sold at a discount to its face value. For example, a $1,000 zero coupon bond with a 10-year maturity might initially sell for $625. At maturity you will receive the face value, $1,000. The effective interest rate in this situation is approximately 4.75%. Zero coupon bonds naturally increase in value over time because they are getting closer to their maturity date. For example, the same bond just described would, after 5 years, be worth about $790.

Mutual Funds

Mutual funds have become far and away the most popular investment vehicle for most people. There's good reason for this. Let's see how mutual funds work.

A *mutual fund* pools the money from a number of investors and buys a portfolio of stocks and/or bonds. As the value of the portfolio goes up or down, so does the value of your shares in the fund. There are two primary advantages of mutual funds over owning individual stocks and bonds:

- **Diversification**—A mutual fund can diversify its investments in a way few individual investors can.
- **Management**—Most mutual funds are managed by a professional money manager who can keep abreast of market news and trends in a way few nonprofessionals can.

The most important downside of mutual funds is the fees involved. The mutual fund management company charges a fee, usually expressed as a percentage of the fund's total value, to cover their expenses and profits. This fee can range from less than 0.5% per year for some very efficient funds to as much as 2% or 2.5%. As a result, when the stocks in the fund go up, the shares of the fund will go up less, and when the stocks in the fund go down, the shares of the fund will go down more. Some funds also charge a *load*, a sales commission you pay when you buy the fund (a *front-end load*) or when you sell it (a *back-end load*). Even so, the advantages of mutual funds outweigh the impact of these fees—at least millions of investors seem to think so.

Most mutual funds are sold directly to investors by the management company. In almost every case, the company offers an entire family of funds designed to various investment goals. Some of the largest mutual fund families are Fidelity, Vanguard, American Century, and Dreyfus. (I am not endorsing these fund families, just mentioning them!) There can be advantages to investing with a fund family, such as a single statement and the ability in some cases to move money from one fund to another in the same family without incurring load fees.

You can also buy most mutual funds in a brokerage account. Usually there are no extra fees beyond what the fund itself charges.

Types of Mutual Funds

Most mutual funds are *open-ended funds*. These funds grow and shrink with demand. If more investors are buying shares in the fund, the fund buys more stocks. If people are redeeming (selling) their fund shares, the fund sells stocks. The *net asset value (NAV)* of the fund is simply the total value of all the stocks and other investments the fund owns divided by the number of fund shares outstanding.

A smaller number of mutual funds are *closed-end funds*. These funds decide at the beginning how many fund shares they will issue. After these shares have been sold to the fund's initial investors, no more shares are created. The existing shares trade on the stock market just like shares of stock. The NAV of a closed-end fund is calculated the same way as for an open-ended fund. The selling price of the shares might be more or less than the NAV, depending on how the market views the investments the fund holds.

Mutual Fund Investment Strategies

Each mutual fund has a specified investment strategy. When you are shopping for a mutual fund, look for a fund with a strategy that matches your investment philosophy and goals. There are so many different strategies that it can become quite confusing. Let's try to sort this out a bit.

Funds might direct their investments according to the size of the companies whose stock they buy. A company's size is usually measured as its *market capitalization*, the number of shares outstanding multiplied by the price per share. Companies are usually divided into large-cap, mid-cap, small-cap, and sometimes micro-cap categories, although there are no strict guidelines as to where the dividing lines fall. Here are some typical guidelines:

- **Large-cap**—More than $5 billion
- **Mid-cap**—$1–5 billion
- **Small-cap**—$250 million to $1 billion
- **Micro-cap**—Less than $250 million

The theory behind investing in a specific size of company is that smaller companies tend to be more volatile—their stock prices go up (or down) more and faster—than larger companies. Thus, investing in smaller companies is generally considered to be riskier but with a chance of higher returns. Investing in the largest companies, on the other hand, is a more conservative approach.

Mutual funds can also differ in how aggressive they are. Some funds make a point of investing in companies that are riskier but have a chance of greater returns. Other funds aim for more conservative investments, settling for generally lower returns in exchange for a smaller chance of losses.

You'll also see funds that use the terms *growth* or *income* in their names. *Growth funds* concentrate their investments in companies whose stock price is predicted to rise without regard to payment of dividends. In contrast, an *income fund* seeks out investments that pay dividends that are then distributed to the owners of mutual fund shares. This does not mean that share prices in an income fund cannot go up or down, of course.

Not Just Stocks

Mutual funds are not limited to investing in stocks, although that's what most of them do. You'll find funds that invest in bonds as well.

Some funds concentrate their investments in a particular country or region. You'll see, for example, Europe funds, Japan funds, Far East funds, Germany funds, and so on.

Other funds limit themselves to particular industries. These are sometimes called *sector funds*. There are sector funds for energy, biotechnology, banking, retail, and just about every other specialty area you can think of.

All of the kinds of funds mentioned so far are *managed funds*. This means that the fund's manager is actively involved in deciding which stocks to buy and which to sell. The manager and her staff research the companies and sometimes pay them visits, study market and economic trends, and employ sophisticated computer models in order to manage the fund's portfolio in the most profitable manner. All this activity means that the fund's expenses, and hence the fees you pay, are higher.

Last but not least are the *index funds*. These funds are not actively managed but rather passively follow one of the many market indexes. So, what is a market index?

A *market index* is sort of an average of the stock market or part of it. It is designed to summarize, in a single number, the overall performance of the market. The oldest and best-known market index is the Dow Jones Industrial Average, a weighted average of the stock prices of 30 large companies. On the evening news you'll hear, "The Dow Jones Average is up 12 points today," and you have a general idea of how the market did overall without having to look at individual prices.

Why "Industrial?"

When the Dow Jones Industrial Average was first developed many years ago, in 1884 to be precise, the largest and most important companies in the United States were almost all manufacturing industries, such as Ford and U.S. Steel. Over the years, nonindustrial companies have assumed greater importance in the economy and so are included in the average as well. However, the original name has been retained. As of this writing, the Dow Jones includes Boeing, Microsoft, McDonald's, Procter & Gamble, and Walt Disney among its 30 component companies.

There are literally dozens of market indexes now, each designed to track some specific or general part of the market. The companies tracked in an index are selected by the organization that publishes the index—for example, the Dow Jones company for the Dow Jones Industrial Average

14

and the other Dow Jones averages. Some that you might have heard of are the NASDAQ Composite Index, the S&P 500, and the Russell 1000.

Now we can get back to the topic of index funds. An index fund is based on a specific market index. Sometimes an extra twist is added, such as an index fund that buys only the ten stocks in the DJIA that pay the highest dividends. In other words, index funds are not actively managed—they automatically buy and sell stocks based on the under-lying index. This translates to lower fund expenses and lower fees paid by you. This is the appeal of index funds.

Socially Responsible Funds

These funds tailor their investments to avoid companies who products or services are found objec-tionable by some people. Before investing in such a fund, investigate to make sure that the fund's definition of "socially responsible" matches your own.

But wait—shouldn't an actively managed fund be able to pick better stocks than a fund that is just based on an index? Thus, you would expect a managed fund to have a better return than an unmanaged index fund, even after the higher fees are taken into account. In theory this sounds reasonable, but in practice many, if not most, actively man-aged funds do not do better than the index funds. Index funds are, I believe, a perfectly viable investment option.

Mutual Funds Fees

When you are shopping for a mutual fund, it is important to be aware of the fees it charges. These fees directly reduce your investment return, and your task is to balance a fund's fees with the fund itself. For exam-ple, people are often willing to pay higher fees for a fund with a long record of good returns or with a specific investment strategy they want to pursue.

All funds charge a management fee. These fees, which are usually expressed as a percentage of the fund's assets, are payment to the fund managers for their management services.

Some funds charge a *12b-1 fee*, named after the Securities and Exchange Commission rule that authorizes such fees. These fees are used for shareholder services, such as marketing and sales literature. They can also be used to pay brokers for their services in marketing the fund.

Some funds also tack a few fees on in the Other category to cover things such as accounting and legal costs.

All these costs are combined into an overall annual fund operating expense, which is the figure you should be concerned with. You'll find this information listed in the prospectus for any fund you are considering. Lower fees are better, of course, and some people are surprised to learn just how much fees can eat into your returns.

Let's look at an example. Suppose you invest $10,000 in a fund and leave it there for 10 years. The fund's return (before fees) is 8% per year. What will you have after 10 years?

- If the fund charges 2% annual expenses, $17,640
- If the fund charges 0.5% annual expenses, $20,530

You can see the fees make a big difference—several thousand dollars in this case.

Another kind of fee charged by some mutual funds is a sales commission or *load*. There are two types of loads:

- A *front-end load* is paid when you purchase the shares.
- A *back-end load* is paid when you sell the shares.

Front-end loads immediately reduce the amount of your investment. For example, if you invest $1,000 in a fund with a 5% front-end load, your actual investment is only $950. In general, load funds are sold by brokers and the load serves, at least in part, to provide the commissions that reimburse the broker for her services. This is perfectly reasonable, and if you are using the professional services of a broker, you should expect and be willing to pay loads when you buy mutual funds. If you are managing your investments on your own, however, there are plenty of no-load funds to choose from and, other factors being equal, these would certainly be a better choice.

Back-end loads are often structured as an incentive to keep your money invested in the fund for the long term. A typical scenario would be a back-end load that starts at 6% if you sell within the first year and then gradually decreases to zero after five or seven years.

Be aware, however, that there is often a complex relationship between loads and fund fees. A fund company will often issue several classes of mutual fund shares, usually called Class A, B, or C shares:

- Class A shares will have a front-end load but the lowest annual operating expenses.

- Class B shares charge a back-end load if you sell within the first five years.

- Class C shares will have no load at either end but impose the highest annual operating expenses.

It can be really difficult to decide which type of shares is best for you. In Chapter 16, "Comparing Mutual Funds," I'll present a calculator that can help with this task. At the risk of oversimplifying, you can say that Class A shares are preferred for long-term investments and Class C shares are better for the short term.

Exchange Traded Funds

Exchange traded funds (ETFs) are a fairly new but increasingly popular investment tool. Sometimes they are referred to as *closed-end funds*. An ETF is like a mutual fund in that it provides an investment in a basket of stocks and hence the benefits of diversification. It is like a stock in that the shares trade on the open market without the high fees and restrictions of a mutual fund. ETFs are not without fees, but these fees are quite low and rival the most efficient mutual funds. You do not pay these fees directly; they are reflected in the price of the ETF.

ETFs exist for almost any market segment you can imagine. Three of the better known ETFs are

- The Dow Diamonds (DIA) that is based on the Dow stocks.

- The QUBEs (QQQ) that mirrors the NASDAQ 100 index.

- The Spyders (SPDR) that track various Standard and Poor indexes.

You can find an ETF for just about any investment goal, including ones for individual foreign countries and specific sectors, such as energy or telecommunications.

ETFs are not without their downsides. A major one is the commission you pay when you buy or sell shares in an ETF, just like any regular stock. These commissions can very quickly negate any fee advantage an ETF might have over a traditional mutual fund. For example, suppose you invest $1,000 in an ETF and hold it for one year. Suppose also that you pay a $20 commission when you buy the ETF and another $20 when you sell. That's equivalent to a 4% annual fee, higher than any no-load mutual fund. Add the 0.5% expenses of the ETF itself and you are way behind.

Treasury Bills

A *treasury bill* is a bond that is issued by the U.S. government. Treasury bills are considered the "gold standard" in terms of safety because your principal and interest are guaranteed by the government. Because there is essentially no risk involved, the return tends to be lower than other bonds. You can buy treasury bills directly or you can invest in mutual funds that specialize in them.

Savings Accounts

Saving accounts have fallen out of favor as true investment vehicles. They offer complete safety because they are insured by the Federal Deposit Insurance Corporation, but they pay very low rates. At best you might use a savings account as a short-term parking place for funds.

Certificates of Deposit

A *certificate of deposit (CD)* is a deposit you make at a bank for a fixed term at a fixed rate. For example, you might see banks advertising a two-year $1,000 CD at 4.5%. You deposit $1,000 and at the end of two years you get your $1,000 back plus the 4.5% interest for the two years. CDs pay higher rates than saving accounts and are guaranteed. You can get your money back early but you'll pay a substantial interest penalty. CDs can be useful for socking away cash that has to be 100% safe and you know you won't need for a year or two.

Money Market Accounts

A *money market account* is a type of checking account. There are so many variations on money market accounts that it is impossible to give the complete picture, but the general features when compared with regular checking accounts are

- They pay a higher interest rate than savings accounts.
- You are limited in the number of checks you can write per month.
- You are limited to writing checks for a certain minimum amount.

A money market account is a good place to put cash you do not need on a day-to-day basis. Many investment accounts come linked to a money market account, which can be very convenient.

Risk Versus Return

With any investment, there are two fundamental questions:

- Is my money at risk?
- What will my return be?

A basic fact of investing is that there is an inverse relationship between these factors. If you want higher returns, you must take more risk. Conversely, if you want low risk, you are limited to lower returns.

Risk is difficult to quantify because it requires predicting the future, something no one has managed to do with any success! Unavoidably, risk is considered in terms of probability. In other words, what's the chance I will lose some or all of the money I have invested?

Take, for example, the safest investment—a bank savings account. Because it is guaranteed by the U.S. government, it is as safe as can be, but the returns are quite small. If you absolutely, positively cannot risk losing a single dollar, this might be the investment for you.

At the other end of the spectrum, consider a new Internet startup company. A few Internet companies, such as eBay and Google, have gone on to make huge profits for their investors. But for every successful Internet company, 50 or 100 have failed, taking all their investors' money down the tubes with them. This investment balances the likelihood that you will lose most or all of your investment with the small chance you will win big. Let's take a look at the relative risks of some popular investments.

As I have mentioned, bank savings accounts are as close to 100% safe as you can get.

Money market accounts pay more return than savings accounts. They are not guaranteed by the government and so, in theory, could decrease in value, but this is very unlikely because it would require a major financial upheaval. To my knowledge it has not happened even once so far.

Bonds offer two risks. One is that the price of the bond will go down. The bond market as a whole fluctuates with interest rates, with higher rates meaning lower bond prices and vice versa. An individual bond will decrease in price if the entity that issued it is in financial trouble. Although it's rare, a bond can lose 100% of its value if the issuing company goes bankrupt and defaults on its bond obligations. Bonds issued by the Federal Government are the safest, followed by bonds issued by Federal agencies and certain types of mortgage-backed bonds. The bonds of large, established companies are the safest of the nongovernmental bonds.

Stocks present a wide range of risk levels. Any stock can go down, of course, and even the largest, most stable companies have historically seen significant decreases in their stock prices. As a general but not infallible rule, a company that pays dividends will experience less stock price volatility than one that does not.

The risk of a mutual fund is tied directly to the risk of the various stocks and/or bonds that it owns as well as to the investment strategy of the fund. Generally speaking, a broad-based fund will have less risk than a fund that specializes in a certain sector or country. There are several popular measures of mutual fund volatility:

- *Beta* is a measure of how the fund compares with a benchmark, usually the S&P 500. A beta of 1.00 means that the fund goes up and down in lockstep with the benchmark. A beta of 1.15 means that if the benchmark goes up or down by a certain amount, the fund goes up or down by 15% more.

- *Alpha* is designed to improve on the beta ranking. It compares a fund's historical beta value with its actual performance. An alpha of zero means that the fund's performance was as expected given its beta rating. A positive alpha means that the fund returned more than expected, and a negative alpha means the reverse.

- *Correlation*, sometimes called *R-squared*, is a measure of how closely changes in the fund's price mirror the changes in an underlying benchmark index. R-squared can vary between 0 and 100, with higher values reflecting a closer relationship between the fund's price and the index.

- *Standard deviation* measures the tendency of a fund's price to change quickly over a short period of time. A more general term for this is *volatility*, but standard deviation more specifically measures the fund's price fluctuations as a function of its long-term return. For example, a fund that returned –6%, 2%, 18%, –7%, and 42% for each of the past five years has an average return of 9.8% and a relatively high standard deviation. In contrast, a find that returned 9%, 13%, 9%, 8%, and 10% also has an average return of 9.8% but has a lower standard deviation.

- *Morningstar risk ratings* are created by Morningstar, a company that specializes in analyzing and reporting on mutual funds. Values of less than or greater than 1 indicate less or more risk than other similar funds (similar in investment goals and strategies).

As you can see, trying to get a fix on the risk of an investment is a tricky business that has stumped even the pros for years.

Your Investment Timeframe

When evaluating investments, it is important to have some idea of your timeframe. In other words, when will you need the money?

Some investments have a known timeframe. For example, if you are saving for a child's college education, you know exactly when you will need the money. Other investments might not have a precise target date but you still know whether they are long or short term. An example would be someone in her 30s or 40s saving for retirement—she does not know exactly when she will retire, but she does know it is many years off.

Why is knowing your timeframe important? It has to do with the volatility of different kinds of investments. In particular, it has to do with the fact that stocks, while the proven best investment over the long term, might go down in the short term. If you need the money, you might have no choice but to sell at the low price.

For example, suppose you invest $10,000 in an index fund. It's a darn good bet that in 5 or 10 years you will have a nice return, but in one year—who knows? The idea is that for the short term, you would invest in low risk, low return vehicles (bonds, money market accounts, treasuries), but for the long term, you are better off in stocks.

What is short term and what is long term? There is no agreed-upon definition of these terms. Generally it seems that two years or less is considered short term, five years or more is considered long term, and the middle period is sort of up for grabs!

When Long Term Becomes Short Term

When you have made a long term investment—a college fund, for example—and are nearing the date when you will need the money, that investment suddenly becomes a short term investment. It might be a good idea to move it from higher-risk to lower-risk. For example, when my daughter was a high school sophomore, I started moving her college fund from stock mutual funds to bond funds.

Choosing a Brokerage Account

If you are going to invest in stocks, you will need a *brokerage account* (but see the following section on dividend reinvestment plans). These accounts offer the ability to buy and sell stocks, bonds, and mutual funds and, in most cases, a linked money market account with check-writing privileges. Other services offered differ depending on the brokerage company and the kind of account. For most accounts, the only cost to you is the commission you pay with each purchase or sale. Some accounts might charge a small yearly fee as well. There are three main types of brokerage accounts:

- A full-service brokerage account provides a personal broker, a trained individual who will—at least in theory—answer your questions, keep an eye on your investments, give investment advice, and take care of problems that might arise. As you might expect, commissions are considerably higher at a full-service broker.

- A wrap-fee account provides a set of account services for a fixed fee, usually determined as an annual percentage of the account balance. You do not pay trading commissions, no matter how many trades you make.

- A discount brokerage account provides buying and selling services only. Your investment decisions are completely up to you. Commissions are significantly less than at a full-service broker.

There are pros and cons to both kinds of accounts, and the kind that's best for you will depend on a lot of factors, such as your investment experience and your willingness to do research. Because you can transfer your account from one brokerage to another at any time, this is not a long-term decision.

Dividend Reinvestment Plans

There is a way to invest in stocks without a brokerage account—a *dividend reinvestment plan (DRIP)*. DRIPs are run by individual companies (or by a transfer agent working for the company) to permit investors to buy shares of the company's stock. Purchases and sales are free in some cases, and a nominal charge is assessed in others. The name of these plans comes from the fact that dividends paid by the stock are automatically invested in new shares. This is unlike a standard brokerage account where dividends are paid to you in cash.

DRIPs offer several advantages. You can start investing in a DRIP for a modest amount because there are usually no minimum purchase requirements, and because fees are nonexistent or low, you do not have to worry about them eating into your investment capital. The automatic reinvestment of dividends helps your money grow. DRIPs are an excellent choice for long-term investments.

Finding DRIPs

You'll find a list of DRIPs, and links to the companies' websites, at this URL: http://www.investorguide.com/dripslist.html.

Knowing the fundamentals of investing is an essential first step on your way to becoming a savvy investor. After you start building up a portfolio, you need to keep track of it. That's the topic of the next chapter.

15

Tracking Your Investments

After you start investing, you need to keep track of things. This might seem obvious, but some people let things slide and do not make a point of always knowing just where they stand with their investments. If you want to take charge of your finances, you must stay aware! After you know exactly how your past investment decisions have affected your investments, you're better armed to make more effective investment decisions in the future.

Why Track Investments?

To some people, the answer to this question will seem obvious. To others, however, it is not at all clear. Why should you go to the bother of following every detail of all your investments on a day-to-day basis? The fact is, you shouldn't. Day-to-day is a bit too obsessive for almost everyone! In fact, there is something to be said in some situations for making an investment and forgetting about it for months on end. I'll talk more about the "buy and forget" strategy in a bit. But for now, let's look at some reasons why you should keep track of things.

The first reason is more emotional than practical, but it can be important nonetheless. It's the simple human desire to see how your money is doing. If you have invested $5,000 of your hard-earned money in the Acme

Cuticle Remover Company, you naturally want to see if its stock is up, down, or unchanged. Sure, it's easy to get stock quotes on any of a hundred websites or by looking in the daily paper, but it's much better to have current information presented together with details about your specific investment. After all, the current price of an investment does not mean that much unless it is compared with how much you paid for it!

From a more practical perspective, the ability to track your investments gives you a day-by-day picture of the value of your portfolio. Although such short-term fluctuations are not important in your overall investment strategy, they are still of interest to most investors. More important is the ability to see how individual investments are doing. This information can be useful in evaluating your portfolio and deciding on changes. What sort of situations might you consider?

Buy and Forget?

It can be easy to get a little obsessive about your investments and start checking the prices daily or even more often. I think this is a bad idea. Not only does it consume your time but it can lead to bad investment decisions. Buying an investment is a bet that the price will increase over the time of your investment horizon. This may be 6 months, 2 years, or 10 years, but it certainly is not tomorrow or the day after! Any investment, even those that turn out to be your most successful, will have price fluctuations on a day-to-day basis. Seeing a stock you bought go down can be nerve-wracking, and all too often people respond with panic selling—only to see the price change reverse and trend upward next week or next month. Relax and trust you judgment. I do not really mean you should literally forget your investments, but check them on a more reasonable schedule—weekly perhaps.

Suppose one of your stocks has gone down quite a bit. That in itself is not a reason to sell—in fact, one of the most common bad investing moves is to sell an excellent company because of a short-term dip in the stock price. Still, such a dip might signal that it's time to reevaluate the stock.

- If you still think the company is strong and has good prospects, a dip in the stock price might be an opportunity to buy more shares. This will decrease your average share cost. For example, if you initially bought 50 shares at $32 and then buy another 50 shares at $24, your average cost per share is now $28.

- If, on the other hand, something fundamental has changed and the company does not seem to be as good an investment as it did when you first bought it, this might be the time to sell and take your losses before the stock price goes down further.

If the stock price has gone up significantly, it is also time for a reevaluation. Is it still a good investment at the new price? A stock you bought at $50 might have been a good choice, but after it has gone up to $80 it might not have much potential for further increases. Of course, a rise in price might signal some good news about a company, such as a strategic acquisition or a terrific new product. The stock might be a better buy at the new, higher price. You have to evaluate each situation on its own merits—a rise or decrease in price does not in and of itself mean anything about the company's future prospects.

The Investment Portfolio Workbook

The Investment Portfolio workbook is designed to enable you to keep track of your stock and mutual fund investments. It allows automated download of stock and fund prices from the Web (this requires an Internet connection, of course). It displays the cost of each of your holdings, as well as the current value and gain or loss based on the current price. The main worksheet of this template is shown in Figure 15.1.

Figure 15.1

The Investment Portfolio template enables you to track current prices on your stock and mutual fund investments.

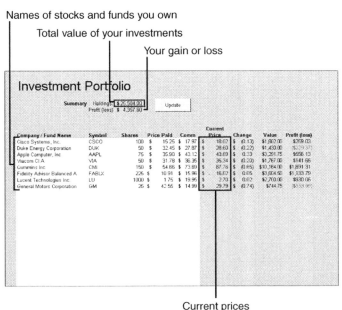

Names of stocks and funds you own

Total value of your investments

Your gain or loss

Current prices

The Holdings Worksheet

Figure 15.1 shows the Holdings worksheet, which is the part of the workbook that shows your holding and summary information. It has four columns where you insert data for each of your holdings:

- Company/Fund Name is the name of the company or mutual fund.
- Shares is the number of shares you own.
- Price Paid is the per-share price you paid. Be sure to enter the actual price paid from your transaction confirmation, which might be slightly different from the market price when you placed your order.
- Comm is the commission you paid plus any other fees, such as a transaction fee. If you paid no commission, enter 0.

It's important to note that the Company/Fund Name entry must be accurate, with no omitted words or misspellings. For example, you cannot enter just Apple but must enter Apple Computer, Inc.. I'll explain why in a moment.

There are also four calculated columns on this worksheet:

- Current price is the latest downloaded price of the stock or fund.
- Change is the change in the price from the start of the trading day (for stocks) or from the previous trading day (funds). This data is downloaded as well.
- Value is the current share price multiplied by the number of shares you own.
- Profit (loss) is the difference between the current value and what you paid, with the commission figured in.

Finally, the worksheet calculates a summary of the total value of your holdings and your overall profit or loss.

What if you need to make changes to your list of holdings, as you most certainly will? Adding a new holding is described above. There are other actions you might need to take, as well. For example, if you sell an entire holding, delete it from the list on the Holdings worksheet as follows:

1. Place the cursor on any cell in the row of the holding you want to delete.

2. Select Edit, Delete to display the Delete dialog box.

3. Select the Entire Row option.

4. Click OK.

If you sell part of a holding—say you own 100 shares of IBM and sell 50 of them—you must adjust the shares number as well as the commission. For example, suppose you paid $24.00 commission when you bought the 100 shares. If you sell 50 of those shares, only half of the original commission is relevant for the 50 shares remaining. Note that any commission you pay to sell the shares does not come into play here. Here's how to adjust the commission amount:

1. Divide the number of shares remaining in the account by the number owned originally. For example, if you sell 100 of 400 shares, you have 300 remaining. Divide 300 by 400 to get 0.75.

2. Multiply this value by the original commission to get the prorated commission.

3. Enter this prorated commission in the Comm column.

In addition to these scenarios, a stock can split, which usually occurs when a company thinks its stock price is too high per share. The stock is *split* so that each existing share becomes two or more new shares at a lower price. In a two-for-one split, for example, each share you own becomes two shares, each worth half as much. You occasionally see reverse splits as well, when a company's stock price has fallen very low. A 1-for–10 reverse split, for example, converts each ten shares of old stock into one share of new stock with ten times the value. A stock split does not involve any gain or loss for the shareholders, but does entail some bookkeeping to keep your holdings information accurate. Such splits and reverse splits affect the way a stock might be viewed by new investors, even though it doesn't change the stock's capitalization value in any way. For example, a company that issues a 1-for-10 reverse split might do so to move its $1.20-per-share stock price to $12.00 per share. Because the number of outstanding shares decreases by 10, the overall value of the stock doesn't change, but new investors looking at the price might be more inclined to purchase a $12.00 stock rather than a $1.20 stock. To handle stock splits, you must first determine the split factor, say 2-for-1 or 3-for-1. For a reverse split, the split factor will be a fractional number. For example, a 1-for-10 reverse split has a factor of 0.1. Then follow these steps:

1. Multiply the number of shares by the split factor.

2. Divide the price paid by the factor.

You don't need to make a change to the commission price when a stock splits.

The final change you might run into is if you buy more shares of a stock or fund you already own. The best way to handle this is to simply enter a separate holding for the new purchase.

The Query Worksheet

The Query worksheet is part of the process when the template downloads current stock prices. It is shown in Figure 5.2. Let's take a look at how this works.

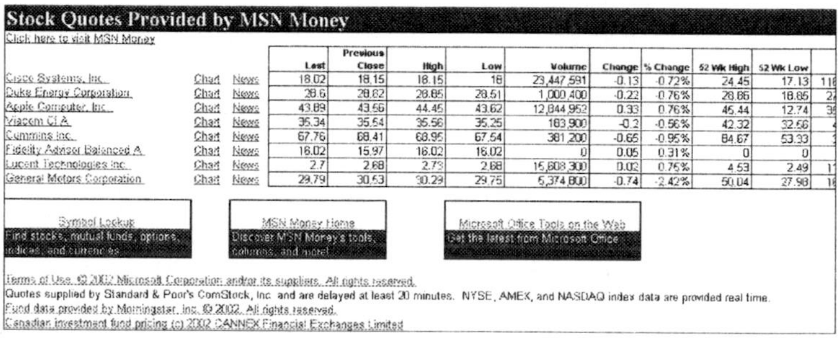

Figure 15.2

The Query worksheet displays the data downloaded from the MSN Money site. (Sample data used for illustrative purposes only.)

Excel includes a capability called *web queries* that is used to retrieve data from a web page and display it in a worksheet. One of the queries that comes with Excel is designed specifically to download stock and mutual fund prices from the MSN website for display in a worksheet, as shown in Figure 5.2. In other words, the data you see in this figure is simply the result of the query. In simplified form, here's how it works each time you update the workbook:

1. The stock symbols are read from column C of the Holdings worksheet.

2. A web query is constructed containing those symbols.

3. The query is executed. Behind the scenes, it retrieves the requested information from the MSN website and places it in the Query worksheet.

4. The individual results in the query are listed in the same order as they are on the Holdings worksheet. This enables the update code to

go through the list a row at time and transfer the price, change, and company name information to the Holdings worksheet.

Using the Investment Portfolio Template

Using the Investment Portfolio template is actually rather simple. To get started, you need to gather information about your investments, specifically the price paid for shares of stocks or mutual funds, the amount of any commission paid, and the symbol. Then enter this information in the relevant columns on the Holdings worksheet. You can enter a company name but do not need to as long as the symbol is correct. The web update will download the full company or fund name and insert it in column B.

You can usually get the symbol for a stock or fund you bought from your confirmation statement. If you do not have this information, here's how to find it:

1. Use your browser to navigate to http://moneycentral.msn.com/ investor/common/find.asp. This page is shown in Figure 15.3.
2. Enter information about the name of the stock or fund whose symbol you want to find.
3. Click Go.

Sometimes the information returned will provide more than one symbol, particularly if you did not know the full name of the fund or company. But you can usually sort out which symbol is the one you are looking for.

When you have all the required information, follow these steps to enter it into the Holdings worksheet:

1. In the Holdings worksheet, move the cell pointer to the first empty cell in the Company/Fund Name column.
2. Enter the company or fund name, or leave it blank and let the workbook update fill it in.
3. Move one column to the right and enter the stock or fund symbol.
4. Move one column to the right and enter the number of shares you bought. Fractional shares, which are common with mutual fund purchases, are perfectly fine.

Select stock or mutual fund

Figure 15.3

If you do not know the symbol for a stock or fund, you can use MSN Money to find it.

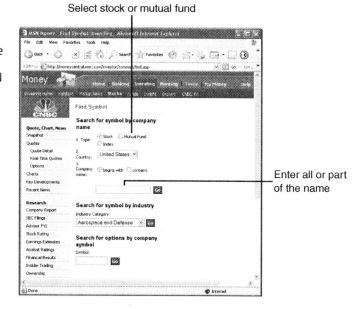

Enter all or part of the name

5. Move one column to the right and enter the price you paid per share.

6. Move one column to the right and enter the commission, if any. If you bought a mutual fund with a front-end load, enter the dollar amount of the load fee here.

Repeat these steps as needed to enter your entire investment portfolio. Then click the Update button to download the current stock information and fill in the other fields in the worksheet.

You can edit the information on the Holdings worksheet as needed. Perhaps you made an error entering the purchase price, or you entered the wrong commission. Making other changes, such as selling all or part of a holding or accounting for a stock split, was explained earlier in the chapter.

Keeping Records

Whenever you sell a stock or fund—assuming that it's not in a tax-sheltered account such as an IRA or 401(k)—you must report any profits on your taxes as capital gains. Likewise, any losses you incur are deductible, within certain limits. Be sure to keep good records of your buy and sell transactions. Your brokerage should send you the necessary information. The Investment Portfolio workbook is not intended for keeping tax records.

The Investment Portfolio workbook is simple and easy to use. But please be aware of the following cautions (some of which have been mentioned before):

- You need a working Internet connection to download current stock prices. If your connection is not working and you click the Update button, the workbook will sit for a few moments and then display an error message.

- There must be no blank rows in the Holdings worksheet, specifically the symbol column. The way the workbook operates is to use the first blank row as the marker for the end of the holding information, so if you include a blank row, the holdings below it will not be updated.

- Be sure to enter company and fund symbols accurately. The Current Price and Change fields will display ??? in the case of an invalid symbol.

Now that you are ready to track your portfolio, we can move to the next chapter where you'll learn some techniques for evaluating and comparing mutual funds.

15

16

Comparing Mutual Funds

When you put money in a unguaranteed investment such as a mutual fund, there is no sure thing. With a little knowledge and help, however, you might be able to improve your chances of picking a winner. This chapter provides some information and tools that should be of help to you.

Choosing Mutual Funds

We have all probably had the experience of reading about a mutual fund that shot up 50%, 100%, or more in the last year, and wishing we had been smart enough (or lucky enough) to have invested in that fund. As they say, hindsight is always 20/20 but it's not any help to the prudent investor. So just how do you go about picking good mutual funds to invest your money in?

There's no easy answer to that question, of course. In particular, I will warn you away from the idea of picking the big winners. Even the most seasoned investment pros cannot predict which funds will do exceptionally well; so why should we ordinary investors expect to? Even so, you should not select funds by throwing darts.

The most important consideration is the type of fund—what kinds of stocks, bonds, or other investment vehicles does it invest in, is it aggressive or conservative, and similar factors. I discussed these in some detail in Chapter 14,

"Learning the Fundamentals of Investing." This choice depends on your investment strategy and goals. After you've selected a type of fund, however, you still have dozens, if not hundreds, of funds to choose from.

Don't Forget Exchange Traded Funds

You learned in Chapter 14 about Exchange Traded Funds (ETFs), sometimes called closed-end funds, that trade on the stock market just like stock shares. These are a valid investment choice for some fund investors. This chapter, however, is focused on traditional mutual funds.

You can also peruse the raft of mutual fund information and evaluations published in almost every personal financial and investing magazine, as well as on numerous websites. These articles can be useful because the writer has already done the work of pulling information about many funds together in one place, making it easier for you to read and evaluate. Note also that Consumer Reports does an extensive mutual fund comparison once a year, and almost any library will have back issues. Some other well-known sources for mutual fund information are Morningstar (www.morningstar.com), Yahoo! Finance (finance.yahoo.com), and MSN Money (moneycentral.msn.com).

Beware, however, of recommendations such as "Ten Top Funds for This Year" or "25 Market Beaters for Your Portfolio." Remember, the people making these recommendations do not have a crystal ball any more than you do! And if they did, they would be making money with their "terrific" investments rather than trying to peddle their advice to you!

Given that it is an essentially hopeless task to predict which funds lead the pack, what can you do? Fortunately, there is one important way to compare funds that is free of guessing and predictions—their expenses. Other things being equal, a fund with lower expenses will provide a higher return to you. Think it will be just a few dollars? Think again.

Suppose you invest $10,000 in a fund that has no load and a 1% annual expense ratio. Assume that the underlying return of the fund's investments is 8% per year. After five years your investment will be worth $13,973 and you will have paid $620 in expenses.

Now take the same scenario but with a 2% expense ratio. After the same period your investment will be worth $13,282 and you will have paid $1,214 in expenses. That's a $691 difference! Add in a 5% front-end load and the difference soars to $1,356. That's a lot of money! With the Mutual Fund Comparator workbook, you can calculate exactly how much impact loads and expenses will have on your bottom line.

The Mutual Fund Comparator

The Mutual Fund Comparator workbook lets you compare any two mutual funds and see how differences in their loads and expense fees will affect your investment return. This workbook is shown in Figure 16.1.

Figure 16.1

Using the Mutual Fund Comparator to see how fund loads and fees affect your return.

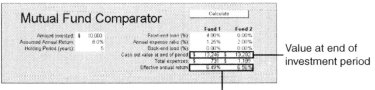

Value at end of investment period

Effective annual investment return

On the left side of this worksheet, you must enter information about the investment, which is assumed to be the same for the two funds you are evaluating:

- **Amount invested**—The total amount of cash you will invest in the fund
- **Assumed annual return**—Your estimate of how the funds' underlying investments will do
- **Holding period**—How long you plan to keep the investment

In the right section of the worksheet, you enter information about the two mutual funds you are comparing:

- **Front-end load**—The percentage front-end load charged by the fund.
- **Annual expense ratio**—The yearly expense ratio charged by the fund.
- **Back-end load**—The back-end load charged by the fund. If the fund has a sliding back-end load, one that decreases the longer you hold the fund, be sure to enter the load amount for the holding period you entered in cell C6.

Be aware that a few funds have a more complex fee schedule in which the annual expense ratio decreases after a certain holding period. The calculator does not take this into account, but you should be aware of this possibility when evaluating a fund's fees.

After all the information has been entered, click the Calculate button to perform the calculations and display the result. Note that the Fund 1 and Fund 2 labels will display in red if you have made any changes and need to recalculate, and in black if the calculations are up to date. The three output calculations are

- **Cash out value**—The amount of cash you'll get if you sell all your shares at the end of the holding period
- **Total expenses**—The total fund expenses you will have paid
- **Effective annual return**—The actual annual investment return you would realize

Look back at the numbers in Figure 16.1. These compare one fund with a 4% front-end load and 1.25% expense ratio to another fund that has no load and a 2% expense ratio. You can see that at the end of five years the results will be essentially identical—the lower expense ratio in Fund 1 offsets the effect of the load.

Now look at a different scenario in Figure 16.2. In this case, which is for a 10-year holding period, neither fund has a load but one has a 0.9% expense ratio while the other is 2.5%. The difference here is quite amazing—almost $3,000!

Figure 16.2

A difference in fund expense ratio can have a major impact on your actual returns.

You might think that the effective annual return calculated by the Mutual Fund Comparator is incorrect. Looking at Figure 16.2, Fund 1 has a base return of 8% with a 0.9% expense ratio—shouldn't the annual return be 8% minus 0.9% or 7.1%? On a strictly annual basis that is true, but for periods of more than one year, the gains are compounded. For example, during year 2 you are earning 7.1% on not only your initial $10,000 investment but also on the $710 gain from the first year, so the gain for year 2 is 7.1% of $10,710 or $760.41. This compounds over the years. The effective annual return displayed by the calculator is the effective return *on your initial investment* over the entire term.

With the next chapter we move to another kind of investing topic — how to plan and save for major expenses such as your children's college years and your retirement years.

17

Planning for College or Retirement

Long-term financial planning is essential when you need to save over an extended period to meet a major financial goal, such as paying for college or funding your retirement. Although precise predictions over periods of years or decades might be unrealistic, there are still techniques you can use to ensure that you are at least in the ballpark.

Long-term Planning

Long-term financial planning is bedeviled by several uncertainties that are not relevant for shorter term situations. If you want your long-term plans to be even reasonably accurate, you must take these uncertainties into account.

Accounting for Inflation

Inflation is the seemingly unstoppable trend for prices to gradually increase over time. We've all heard the stories from old-timers about how you used to be able to get a cup of coffee for 5 cents and a good car for $2,500. On a year-to-year basis, the effects of inflation are almost impossible to notice, but when you are planning for something 10, 20, or even 30 years down the road, it becomes an important factor. Let's look at a hypothetical example.

Suppose you are 35 years old and are starting to give some serious thought to your retirement planning. You plan to retire at age 65, 30 years down the road. Also suppose that inflation has been at a relatively modest 3% per year and you expect it will remain at or near that level until you retire. Well, guess what? You will need almost $2.50 when you retire to have the buying power of $1.00 today. Inflation will continue to exert its effects during your retirement. These factors will, of course, have a major impact on your retirement finances. You can use the Inflation Effects Calculator presented in the next section to determine the future effects of inflation on your buying power.

The Inflation Effects Calculator

Using the Inflation Effects Calculator, it's easy to determine the effects of inflation. You enter the predicted annual inflation rate as a percentage and the number of years, and the calculator shows you how much you will need to equal the buying power of $1.00 today. The calculator is shown in Figure 17.1.

Figure 17.1

The Inflation Effects Calculator helps you determine the effects of inflation on your future buying power.

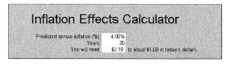

Take a look at the example shown in Figure 17.1. You can see that if inflation averages 4% per year, 20 years down the road you will need $2.19 to equal the buying power of $1.00 today.

What has inflation been historically? I caution against making predictions for the future based on past history, but it is interesting to note that on average, with the exception of the 1910's and 1970's, inflation has remained low for the past 100 years, rarely rising above five percent. (For more details, see inflationdata.com.)

Predicting Your Needs

Another uncertainty when planning for something far in the future is deciding how much money you will actually need when the time comes. Of course, inflation plays a role here, as discussed in the previous section, but it's not the only factor. For example, when planning for retirement, you need to have some idea of the standard of living you want and plan accordingly. Likewise, college costs have historically increased faster than general inflation. These matters will be discussed further in the sections about college and retirement planning.

Not Over-Saving

Saving money is generally a good thing, but it can be overdone. Yes, you need to plan for the future, but you also need to live your life now, in the present. On the one hand, you certainly do not want to ignore retirement planning and find yourself scraping by on just your Social Security check in your golden years. On the other hand, neither do you want to live "on the cheap" for most of your life, foregoing vacations and other pleasures just so you can have a luxurious retirement. Finding some sensible middle ground is certainly the best approach.

Saving for College

Planning for your children's college educations can be a daunting task. Never mind grades, SAT scores, and getting accepted at the right place—just paying for it is a major undertaking. Very few people can count on being able to pay college costs out-of-pocket when they occur. Rather, it is a matter of a long-term saving plan that might start when the child is still in diapers.

College costs vary widely. Some exclusive private universities have annual costs that approach and even exceed $40,000. At the other end of the scale, some state universities have costs less than $10,000 a year for in-state students. Looking at average annual costs, as determined by the College Board, can be instructive (these figures are for 2004):

Private four year—$27,677

Public four year (in state)—$12,841

Public four year (out of state)—$19,188

Public two year—$10,458

These figures include tuition, room, board, and fees, but not personal expenses or travel.

17

Tax-Advantaged College Savings

Many people take advantage of special college saving plans, such as the 529 plans, for their college savings. These plans offer various tax advantages that let your education savings grow at a faster rate than they would in a regular taxable account. Also, many states offer special savings plans that are applicable to the state university system. These plans have disadvantages as well. They typically offer a very limited range of investment options. Also, in the unlikely event that you save more than you need—maybe your daughter will get a nice fat scholarship—you cannot simply take the extra money back without tax considerations.

Setting up a college savings plan has three related parts:

- Estimating how much money you will need in today's dollars
- Estimating the dollar amount you will need when your son or daughter actually starts college
- Determining the amount you will have to save to meet this goal

The first of these items might sound easy but it can be difficult. It's easy because you can go to any college or university's website, or to one of the many published or web-based college guides, and find figures on its total annual cost. It's difficult because it's almost impossible to predict which college your 3-year-old son will want to attend 15 years down the road!

Determining the dollar amount you will need when your child actually starts college is a simple matter of applying inflation to the amount you need in today's dollars. The problem is that college costs typically rise at a faster rate than general inflation. In recent years these costs have been increasing in the range of 5%–8% a year. When calculating the dollar amount you will need in the future, you should use a figure in this range rather than an estimate of general inflation. Also remember that inflation in college costs will not stop when your child starts college but will continue over the years he attends.

Another thing to consider is the fact that very few people pay all college costs from savings. Most people pay at least a part of college costs out-of-pocket at the time they come due. Scholarships, financial aid, and student loans are another factor that might come into play, although it is essentially impossible to predict years in advance.

All these factors mean that estimating the dollar amount you should have saved by the time your child starts college is fraught with uncertainty. This does not mean you should abandon the task as impossible. It does mean that you should remain aware of the uncertainties involved and expect to make adjustments to your plan as time passes.

After you have estimated the dollar amount you want to have in the future, calculating the amount you will have to save regularly is an easy matter for Excel.

The College Cost Calculator

The College Cost Calculator enables you to get a handle on how much you will need to have saved by the time your child goes to college. This workbook is shown in Figure 17.2. You might notice the College Savings tab in this workbook—that's a related calculator I will get to in the next section.

Annual college cost today

Figure 17.2

Use the College Costs Calculator to predict how much you will need to save for college expenses.

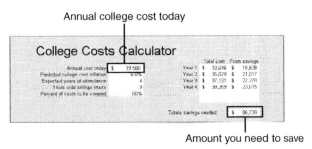

Amount you need to save

The inputs to this calculator, in cells C4:C8 are as follows:

- **Annual cost today**—The current annual cost of the college of interest. You can also use one of the average cost figures presented earlier in the chapter.

- **Predicted college cost inflation**—Your prediction of how much college costs will increase per year. I recommend you use a figure in the 5%–8% range.

- **Expected years of attendance**—How many years your child will attend college. The worksheet can handle values from 2 to 6.

- **Years until college starts**—How many years until your child will start college.

- **Percent of costs to be covered**—What percentage of college costs you want to cover from your savings.

17

The output of the calculator shows you the predicted total costs per year, as well as the amount you will need from savings. It also calculated the total amount of savings you will need. In the example shown in the figure, you can see that you will need about $87,000 in savings to meet 60% of the projected college costs for a college whose current costs are $19,560 per year.

After you have estimated how much savings you will need for college, how can you save to meet that goal? That's what the College Savings Calculator helps you determine.

The College Savings Calculator

Knowing how much you need to save for college is one thing—but how do you go about it? Most people would like to set up a system whereby they put aside a fixed amount each month. But how much? The College Savings Calculator can tell you. This calculator is a separate worksheet in the College Costs workbook. This combination makes sense because the College Savings Calculator uses figures that are already entered in the College Costs Calculator. The College Savings worksheet is shown in Figure 17.3.

Figure 17.3

The College Savings Calculator helps you determine how much to save per month to meet your goal.

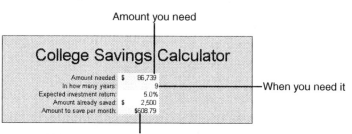

Amount you need

College Savings Calculator

Amount needed:	$	86,739
In how many years:		9
Expected investment return:		5.0%
Amount already saved:	$	2,500
Amount to save per month:		$608.79

When you need it

How much you need to save per month

The first two inputs to this calculator, the amount needed and in how many years, are automatically carried over from the College Costs worksheet. You must be sure to enter data in the College Costs worksheet before using the College Savings worksheet. If however you plan to save a fixed dollar amount rather than relying on the figure calculated by the College Costs calculator, you can enter it in cell D4.

The two inputs you enter are

- **Expected investment return**—The amount you expect your investment to grow annually
- **Amount already saved**—The amount, if any, you already have saved for college costs

The output of this calculator is the amount you will need to put away each month to meet your goals. The calculations assume that savings will continue until the start of college. Two values are displayed, one in cell C8 for the goal carried over from the College Costs Calculator and another in cell D8 for the fixed amount you entered in cell D4 (if any).

Remember that using this calculator involves a lot of uncertainties, as I have discussed earlier in this chapter. I highly recommend rerunning it once a year or so as updated information becomes available, particularly if you will be increasing your savings amount over the years as your child nears college age and your income increases.

Saving for Retirement

Retirement is the big pie in the sky for a lot of people. We are living longer, healthier lives these days, and most people who are currently working can look forward to at least 15 or 20 years of active retirement. To really enjoy your retirement, however, you need adequate financial resources. Where's the fun in spending your golden years on a strict budget, unable to afford the golf, travel, fishing, or whatever you love to do?

Of course, retirement is not a simple as it used to be. It was once common for people to work full-time until they were 65 and then retire on Social Security and a pension that paid a fixed benefit for the rest of their lives. This kind of pension is called a *defined benefit plan* because the amount you receive per month is fixed at the time you retire, usually based on your length of service and the amount your were paid for the last few years of employment. Such plans are less and less common these days.

Nowadays, your retirement finances are much more likely to involve a *defined contribution plan* such as a 401(k) or SEP. These plans involve your employer and you putting a certain amount of money away each month, tax deferred. You invest this money as you see fit (with certain limitations). Then when you retire, this money is available for you to live on or to purchase an annuity that pays you a regular income.

While there are various kinds of defined contribution plans with varying details, the bottom line is the same for all of them: You must save enough for retirement. The question "What is enough?" is important, of course, and I will get to that in due time. Regardless, the amount you put away, plus any contributions from your employers, plus investment gains, must meet your retirement needs.

What About Social Security?

Most Americans who have worked for at least part of their adult life will be eligible for Social Security retirement benefits. The amount you will receive depends on several factors, including your work history and the age at which you start taking the benefits. Many people receive a yearly statement from the Social Security Administration with details of their Social Security account and estimates of the benefits they will be eligible for. If you do not receive this statement, you can request one by going to www.ssa.gov and clicking on the Your Social Security Statement link.

Should you include your projected Social Security retirement income in your planning? I cannot answer that question for you. There has been a lot of political talk lately about the system's financial woes, with dire predictions that benefits might have to be cut for future retirees. I don't think that anyone can really predict what will happen. One suggestion is to take a conservative approach and include only part of your projected Social Security income in your planning. One reasonable approach is to cut your projected benefits by 2% for each year you are younger than 55. Therefore:

> Projected benefits = official projected benefits x (100% – 2 x (55 – your age)%)

For example, if you are 48 and your official projected benefits are $1,850, you would calculate as follows:

> $1,850 x (100% – 2 x (55 – 48)%)
>
> which reduces to
>
> $1,850 x (100% – 14%)
>
> or
>
> $1,850 x 86% = $1,591

How Much Retirement Income Will You Need?

This can be a difficult question to answer. How can you predict your needs and desires 20, 30, or 40 years in the future? Many people think it is best to figure your needed retirement income as a percentage of your current income. The figures used most often are 70% or 80%. They are based on the assumption that you will have fewer expenses when you retire than you do now. For example, you might have paid off your mortgage or moved to a smaller place with lower payments. Also, you will probably be finished with college and other expenses for your children.

But there can be scenarios when taking 70%–80% of current income as a projection for your desired retirement income can be problematic. For instance, maybe you are still in your 30s and at a relatively early stage in your career. Your income might have a lot of growing to do over the next couple of decades, so projecting your retirement needs based on current income might not be a good idea. Or maybe your goals for retirement include some relatively costly activities, such as lots of travel or your own yacht. Then you might need more than your current income to have the lifestyle you want during retirement.

The bottom line is that there is no one correct way to estimate the income you will need during retirement. You need to think about your own situation, your goals and desires, and estimate accordingly. If you are really at a loss, I recommend taking 80% of your current income as a starting point and then adjusting it up or down if any special situations apply.

How Much Do You Need to Save?

After you have estimated the amount of retirement income you will need, your next step is to calculate how much you need to save by the time you retire in order to realize that projected income. Bear in mind, this process is fraught with uncertainties for several reasons. Suppose you saved $X by the time you retire. Then what do you do with that money? There are several possible ways to use that money to provide a retirement income.

One approach is to leave the money invested and live off the interest. This sounds like a conservative approach because the principal remains untouched, but remember, inflation does not stop just because you retire and inflation will continue to erode your buying power throughout your retirement years. With today's increased life expectancies, this could easily be 25 or 30 years or more, enough time to see the buying power of a fixed income cut in half by even low inflation.

17

Then there's the question of how to invest your retirement funds. A lot of people think first about safe investments such as certificates of deposit and government securities, but the relatively low return on these investments will have a serious negative effect on your income. Inflation often outperforms the return on these financial instruments.

More and more financial advisors are recommending keeping a good portion of your money invested in the stock market to take advantage of its higher returns. But while the market reliably has higher *average* returns over the long term, it does not necessarily have better returns on a year-to-year basis. You might face one or more years of a bear market with very small or even negative returns at some point during your retirement, and your financial strategy should take this possibility into account.

Pre-tax Versus After-tax Savings

Most people's retirement savings are pre-tax, such as individual retirement accounts, Keoghs, SEPS, and 403b accounts. You do not pay income tax on money you contribute to the account or on gains in the account. At retirement, however, all withdrawals from the account are fully taxable as income. If you have retirement savings that are after-tax rather than pre-tax, as is the case with standard brokerage accounts, withdrawals are not subject to income tax. In terms of generating spendable retirement income, therefore, after-tax savings are worth considerably more than the same dollar amount of pre-tax savings.

Annuities

Given the uncertainties of generating income from retirement savings, many people turn to annuities. In a nutshell, an annuity is when you pay a large chunk of money to a company in return for a promise to return to you a certain income for the rest of your life. In reality, the subject of annuities is very complex and I can only scratch the surface here.

Annuities are usually sold by insurance companies. Because they sell to large numbers of people, they can take a probability approach. They do not know exactly how long you will live, but they can estimate with very good accuracy how long their customers will live on average. The payments you will receive are based on this estimate.

Let's see how this works in simplified form. Suppose you buy a $250,000 annuity. The insurance company has your $250,000, plus the gains they will make from investing it. In theory, the total of payments they will make to you equals this initial amount plus the anticipated investment gains less their profit. If you should live much longer than expected, your payments will be balanced out by someone who lives a much shorter time that predicted.

Annuities are further complicated by the fact that there are so many different payment options available. A few of the choices you will have are

- Do the payments stop when you die or will they continue to your spouse if he or she survives you?
- Do the payments increase to account for inflation?
- Is there a death benefit paid when you die?

As a final complicating factor, the level of payments you will receive is, of course, higher the older you are when you start receiving them.

The Retirement Planner Workbook

Despite all the uncertainties that surround retirement planning, there's no reason why you cannot do some planning. At the very least, such planning can give you an idea if you are way off base or if you are at least somewhere near the right track. The Retirement Planner workbook can help with this task. It is shown in Figure 17.4.

In the About You section, enter information about your age, desired retirement age, and years of retirement. This last number is how long you expect to be retired—in other words, how long you expect to live after retirement. You also enter your desired income at retirement, in current dollars. If you want to include your Social Security retirement benefits in the calculations, enter them in the designated field. If you will receive a defined benefit pension, enter it, too.

In the Projections section, you enter your guesses at the level of inflation and the annual return you will earn on your investments. Be realistic with these numbers. Entering an unreasonably low inflation rate or an unreasonably high return will give you a falsely rosy picture of your retirement plans.

17

Information about your retirement savings

Information about you

Figure 17.4

The Retirement Planner can help you match your retirement savings plan to your goals.

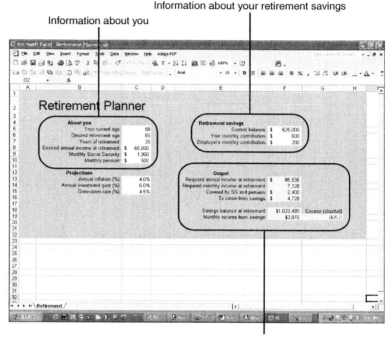

Result of analysis

The Projections section also contains a field labeled Draw-down Rate. This is the percentage you withdraw from your account each year as income. Your draw-down is an important figure so you can maintain your retirement lifestyle, and it is essential that you enter a realistic value here if the workbook is to provide valid projections. The consensus among financial planners is to use a figure of 3.5%–4.5%, and never any more than 5%. The theory behind this is that by withdrawing from the account at a rate lower than the projected investment gain, the principal amount will grow over the years and provide an increase that protects you, at least partially, against larger-than-expected inflation.

The Retirement Savings section contains fields for the current balance in your retirement accounts and the monthly contributions made by you and by your employer. If you have more than one retirement savings plan, combine the numbers for all of them here.

The Output section provides several kinds of information. They are

- **Required annual income at retirement**—The annual income, in future dollars, you will need at retirement to match the buying power of the desired income you specified in current dollars

- **Required monthly income at retirement**—The annual income projection divided by twelve

- **Covered by SS and pension**—The amount of your monthly income that your Social Security and pension will cover

- **To come from savings**—The amount of your required monthly retirement income that must come from your savings

- **Savings balance at retirement**—The total amount you will have saved when you retire

The next output value is the calculated amount you can expect to receive per month from your savings based on the draw-down rate in cell C15. Finally, the worksheet calculates the amount your projected income exceed or falls short of your projected required income.

This is the final chapter in the book, and I hope you have found the reading to be informative and enjoyable. Now you can sit back and relax about your finances, right? Wrong! Staying on top of your finances is a never-ending process. The world changes, your situation changes, your goals change—all though your life you will need to keep attuned to your finances and make adjustments and changes as needed. With the proper knowledge and tools, it is not particularly difficult or time-consuming, and believe me—it is well worth it!

Appendices

A

Workbook Reference

This appendix provides additional details about the inner workings of the workbooks presented in this book. If you just want to use these workbooks, you will not need this information. But if you are interested in modifying some of the templates or simply want to learn more about how Excel works, you will find these details valuable.

The explanations I provide here assume you have some familiarity with Excel formulas and functions and also with VBA programming. It would be impractical to provide all the background information a beginner would need to understand these topics—after all, entire books have been written on these subjects! I also assume you have already read the chapter material on using the workbooks.

The workbooks are all protected to prevent the user from making accidental changes. Only those cells where data should be entered are unlocked. If you want to modify the workbooks (to experiment with different formulas, for example), you will have to unlock each worksheet by selecting Tools, Protection, Unprotect Sheet.

Chapter 4: Net Worth Calculator

The Net Worth Calculator might appear complex but the underlying worksheet functionality is relatively simple. This worksheet is shown in Figure A.1.

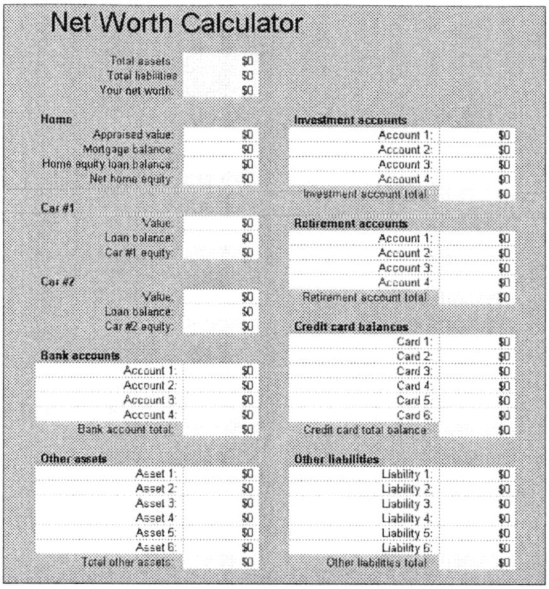

Figure A.1

The Net Worth Calculator.

Net Worth Calculator

Let's start by looking at row 7 and below where you enter your financial details. Each section deals with a particular part of your assets or liabilities. For example, in the Home section you enter the appraised value in cell C8, the mortgage balance in C9, and the home equity loan balance in C10. Your new equity is calculated in cell C11 with this formula:

```
=C8-C9-C10
```

Other sections work in much the same way, using a simple formula to determine the total asset or liability for that section.

The summary section near the top simply pulls together the data from the various parts of the worksheet. Total assets in cell C3 are calculated with this formula:

```
=C11+C16+C21+C28+C37+F12+F19
```

Likewise, total liabilities in cell C4 are calculated with this formula:

```
=F28+F37
```

And finally, your net worth in C5 is simply the difference between these two amounts:

```
=C3-C4
```

Some net worth calculators do things in a slightly different way. The total value of your house and cars would be included as part of your assets, and the amounts owed on a mortgage and loans would be included in your liabilities. The method used here, however, gives the same final net worth value, which is what you are interested in, after all.

Chapter 5: Budget Workbook

This is one of the more complex templates presented in this book. It relies not only on worksheet formulas but also on macros (VBA code) to perform its tasks. There are several separate worksheets in this workbook. The main one, named Overview, is shown in Figure A.2.

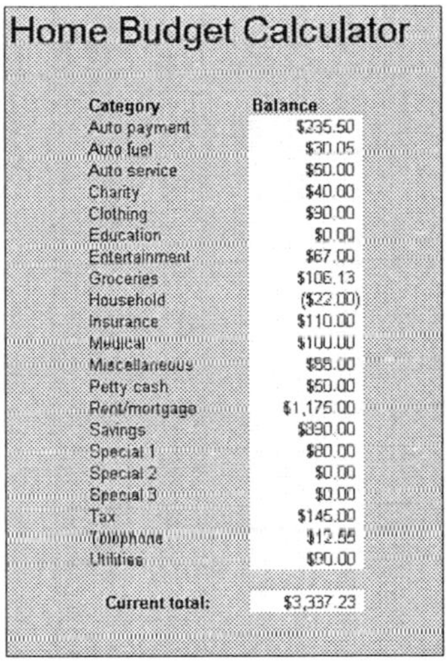

Figure A.2

The Overview worksheet of the Home Budget workbook.

Home Budget Calculator

Category	Balance
Auto payment	$235.50
Auto fuel	$30.05
Auto service	$50.00
Charity	$40.00
Clothing	$90.00
Education	$0.00
Entertainment	$67.00
Groceries	$106.13
Household	($22.00)
Insurance	$110.00
Medical	$100.00
Miscellaneous	$55.00
Petty cash	$50.00
Rent/mortgage	$1,175.00
Savings	$390.00
Special 1	$80.00
Special 2	$0.00
Special 3	$0.00
Tax	$145.00
Telephone	$12.55
Utilities	$90.00
Current total:	$3,337.23

The Budget Menu

Note that the menu bar has a new item on it—Budget. Adding custom menu items to templates is one of Excel's more advanced capabilities.

Viewing Macro Code

When you are working with a workbook that contains macro code, you can press F11 to open the Visual Basic Editor to view and, if desired, modify the code. The Visual Basic Editor is shown in Figure A.3.

A

Figure A.3

You use the Visual Basic Editor to enter and modify macro code.

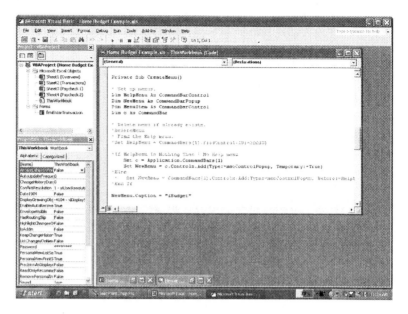

The menu is created by the code shown in Listing A.1. It creates the top-level Budget menu and then adds three menu commands to it, named Transactions, Paycheck 1, and Paycheck 2. Each of these commands is connected to another macro (which I will get to soon). When you select the menu command, the macro is run.

The code that creates the menu is called from the Workbook_Open event that is triggered whenever the workbook is opened.

Listing A.1 The Code That Creates the Custom Budget Menu

```
Private Sub CreateMenu()

' Set up menus.
Dim HelpMenu As CommandBarControl
Dim NewMenu As CommandBarPopup
Dim MenuItem As CommandBarControl
Dim c As CommandBar

Set c = Application.CommandBars(1)
Set NewMenu = c.Controls.Add(Type:=msoControlPopup, Temporary:=True)
NewMenu.Caption = "&Budget"

' Add sub menu items.
Set MenuItem = NewMenu.Controls.Add(Type:=msoControlButton)
With MenuItem
    .Caption = "&Transactions"
    .OnAction = "ThisWorkbook.ShowTransactionForm"
End With

Set MenuItem = NewMenu.Controls.Add(Type:=msoControlButton)
```

A

```
With MenuItem
    .Caption = "Paycheck &1"
    .OnAction = "ThisWorkbook.EnterPaycheck1"
End With

Set MenuItem = NewMenu.Controls.Add(Type:=msoControlButton)
With MenuItem
    .Caption = "Paycheck &2"
    .OnAction = "ThisWorkbook.EnterPaycheck2"
End With

End Sub
```

Of course, I did not want to leave the menu in place when you have finished using the Home Budget template and closed it! It is necessary to remove the menu when the workbook is closed. This is accomplished by the code shown in Listing A.2. This code is called from the Workbook_BeforeClose event.

Listing A.2   The Code That Deletes the Budget Menu

```
Private Sub DeleteMenu()
    On Error Resume Next
    Application.CommandBars(1).Controls("Budget").Delete
End Sub
```

The Transactions Worksheet

All of your budget data for income and expenses is stored on the Transactions worksheet, shown in Figure A.4. Each individual transaction consists of a date, a category, an amount (positive for income, negative for expenses), and an optional note. The information on the Overview worksheet, shown in Figure A.4, is calculated from the data on the Transactions worksheet.

Although you could enter your transactions directly into the Transactions worksheet, you should not. To simplify the task and to lessen the chance of errors, the template includes a data entry form, discussed next.

The Transaction Entry Form

Excel gives you the capability of designing custom forms for use in your workbooks. Each form can contain a variety of items, called *controls*, such as buttons, text boxes, lists, and option buttons. The transaction entry form for the Home Budget workbook is shown in Figure A.5. You can see that it provides places for you to enter all the required details for a transaction.

Figure A.4

Budget transactions are kept on the Transactions worksheet.

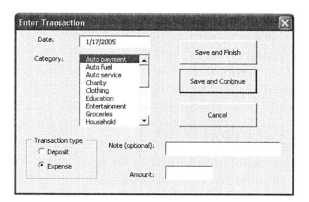

Figure A.5

The Enter Transaction form simplifies the task of entering budget transactions.

You can see that the list on the form presents all the permitted budget categories. These items are inserted into the list when the form is first displayed by the code shown in Listing A.3. This code is part of the form itself. If you want to include more categories in your budget, you can add them here.

Listing A.3   Creating the List of Budget Categories

```
Private Sub UserForm_Initialize()

txtDate.Text = Date

lstCategories.AddItem "Auto payment"
lstCategories.AddItem "Auto fuel"
lstCategories.AddItem "Auto service"
lstCategories.AddItem "Charity"
lstCategories.AddItem "Clothing"
lstCategories.AddItem "Education"
lstCategories.AddItem "Entertainment"
lstCategories.AddItem "Groceries"
```

A

```
lstCategories.AddItem "Household"
lstCategories.AddItem "Insurance"
lstCategories.AddItem "Medical"
lstCategories.AddItem "Miscellaneous"
lstCategories.AddItem "Petty cash"
lstCategories.AddItem "Rent/mortgage"
lstCategories.AddItem "Special 1"
lstCategories.AddItem "Special 2"
lstCategories.AddItem "Special 3"
lstCategories.AddItem "Tax"
lstCategories.AddItem "Telephone"
lstCategories.AddItem "Utilities"

End Sub
```

The Transaction Entry form also includes code to process the data you enter on the form—in other words, to enter it in the proper locations on the Transactions worksheet. This code is shown in Listing A.4. The actions it carries out are

1. Makes sure a valid date was entered and, if not, displays a message to you

2. Makes sure a category was selected from the list and, if not, displays a message to you

3. Makes sure an amount greater than zero was entered and, if not, displays a message to you

4. Changes the amount to a negative value if the Expense option is selected

5. Passes the entered data to the EnterTransaction macro that is a part of the workbook itself and not a part of the form

Listing A.4   Processing a Transaction

```
Private Sub ProcessTransactionData()

Dim d As Date
Dim cat As String
Dim amt As Currency
Dim note As String

On Error Resume Next
d = DateValue(txtDate.Text)
If Err = 13 Then
    MsgBox "Please enter a valid date."
    txtDate.SetFocus
    Exit Sub
End If

cat = lstCategories.Text
If cat = "" Then
```

A

Listing A.4   Continued

```
    MsgBox "You must select a category"
    lstCategories.SetFocus
    Exit Sub
End If

amt = Val(txtAmount.Text)
If amt <= 0 Then
    MsgBox "Please enter an amount greater than 0"
    txtAmount.SetFocus
    Exit Sub
End If

If optExpense Then amt = -amt

note = txtNote.Text

ThisWorkbook.EnterTransaction d, cat, amt, note
txtAmount.Text = ""
txtNote.Text = ""

End Sub
```

The code shown in Listing A.4 processes the transaction data you enter on the Transaction Entry form and then passes it to the workbook macro EnterTransaction. This code is shown in Listing A.5. It starts in cell B2 of the transactions worksheet and then moves down a row at a time looking for a blank cell. When it finds one, this is the next empty row in the transactions table and is where the new data should go.

Listing A.5   Entering Transaction Data in the Transactions Worksheet

```
Public Sub EnterTransaction(d As Date, cat As String, _
    amt As Currency, note As String)

Dim r As Range
Dim w As Worksheet

Set w = Application.Worksheets("Transactions")
Set r = w.Cells(2, 2)

Do While r.Value <> ""
    Set r = r.Offset(1, 0)
Loop

r.Value = d
r.Offset(0, 1).Value = cat
r.Offset(0, 2).Value = amt
r.Offset(0, 3).Value = note

End Sub
```

The Transaction Entry form is displayed when you select Transactions from the Budget menu. The menu command is connected to the macro shown in Listing A.6. This connection between the menu command and macro is established when the menu is created, as was shown in Listing A.1.

Listing A.6   Displaying the Transaction Entry Form

```
Public Sub ShowTransactionForm()

' Called to enter a budget expense or deposit
frmEnterTransaction.Show

End Sub
```

Entering Paychecks

The Home Budget workbook has the capability of automatically apportioning your paycheck among the various budget categories. There are two parts to this. The first is the Paycheck 1 worksheet (Paycheck 2 is for a second paycheck and works the same way). This is shown in Figure A.6. You enter the amount to go into each budget category from each paycheck. The total, calculated in cell C3, should be equal to the take-home pay.

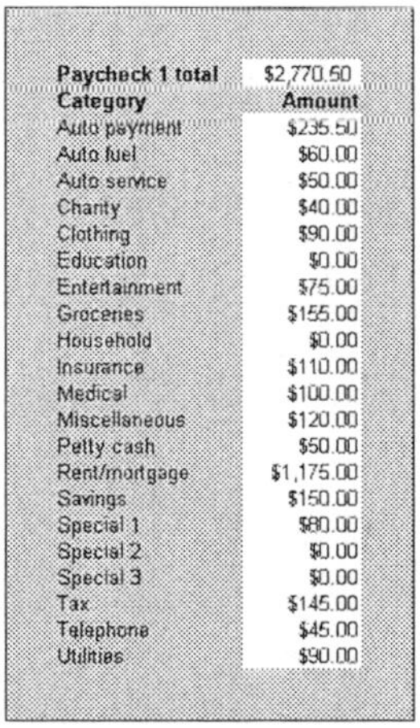

Figure A.6

You apportion your paycheck among the budget categories on the Paycheck work-sheet.

Paycheck 1 total	$2,770.50
Category	Amount
Auto payment	$235.50
Auto fuel	$60.00
Auto service	$50.00
Charity	$40.00
Clothing	$90.00
Education	$0.00
Entertainment	$75.00
Groceries	$155.00
Household	$0.00
Insurance	$110.00
Medical	$100.00
Miscellaneous	$120.00
Petty cash	$50.00
Rent/mortgage	$1,175.00
Savings	$150.00
Special 1	$80.00
Special 2	$0.00
Special 3	$0.00
Tax	$145.00
Telephone	$45.00
Utilities	$90.00

The second part of the paycheck process is done by a macro. When you select Paycheck 1 from the Budget menu, this macro reads the category amounts from the Paycheck 1 worksheet and enters transactions that deposit these amounts into their respective budget categories. This code is shown in Listing A.7. You can see that after retrieving the data from the Paycheck 1 worksheet, it calls the EnterTransaction macro to enter

A

the transaction on the Transactions worksheet. This macro, presented earlier in Listing A.5, is the same one used to enter data from the Enter Transaction form.

Listing A.7   Transferring Data from a Paycheck Worksheet to the Transactions Worksheet

```
Private Sub EnterPaycheck(paycheck As String)

Dim w As Worksheet
Dim r As Range
Dim d As Date
Dim n As String
Dim amt As Currency
Dim cat As String
Dim row As Integer

n = "From " & paycheck
d = Date

Set w = Application.Worksheets(paycheck)
Set r = w.Cells(4, 2)

For row = 1 To 20
    cat = r.Offset(row, 0).Value
    amt = Val(r.Offset(row, 1).Value)
    If amt > 0 Then EnterTransaction d, cat, amt, n
Next

End Sub
```

The Overview Worksheet

The main worksheet in the Home Budget Calculator is the Overview worksheet. This was shown earlier in Figure A.2. You can see it consists of a list of the budget categories, each one adjacent to the current balance for that category. A grand total is calculated at the bottom.

How does the worksheet calculate the total for each category? This seemed like a difficult problem until I realized that the current balance for a category is easily calculated by simply summing all the deposits to and withdrawals from the category. Because withdrawals are entered as negative numbers, this is a task for Excel's SUMIF function.

SUMIF calculates a sum from a column of numbers, but includes only those rows that meet a specified criterion. Thus, to get the current total for the Clothing category, for example, I would use SUMIF to add all the values in column D of the Transactions worksheet where column C contains the entry Clothing.

Let's dissect the formula used in column C of the Overview worksheet. This is the formula from cell C5; it is essentially identical for the other category rows:

```
=SUMIF(Transactions!$C$3:$C$60000,Overview!B5, _
    Transactions!$D$3:$D$60000)
```

Let's look at the three arguments:

- `Transactions!$C$3:$C$60000`—This argument tells the function where to compare the criterion; in this case, in cells C3:C60000 on the Transactions worksheet.

- `Overview!B5`—This argument tells the function what the criterion is. Here it is the category name in cell B5 on the Overview worksheet.

- `Transactions!$D$3:$D$60000`—The final argument tells the function where the values are located that are to be summed if the criterion is met. In this case it is cells D3:D60000 on the Transactions worksheet.

Because of the way Excel formulas work, the totals on the Overview worksheet are updated immediately when transactions are entered, edited, or deleted.

Note that if you want to add more categories to the budget workbook, you will have to enter them in the list on the Overview worksheet. This is in addition to changing the code shown earlier in Listing A.3 that adds the categories to the list in the Enter Transaction form.

Chapter 6: Checkbook Register Workbook

The Checkbook Register workbook, shown in Figure A.7, looks relatively simple but has some complexities under the hood. The single worksheet in this template consists mainly of a list of all checking account transactions—deposits, checks, ATM withdrawals, and so on—with summary cells (D4 and D5) to display totals.

The Register Menu

Like the Home Budget workbook discussed earlier in this appendix, the Checkbook Register workbook has a custom menu item called Register added to the menu bar. Because I discussed the creation of custom menus already, I will not go into any detail here but will just present the code for creating and removing the Register menu in Listing A.8.

Cleared and current balances

Figure A.7

The Checkbook
Register workbook.

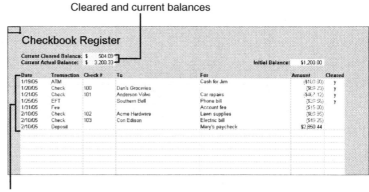

Transactions

Listing A.8 Creating and Removing the Custom Register Menu

```
Private Sub CreateMenu()

' Set up menus.
Dim HelpMenu As CommandBarControl
Dim NewMenu As CommandBarPopup
Dim MenuItem As CommandBarControl
Dim c As CommandBar

' Delete menu if already exists.
 DeleteMenu
    Set c = Application.CommandBars(1)
    Set NewMenu = c.Controls.Add(Type:=msoControlPopup, Temporary:=True)

NewMenu.Caption = "&Register"

' Add sub menu items.
Set MenuItem = NewMenu.Controls.Add(Type:=msoControlButton)
With MenuItem
    .Caption = "&Transactions"
    .OnAction = "ThisWorkbook.ShowTransactionForm"
End With

Set MenuItem = NewMenu.Controls.Add(Type:=msoControlButton)
With MenuItem
    .Caption = "Sort by &Date"
    .OnAction = "ThisWorkbook.SortByDate"
End With

Set MenuItem = NewMenu.Controls.Add(Type:=msoControlButton)
With MenuItem
    .Caption = "Sort by Check &Number"
    .OnAction = "ThisWorkbook.SortByCheckNum"
End With

Set MenuItem = NewMenu.Controls.Add(Type:=msoControlButton)
With MenuItem
    .Caption = "Sort by &To"
    .OnAction = "ThisWorkbook.SortByTo"
End With
```

A

```
End Sub

Private Sub DeleteMenu()
    On Error Resume Next
    Application.CommandBars(1).Controls("Register").Delete
End Sub
```

Entering Transactions

In another parallel with the Home Budget workbook, the Checkbook Register employs a custom form for entering transactions. This form is shown in Figure A.8. You can see that it includes entry fields for all the required information and a list of transaction types to choose from. Amounts are always entered on the form as positive values and then converted to negative values for entry into the Register worksheet for those transactions that take money out of the account.

Figure A.8

This custom form is used to enter transactions into the Check Register.

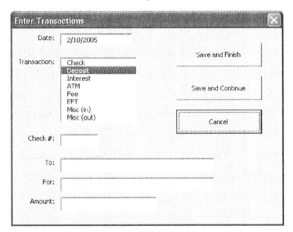

The form itself includes macro code to process the transaction data when you click either the Save and Continue or Save and Finish button. This code, shown in Listing A.9, consists mostly of checking to see that appropriate data was entered. If the code detects a problem, you are prompted to fix it.

Listing A.9   Processing Data You Entered

```
Private Sub ProcessTransactionData()

Dim d As Date
Dim trans As String
Dim amt As Currency
Dim note As String

On Error Resume Next
d = DateValue(txtDate.Text)
```

Listing A.9 Continued

```
If Err = 13 Then
    MsgBox "Please enter a valid date."
    txtDate.SetFocus
    Exit Sub
End If

trans = lstTransaction.Text
If trans = "" Then
    MsgBox "You must select a transaction type."
    lstTransaction.SetFocus
    Exit Sub
End If

If trans = "Check" And Val(txtCheckNum.Text) <= 0 Then
    MsgBox "Please enter a check number."
    txtCheckNum.SetFocus
    Exit Sub
End If

amt = Val(txtAmount.Text)
If amt <= 0 Then
    MsgBox "Please enter an amount greater than 0"
    txtAmount.SetFocus
    Exit Sub
End If

' Adjust for payments out.
If trans = "Check" Or trans = "ATM" Or trans = "Fee" _
    Or trans = "EFT" Or trans = "Misc (out)" Then
    amt = -amt
End If

If trans = "Check" Or trans = "EFT" Then
    If txtTo.Text = "" Then '
    MsgBox "You must enter something in the To field."
    txtTo.SetFocus
    Exit Sub
    End If
End If

ThisWorkbook.EnterTransaction d, trans, txtCheckNum.Text, txtTo.Text,
txtFor.Text, amt

txtAmount.Text = ""
txtFor.Text = ""
txtTo.Text = ""
txtCheckNum.Text = ""

End Sub
```

After the code in ProcessTransactionData has verified that the data is okay, the data is passed to the EnterTransaction macro. This macro, shown in Listing A.10, performs the actual task of entering the data in the cells of the Checkbook Register worksheet. The code works by starting at the top of the transaction list and moving down until it finds the first blank row. Then it moves across and enters each item of data in the appropriate column.

Listing A.10   Entering the Verified Transaction Data

```
Public Sub EnterTransaction(d As Date, trans As String, num As String, _
    payee As String, whatfor As String, amt As Currency)

Dim r As Range
Dim w As Worksheet

Set w = Application.Worksheets("Register")
Set r = w.Cells(7, 2)

Do While r.Value <> ""
    Set r = r.Offset(1, 0)
Loop

r.Value = d
r.Offset(0, 1).Value = trans
r.Offset(0, 2).Value = num
r.Offset(0, 3).Value = payee
r.Offset(0, 4).Value = whatfor
r.Offset(0, 5).Value = amt

Set w = Nothing
Set r = Nothing

End Sub
```

Sorting the Transactions

The Checkbook Register gives you the option of sorting the transactions by date, check number, or payee (the To column). These actions are done with the corresponding commands on the Register menu. Each menu command is connected to the corresponding macro by the code that creates the custom menu (refer to Listing A.8). Because of Excel's built-in sorting capabilities, these macros are quite short. The three sorting macros are shown in Listing A.11.

Listing A.11   Three Macros Used to Sort the Register Transactions

```
Private Sub SortByCheckNum()

Dim r As Range
Dim w As Worksheet

Set w = Application.Worksheets("Register")
Set r = w.Cells(7, 2)
r.CurrentRegion.Sort Key1:="Check #", Header:=xlYes
```

A

Listing A.11 Continued

```
Set r = Nothing
Set w = Nothing

End Sub

Private Sub SortByTo()

Dim r As Range
Dim w As Worksheet

Set w = Application.Worksheets("Register")
Set r = w.Cells(7, 2)
r.CurrentRegion.Sort Key1:="To", Header:=xlYes

Set r = Nothing
Set w = Nothing

End Sub

Private Sub SortByDate()

Dim r As Range
Dim w As Worksheet

Set w = Application.Worksheets("Register")
Set r = w.Cells(7, 2)
r.CurrentRegion.Sort Key1:="Date", Header:=xlYes

Set r = Nothing
Set w = Nothing

End Sub
```

Calculating the Totals

The Checkbook Register displays two totals, one for the cleared balance and one for the actual balance. Let's see how these are done.

The actual balance is the easier one to calculate. It is simply the sum of the initial balance (cell G5) and all of the individual transactions. The formula is

```
=G5+SUM(G8:G60000)
```

Calculating the cleared balance is a bit more complicated. The cleared balance is the sum of the initial balance plus all transactions that have been marked as cleared. Cleared transactions are marked with a *y* (or any other character) in the Cleared column. The formula uses the SUMIF function to sum only those values in column G where column H is not blank. The formula is

```
=G5+SUMIF(H8:H60000,"<>",G8:G60000)
```

A

Chapter 7: Real Cost Calculator

The Real Cost Calculator is designed to tell you how much it will really cost to buy something on a credit card and pay it off over time. This workbook is shown in Figure A.9. You enter the items' cost, the credit card interest rate, and the intended monthly payment in cells C4:C6. The worksheet calculates how long it will take to pay off the balance and the final total cost.

Item's price sticker

Figure A.9

The Real Cost Calculator determines the real cost of credit card purchases.

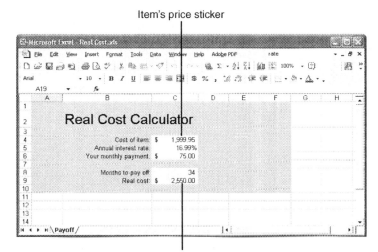

Actual cost of charging item

The Months to Pay Off value is calculated using Excel's NPER function. This function is given the principal amount, interest rate, and payment amount for your credit card and returns the number of periods it will take to pay off. Because the return value might be fractional—for example, 28.46 months—the result is plugged into the INT function to get the next lowest integer and then 1 is added. This results in the displayed answer being the next higher integer than the answer supplied by NPER. The final formula in cell C8 is

```
=INT(NPER(C5/12,C6,-C4)) + 1
```

The total cost displayed in cell C9 is easily calculated as the number of months to pay off the debt times the monthly payment. This amount is not precise to the penny because the final payment will almost always be less than the earlier ones, but it is close enough for our purposes.

A

Chapter 7: Payoff Calculator

The Credit Card Payoff Calculator from Chapter 7, "Getting the Most from Your Credit Cards," helps you calculate how much interest you will save by paying off a credit card balance now instead of paying it off over time. This calculator, shown in Figure A.10, has three inputs: the amount you owe, the interest rate the card charges, and the amount you propose to pay each month.

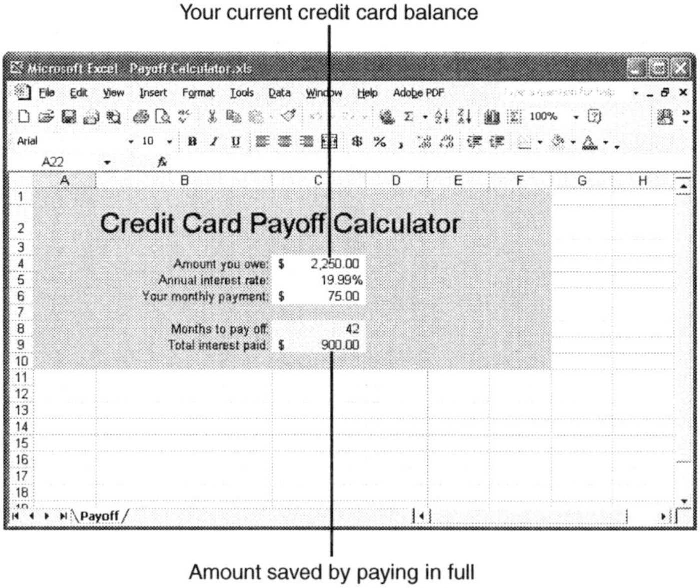

Figure A.10

The Credit Card Payoff Calculator shows you how much you will save by paying off a credit card balance now.

Your current credit card balance

Amount saved by paying in full

The first calculation, in cell C8, determines how long it will take to pay off the balance using Excel's NPER function. The arguments to this function are the three input values in cells C4:C6. Please note that

- The annual interest rate is divided by 12 to get the monthly interest rate, which is necessary because you are making monthly payments.

- The amount you owe is entered into the formula as a negative amount in accord with the way Excel handles cash flows.

NPER can return a fractional value, so to round off to the next lowest integer, the INT function is used. Then 1 is added to get the final result. The formula is shown here:

```
=INT(NPER(C5/12,C6,-C4)) + 1
```

The amount in cell C9 is the total interest paid. This is easily calculated as the sum of all payments minus the original balance. The formula is

=((C8*C6) - C4)

Chapter 7: Cash Advance Cost Calculator

The Cash Advance Cost Calculator is used to determine the total cost of taking a cash advance from your credit card and paying it back over time. This calculation is complicated by the fact that not only do you pay interest on cash advances but also a one-time fee of a certain percentage of the advance amount. This calculator is shown in Figure A.11.

Figure A.11

Use the Cash Advance Cost Calculator to determine the total cost of a cash advance.

Cost of advance over the full payback period

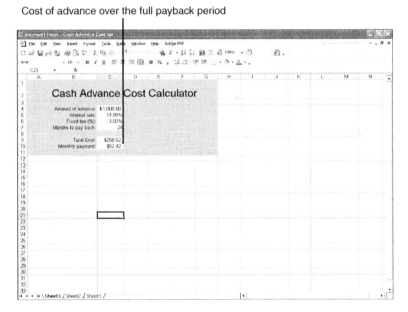

There are four inputs to this calculator:

- The amount of the advance
- The card's interest rate for advances
- The fixed fee as a percentage
- The number of months over which you will pay the advance back

The cost of the advance is, in principle, easily calculated by summing the payments you will make and subtracting the original advance amount. The amount put on your credit card account will actually be the advance amount itself, plus the one-time fee. In the example shown in Figure A.11, you will get $1,000 cash but your account will be charged $1,030—the $1,000 plus 3%.

The formula in cell C9 uses the PMT function to calculate the monthly payment on this total amount, which is calculated as C4+(C4*C6). This monthly payment amount is multiplied by the number of months to get the total you will pay. Then by subtracting the advance amount in cell C4, the total cost is determined. The formula in cell C9 is

`=-PMT(C5/12,C7,C4+C4*C6)*C7-C4`

Note the leading minus sign. The return value of the PMT function will be negative because it represents money you are paying out. It makes more sense, however, to display the answer as a positive value in the worksheet.

Chapter 8: Mortgage Payment Calculator

The Mortgage Payment Calculator is shown in Figure A.12. This calculator does two things: It shows you the monthly payment on a specific house purchase, and estimates how much house you can afford based on a given monthly payment.

Calculate payment for a specific house

The house you can buy with that payment

Figure A.12

The Mortgage
Payment Calculator.

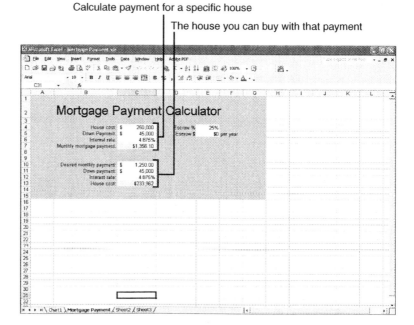

Both calculations use the escrow information entered in cells E4:E5. If you enter a dollar amount in cell E5, that amount is used in the calculations (I'll show how that's done soon). If you enter 0 in cell E5, the percentage value in cell E4 is used.

The first part of the calculator is in cells C4:C7. The first three cells are for entering the house price, the down payment amount, and the mortgage interest rate (a 30-year mortgage is assumed. If you want to calculate for another term, change the formula in cell C7, substituting the new term in months for the 360 value that occurs twice in the formula. The same applies for the other formulas given below). The resulting monthly payment based on this information and the escrow information is calculated in cell C7. Because of the need to use one or the other escrow amount, this formula uses the IF function and is rather long:

```
=IF(E5>0,-PMT(C6/12,360,C4-C5)+E5/12,-PMT(C6/12,360, _
    C4-C5)*(1+E4))
```

The first part of the formula (E5>0) is the condition. If this is true—if the value in cell E5 is greater than zero—the payment is calculated using the PMT function and adding one-twelfth of the annual escrow amount:

```
-PMT(C6/12,360,C4-C5)+E5/12
```

If, however, cell E5 is zero, the payment is calculated using the PMT function and applying the percentage factor from cell E4:

```
-PMT(C6/12,360,C4-C5)*(1+E4)
```

The second part of the calculator is in cells C10:C13. You enter the desired monthly payment, the down payment amount, and the mortgage interest rate. Then cell C13 calculates the maximum house price you could afford based on this information and the escrow data from cells E4:E5. Again, the IF function is used as described previously to use one or the other escrow fields:

```
=IF(E5>0,C11+ABS(PV(C12/12,360,
    C10-(E5/12))),C11+ABS(PV(C12/12,360,C10/(1+E4))))
```

Chapter 8: Mortgage Points Comparator

The Mortgage Points Comparator, shown in Figure A.13, enables you to compare two mortgages that differ in terms of the interest rates and points charged.

Figure A.13

The Mortgage Points Comparator collates two mortgages.

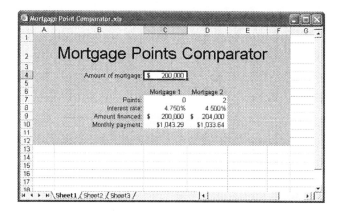

To use this calculator, you enter the mortgage amount in cell C4. For each mortgage, the interest rate and number of points are entered in the indicated fields. The algorithm assumes that any points are rolled into the financed amount.

For each mortgage, the amount financed is simply the amount of the mortgage plus the amount of the points. This is calculated in cell C9 with this formula:

```
=$C$4+((C7/100)*$C$4)
```

Cell D9 has an equivalent formula. Then the monthly payment (not including escrow) is calculated in cell C10 with the PMT function:

```
=-PMT(C8/12,360,C9)
```

You'll note that a 30-year mortgage term is assumed.

Chapter 8: Mortgage Tax Savings Calculator

Because mortgage interest and property tax payments are tax deductible, the resulting tax savings often mean that the true cost of buying a house is significantly less than it seems. The Mortgage Tax Savings Calculator is designed to show you just how much less the cost is. It is shown in Figure A.14.

Cells C4 through C11 are for you to enter information about your federal and state marginal tax rates, the house, the mortgage, the property tax, and the insurance cost. The output data in cells C13:C20 are calculated based on this information as described next.

A

Figure A.14

The Mortgage Tax
Savings Calculator.

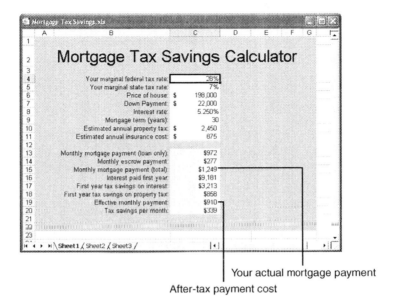

Your actual mortgage payment

After-tax payment cost

Cell C13 is the monthly mortgage payment (not including escrow) that is calculated using the PMT function:

```
=-PMT(C8/12,C9*12,C6-C7)
```

Cell C14 is the monthly escrow payment, which is the sum of the annual property tax and insurance costs divided by 12:

```
=(C10+C11)/12
```

Cell C15 is the total monthly PITI payment that is simply the sum of cells C13 and C14:

```
=C13+C14
```

Cell C16 calculates the total mortgage interest that will be paid the first year. It uses the IPMT function. The payments are monthly, so the formula in this cell must calculate the interest for each month and then add them together. For example, the interest for the first month is calculated as

```
IPMT(C8/12,1,C9*12,C6-C7)
```

The entire formula in cell C16 simply does this for each month and adds them together:

```
=-(IPMT(C8/12,1,C9*12,C6-C7)+IPMT(C8/12,2,C9*12, _
    C6-C7)+IPMT(C8/12,3,C9*12,C6-C7)+IPMT(C8/12,4,C9*12, _
    C6-C7)+IPMT(C8/12,5,C9*12,C6-C7)+IPMT(C8/12,6,C9*12, _
    C6-C7)+IPMT(C8/12,7,C9*12,C6-C7)+IPMT(C8/12,8,C9*12, _
    C6-C7)+IPMT(C8/12,9,C9*12,C6-C7)+IPMT(C8/12,10,C9*12, _
    C6-C7)+IPMT(C8/12,11,C9*12,C6-C7)+IPMT(C8/12,12,C9*12,C6-C7))
```

A

Cell C17 calculates your tax savings for the first year based on the interest paid. This is equal to the total interest paid in the first year multiplied by the federal and state marginal tax rates:

```
=C16*C4+C16*C5
```

Cell C18 calculates the tax savings due to your property tax payment:

```
=C4*C10+C5*C10
```

Cell C19 calculates the effective monthly PITI payment. This is done by adding the annual tax savings (from cells C17 and C18) and dividing by 12 to get the monthly savings, and then subtracting this from the PITI payment in cell C15:

```
=C15-(C18+C17)/12
```

Finally, cell C20 shows you the estimated monthly tax savings:

```
=C15-C19
```

Chapter 8: Maximum Mortgage Calculator

The Maximum Mortgage Calculator presents estimates of the mortgage amount you could get at various interest rates. This calculator is shown in Figure A.15.

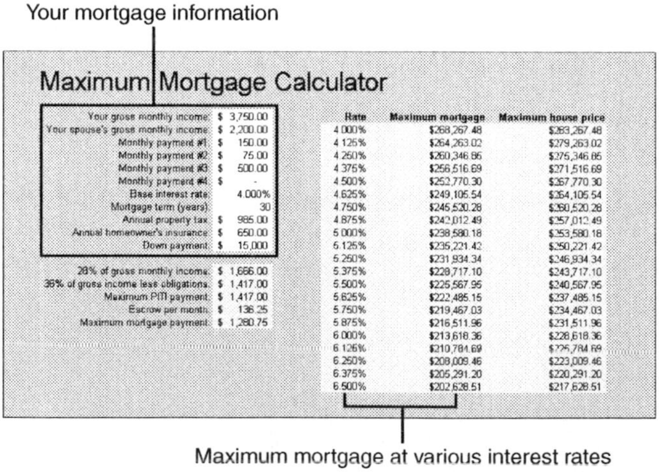

Your mortgage information

Figure A.15

The Maximum Mortgage Calculator helps you estimate how much of a mortgage you can qualify for.

Maximum mortgage at various interest rates

As explained in the chapter, the calculations employ a formula that is widely used in the mortgage industry, and that is based on your gross income (and your spouse's, if applicable) and your other obligations. This formula says that your maximum monthly PITI payment is the lesser of

(a) 28% of your gross monthly income, or (b) 36% of your gross monthly income, less other monthly obligations (car payments and so forth).

In the workbook, cells C4 through C14 provide fields for entry of user information. Calculations for output values are as follows.

Cell C16 calculates 28% of gross monthly income with the formula

```
=(C4+C5)*0.28
```

Cell C17 calculates 36% of gross income, less obligations, with this formula:

```
=(C4+C5)*0.36-SUM(C6:C9)
```

Cell C18 uses the IF function to display the lower of the values in cells C16 and C17:

```
=IF(C17>C16,C16,C17)
```

Cell C19 calculates your monthly escrow payment by adding the annual property tax and insurance costs and dividing by 12:

```
=(C12+C13)/12
```

Finally, cell C20 displays the maximum mortgage payment you could afford under the guidelines by subtracting the monthly escrow payment from the maximum PITI payment:

```
=C18-C19
```

The really interesting information is shown in the table in cells E4:G25. The first column displays a range of interest rates starting with the base value you entered in cell C10. Cell E5 simply copies this value with the formula

```
=C10
```

Each subsequent cell in the column adds 1/8% to the value above it. Thus the formula in cell E6 is

```
=E5+0.00125
```

Column F displays the maximum mortgage you could get at the interest rate in column E, the mortgage term in cell C11, and the payment amount in cell C20. This calculation uses the PV function as shown here (for cell F5):

```
=-PV(E5/12,$C$11*12,$C$20)
```

Finally, column G displays the maximum house price you could afford by adding the down payment in cell C14 to the maximum mortgage amount in column F.

Chapter 8: Mortgage Detail Calculator

The Mortgage Detail Calculator is designed to provide a complete analysis of all the details of a mortgage. It is shown in Figure A.16.

Figure A.16

The Mortgage Detail Calculator provides the most complete look at the details of a mortgage.

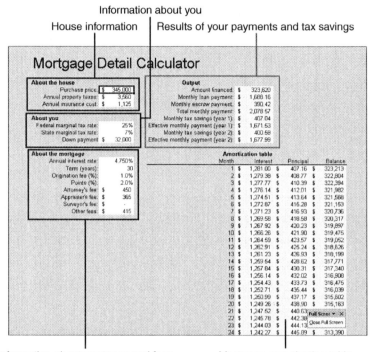

Information about you

House information | Results of your payments and tax savings

Information about mortgage and fees | Mortgage amortization table

The left side of this workbook provides input cells for all the relevant information. These were explained in Chapter 8, "Understanding Mortgages—And Getting the One That's Best for You." The algorithms used for the calculations assume that all the costs, such as attorney's fees, will be rolled into the mortgage.

Cells F5 through F12 provide summary calculations from the data you entered.

Cell F5 displays the total amount financed. It is calculated as the house price minus the down payment plus the amounts added for the origination fee and points and the various miscellaneous fees from cells C19:C22. The formula is

`=(C5-C12)+(C17+C18)*(C5-C12)+SUM(C19:C22)`

Cell F6 displays the monthly loan payment (not including escrow). It is calculated using the PMT function:

```
=-PMT(C15/12,C16*12,F5)
```

Cell F6 is your monthly escrow payment, calculated as 1/12 of the sum of the annual insurance and property tax amounts:

```
=(C7+C6)/12
```

Cell F7 is your total PITI payment, the sum of the mortgage payment and the escrow payment:

```
=F7+F6
```

Cell F9 estimates your monthly tax savings for the first year. It does this by adding together the annual property tax payment with the sum of the monthly interest payments for the first year (obtained from the amortization table I'll get to in a moment). This amount is multiplied by the sum of the federal and state marginal tax rates, and the result is divided by 12 to get a monthly amount. The formula is

```
=(C10+C11)*(SUM(F16:F27)+C6)/12
```

Cell F10 displays the effective monthly payment for year one, which is simply the actual PITI payment from cell F8 minus the tax savings from F9:

```
-F8-F9
```

Cells F11 and F12 do the same thing for the second year, and their formulas are essentially the same as just described.

This workbook also includes an amortization table. This table shows the interest amount, principal amount, and balance for each payment over the life of the mortgage.

The Month column displays the numbers 1 through 360, enough to handle a 30-year mortgage. For shorter term mortgages, only the relevant rows will be filled in.

The Interest column uses the IPMT function to calculate the interest for the specified payment. The payment number is taken from the Month column, and the other information IPMT needs is taken from the relevant input fields elsewhere on the worksheet.

```
-IPMT($C$15/12,E16,$C$16*12,$F$5)
```

This formula could have been copied down to fill all 360 rows of the table. But what if the mortgage is not for 30 years but for a shorter period? I did not want nonsense data being displayed for the months after the mortgage ends. To avoid this, I used the IF function to display a result in the cell only if the month (from the Month column) was within the term of the mortgage. Otherwise, the cell display is blank. Thus the entire formula in cell F16, and copied to all rows below, is

```
=IF(E16<=($C$16*12),-IPMT($C$15/12,E16,$C$16*12,$F$5),"")
```

The Principal column determines the amount of the payment that goes toward the principal by subtracting the interest payment in the Interest column from the total payment amount in cell F6. The same technique with the IF function is used to display the result only in rows that fall within the mortgage term:

```
=IF(E16<=$C$16*12,$F$6-F16,"")
```

The Balance column is a little trickier. In the first row, for month 1, the balance is the initial amount of the mortgage from cell F5, less the first month's principal payment from cell G16. The formula in cell H16 (again using IF as described before) is

```
=IF(E16<=($C$16*12),$F$5-G16,"")
```

For months 2 and onward, the balance is the previous month's balance less that month's principal payment. Thus the formula in cell H17 is

```
=IF(E17<=($C$16*12),H16-G17,"")
```

This is the formula that is copied down to all the lower rows in the table.

Chapter 9: Home Equity Line of Credit Calculator

The Home Equity Line of Credit Calculator lets you view the payment and amortization schedule for this kind of loan. It is shown in Figure A.17.

Most home equity loans figure the minimum payment two ways—as a percentage of the balance and as a fixed dollar amount. For any given month, your minimum payment is the larger of these two amounts. The calculator takes this into account.

A

Figure A.17

The Home Equity Line
of Credit Calculator.

Equity line details   Total interest

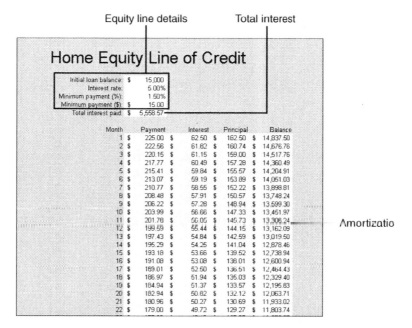

Cells C4 through C7 are for input of information about the loan. Cell C8 calculates the total interest you will pay, based on the interest payments in the amortization table. This calculator assumes you will make the minimum required payment each month, which might not be the case. If you want to get results for a payment that is larger than the minimum, enter your proposed payment amount in cell C7 as the minimum payment amount.

The amortization table that starts in row 11 provides the main results of the workbook. It follows a strategy similar to that used in some of the earlier calculators. The first row uses different formulas than subsequent rows.

Cell C11 displays the first payment as the greater of (a) the minimum payment percent times the initial balance or (b) the minimum payment dollar amount (cell C7). This is done using the IF function:

```
=IF(C6*C4>C7,C6*C4,C7)
```

Cell D11 calculates the first month's interest payment as simply the annual interest (cell C5) divided by 12 and then multiplied by the initial balance:

```
=C5/12*C4
```

Cell E11 calculates the principal component of the first payment by subtracting the interest component from the total payment:

```
=C11-D11
```

Finally for the first row, the first month balance is determined by subtracting the first month's principal payment from the initial balance:

`=C4-E11`

The second row uses different formulas and is copied down for the entire table. The formula in cell C12 uses the IF function to determine if the previous month's balance—from the cell in column F one row up—is greater than 0. If not, 0 is displayed. If it is greater than 0, another nested IF function determines the actual payment based on the greater of the two minimums. The formula is

`=IF(F11>0,IF($C$6*F11>$C$7,$C$6*F11,$C$7),0)`

Cell D12 again uses an IF function to display a result only if the previous month's balance is greater than 0. If it is, the interest portion of the current month's payment is calculated as before:

`=IF(F11>0,$C$5/12*F11,0)`

Cell E12 calculates the principal portion of the current payment by subtracting the interest part from the total payment. A result is displayed only if a payment is due, again using the IF function:

`=IF(F11>0,C12-D12,0)`

Finally, the balance in cell F12 is calculated as the previous month's balance less the principal component of the current month's payment:

`=IF(F11>0,F11-E12,0)`

Chapter 10: Mortgage Refinance Breakeven Calculator

The Mortgage Refinance Breakeven Calculator is designed to help you determine if refinancing your primary home mortgage makes sense financially. It is shown in Figure A.18.

Cells C5:C9 are for information about the current mortgage. The remaining year's figure should be entered to the nearest year, even if a partial year is involved. This rounding will cause minor inaccuracies in the output but they are so small as to not influence the results in any meaningful way. Note that this calculator ignores escrow, which would probably be the same before and after a refinance, in any case.

A

New mortgage information

Current mortgage information

Figure A.18

The Mortgage
Refinance Breakeven
Calculator.

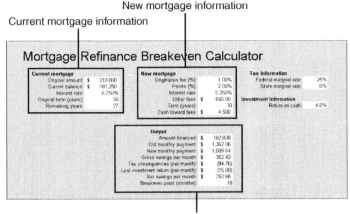

Refinance evaluation

The New Mortgage section provides input fields for information about the new mortgage. The Other Fees field is for the total of other fees involved, such as survey and appraisal. The Cash Toward Fees field is for the amount of cash you will put toward points and fees (as opposed to rolling them into the principal of the new mortgage).

The output fields are as described next.

Cell E14 is the total amount you will borrow on the new mortgage. It is calculated as the sum of the balance due on the old mortgage, the origination fee, points, and fees. Then the Cash Toward Fees is subtracted. The formula is

```
=C6+(E5+E6)*C6+E8-E10
```

The old monthly payment is calculated using the PMT function:

```
=-PMT(C7/12,C8*12,C5)
```

Likewise, the new mortgage payment uses this formula:

```
=-PMT(E7/12,E9*12,E14)
```

Gross Savings per Month in cell E17 is simply the difference between the old and new payments:

```
=E15-E16
```

The Tax Consequences result is calculated as the tax savings you will lose or gain because you are paying less or more interest on the refinanced mortgage. This figure is based on interest payments for the first 12 months after the refinance. Note that this formula references the Hide Me worksheet—I'll explain this in a moment.

```
=-((G5+G6)*('Hide Me'!F17-'Hide Me'!C17))/12
```

A

The Lost Investment Return result is a calculation based on any cash you would put toward fees (cell G9) and the predicted investment return you would have earned on that cash (cell E10):

```
=-(G9*E10)/12
```

The Net Savings per Month is a simply addition of the mortgage payment savings less any tax and investment consequences:

```
=E17+E18+E19
```

Finally, the Breakeven Point (Months) is a determination of how long your savings will take to make up the cash you put toward the refinance. The formula uses the IF function to display NA if the cash amount is zero.

```
=IF(E10>0,INT(E10/E20) + 1,"NA")
```

The Hide Me worksheet is shown in Figure A.19. This worksheet contains formulas whose results are used by the main worksheet but you do not need to see. If you want to display this worksheet, select Format, Sheet, Unhide.

Figure A.19

The Mortgage Refinance Breakeven Calculator includes this hidden worksheet for calculating interest payments.

	A	B	C	D	E	F	G	H
1		This worksheet is used for background calculations.						
2		Do not make any changes!						
3								
4		New mortgage interest			Old mortgage interest			
5		1	$799.91		37	$1,140.79		
6		2	$799.00		38	$1,139.55		
7		3	$798.07		39	$1,138.30		
8		4	$797.15		40	$1,137.04		
9		5	$796.22		41	$1,135.77		
10		6	$795.29		42	$1,134.50		
11		7	$794.35		43	$1,133.22		
12		8	$793.41		44	$1,131.93		
13		9	$792.46		45	$1,130.64		
14		10	$791.51		46	$1,129.33		
15		11	$790.56		47	$1,128.03		
16		12	$789.60		48	$1,126.71		
17			$9,537.52			$13,605.80		
18								
19								
20								

Columns B and C calculate the interest portion of each of the first 12 payments on the new mortgage. This is done using the IPMT function as shown here for month 1:

```
=-IPMT(Refinance!$E$7/12,'Hide Me'!B5,
    Refinance!$E$9*12,Refinance!$E$14)
```

Columns E and D do the same for the next 12 payments on the old mortgage. The month number is calculated based on the Remaining

Years field (cell C9) on the main worksheet as follows (for cell E5 on the hidden worksheet):

```
=(Refinance!C8*12-Refinance!C9*12) + 1
```

Subsequent rows just add 1 to the value in the above cells to get the next month value. Then the interest on that month's payment for the old mortgage is calculated using the IMPT function:

```
=-IPMT(Refinance!$C$7/12,'Hide Me'!E5,
    Refinance!$C$8*12,Refinance!$C$5)
```

The interest totals in cells C17 and F17 are used in formulas in the main worksheet to calculate the tax consequences of the refinance.

Chapter 11: Escrow Cancellation Calculator

The Escrow Cancellation Calculator helps you determine the financial payback for canceling your escrow account and managing your insurance and property tax payments yourself. It is shown in Figure A.20.

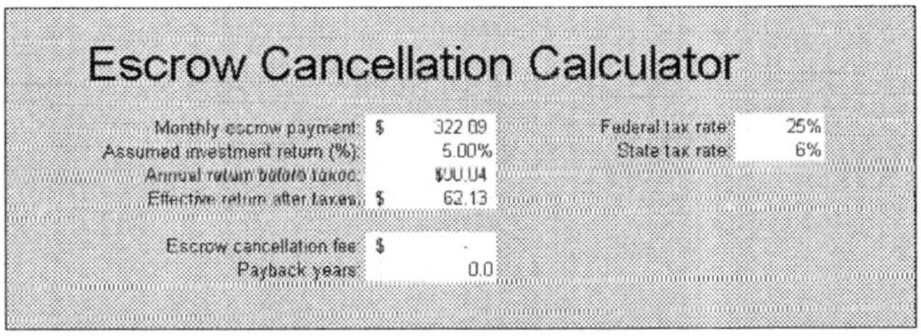

Figure A.20

The Escrow Cancellation Calculator.

You input your monthly escrow payment, marginal tax bracket information, and the estimated return that would be obtained if the escrow payment were invested each month for a year. The Annual Return Before Taxes calculates the amount you would earn over the year at the projected rate by determining the future value (using the FV function) of the account in one year and then subtracting the amount actually put into the account. This difference is, of course, the gain. The formula is

```
=-FV(C5/12,12,C4)-(C4*12)
```

The Effective Return After Taxes calculates your actual return after you pay taxes on it, as follows:

```
=C6-(C6*(E5+E4))
```

If there is a fee for canceling your escrow account, this amount can be entered in cell C9. Then cell C10 displays the payback period by dividing the fee amount by the effective annual return:

```
=C9/C7
```

Chapter 12: Rent Versus Buy Calculator

The Rent versus Buy Calculator will help people who are trying to decide whether to keep renting their home or to take the plunge and buy their own place. This workbook has three worksheets.

The Input Worksheet

The worksheet where you enter information, named Rent versus Buy, is shown in Figure A.21.

Figure A.21

You enter your information on this worksheet of the Rent versus Buy Calculator.

Purchase price of house   Amount financed

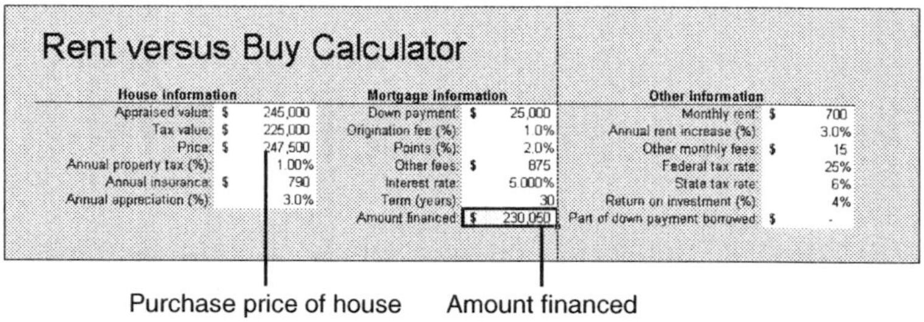

The input fields on this worksheet were explained in Chapter 12, "Renting Versus Buying Your Home—Making the Right Choice," so I will not go into them here. The one calculated field, cell E11, determines the total amount that would be financed by adding the price, points, origination fee, and other fees and then subtracting the down payment:

```
=C7+(E6+E7)*(C7-E5)+E8-E5
```

The Output Worksheet

The Output worksheet of this calculator displays the results in a tabular format, as shown in Figure A.22.

The formulas used on this worksheet mostly reference input fields on the Rent versus Buy worksheet. The sample formulas shown here are all from the first row of results.

The Buying Section

Columns B through I present data based on the buying scenario entered on the input worksheet. The PI (principal and interest) payment in column D is calculated using the PMT function:

```
=-PMT('Rent versus Buy'!$E$9/12,'Rent versus Buy'!$E$10*12,
    'Rent versus Buy'!$E$11)
```

Equity if buying   Equity if renting

Figure A.22

The results of the Rent versus Buy Calculator.

Month	PITI Payment	PI Payment	Principal	Interest	Effective PITI Payment	Balance	Equity	Rent Payment	Equity
1	$1,488.29	$1,234.96	$276.42	$958.54	$ 1,191.14	$229,774	$15,225	$ 715.00	$ 25,000
2	$1,488.29	$1,234.96	$277.57	$957.39	$ 1,191.50	$229,496	$16,415	$ 715.00	$ 25,560
3	$1,488.29	$1,234.96	$278.72	$956.23	$ 1,191.86	$229,217	$17,306	$ 715.00	$ 26,122
4	$1,488.29	$1,234.96	$279.89	$955.07	$ 1,192.22	$228,937	$17,906	$ 715.00	$ 26,686
5	$1,488.29	$1,234.96	$281.05	$953.91	$ 1,192.58	$228,656	$18,303	$ 715.00	$ 27,253
6	$1,488.29	$1,234.96	$282.22	$952.73	$ 1,192.94	$228,374	$19,004	$ 715.00	$ 27,822
7	$1,488.29	$1,234.96	$283.40	$951.56	$ 1,193.31	$228,091	$20,607	$ 715.00	$ 28,393
8	$1,488.29	$1,234.96	$284.58	$950.38	$ 1,193.67	$227,806	$21,514	$ 715.00	$ 28,966
9	$1,488.29	$1,234.96	$285.77	$949.19	$ 1,194.04	$227,520	$22,423	$ 715.00	$ 29,541
10	$1,488.29	$1,234.96	$286.96	$948.00	$ 1,194.41	$227,233	$23,335	$ 715.00	$ 30,119
11	$1,488.29	$1,234.96	$288.15	$946.81	$ 1,194.78	$226,945	$24,249	$ 715.00	$ 30,700
12	$1,488.29	$1,234.96	$289.35	$945.61	$ 1,195.15	$226,656	$25,166	$ 715.00	$ 31,282
13	$1,493.92	$1,234.96	$290.56	$944.40	$ 1,201.15	$226,365	$26,087	$ 736.00	$ 31,851
14	$1,493.92	$1,234.96	$291.77	$943.19	$ 1,201.53	$226,074	$27,009	$ 736.00	$ 32,423
15	$1,493.92	$1,234.96	$292.98	$941.97	$ 1,201.90	$225,781	$27,935	$ 736.00	$ 32,997
16	$1,493.92	$1,234.96	$294.21	$940.75	$ 1,202.28	$225,486	$28,864	$ 736.00	$ 33,573
17	$1,493.92	$1,234.96	$295.43	$939.53	$ 1,202.66	$225,191	$29,795	$ 736.00	$ 34,152
18	$1,493.92	$1,234.96	$296.66	$938.30	$ 1,203.04	$224,894	$30,729	$ 736.00	$ 34,733
19	$1,493.92	$1,234.96	$297.90	$937.06	$ 1,203.43	$224,596	$31,666	$ 736.00	$ 35,316
20	$1,493.92	$1,234.96	$299.14	$935.82	$ 1,203.81	$224,297	$32,606	$ 736.00	$ 35,902
21	$1,493.92	$1,234.96	$300.39	$934.67	$ 1,204.20	$223,997	$33,548	$ 736.00	$ 36,489
22	$1,493.92	$1,234.96	$301.64	$933.32	$ 1,204.59	$223,695	$34,494	$ 736.00	$ 37,080
23	$1,493.92	$1,234.96	$302.89	$932.06	$ 1,204.98	$223,392	$35,442	$ 736.00	$ 37,672
24	$1,493.92	$1,234.96	$304.16	$930.80	$ 1,205.37	$223,088	$36,394	$ 736.00	$ 38,267
25	$1,499.71	$1,234.96	$305.42	$929.53	$ 1,211.55	$222,783	$37,348	$ 757.63	$ 38,849
26	$1,499.71	$1,234.96	$306.70	$928.26	$ 1,211.95	$222,476	$38,306	$ 757.63	$ 39,432
27	$1,499.71	$1,234.96	$307.97	$926.98	$ 1,212.35	$222,168	$39,266	$ 757.63	$ 40,019
28	$1,499.71	$1,234.96	$309.26	$925.70	$ 1,212.74	$221,859	$40,227	$ 757.63	$ 40,607
29	$1,499.71	$1,234.96	$310.55	$924.41	$ 1,213.14	$221,548	$41,192	$ 757.63	$ 41,198

The interest portion of the payment (column F) is calculated using the IPMT function:

```
=-IPMT('Rent versus Buy'!$E$9/12,B4,
    'Rent versus Buy'!$E$10*12,'Rent versus Buy'!$E$11)
```

The principal portion of the payment in column E is simply the difference between the total PI payment and the interest portion:

```
=D4-F4
```

The PITI payment in column C is the PI payment plus the escrow payment. The tax portion of the escrow payment relies on data in the hidden column O that I will explain shortly:

```
=-PMT('Rent versus Buy'!$E$9/12,'Rent versus Buy'!$E$10*12, _
    'Rent versus Buy'!$E$11)+'Rent versus Buy'!$C$9/12+ _
    ('Rent versus Buy'!$C$8*O4)/12
```

The effective PITI payment displayed in column G is the actual PITI payment less any tax savings:

```
=C4+('Rent versus Buy'!$G$8+'Rent versus Buy'!$G$9)*IPMT('Rent _
    versus Buy'!$E$9/12,B4,'Rent versus Buy'!$E$10*12, _
    'Rent versus Buy'!$E$11)
```

The Balance column in the first row is calculated by subtracting the first month's principal payment from the total amount financed on the Rent versus Buy worksheet:

```
='Rent versus Buy'!E11-E4
```

A

For the second and subsequent months, the balance is calculated as the last month's balance minus this month's principal payment. For example, the second month's formula is

```
=H4-E5
```

The last column in the Buying section, Equity, is calculated by subtracting the current balance owed on the mortgage (column H) from the current value of the house. This latter figure is calculated in some hidden columns I'll explain soon. The formula is

```
-P4-H4
```

The Renting Section

The Renting section in columns K and L is relatively simple. Column K calculates that month's rent and fees based on information you entered on the input worksheet, including projected annual increases:

```
='Rent versus Buy'!$G$5*(1+'Rent versus Buy'!$G$6)^ _
    (INT((B4-1)/12))+'Rent versus Buy'!$G$7
```

The Equity column represents the amount of money you would have if you invested the cash that would have gone for the down payment on the house (less any part of this that is borrowed) as well as the difference between the rent payment and the mortgage payment. The formula for the first row is

```
='Rent versus Buy'!E5-'Rent versus Buy'!G11
```

For subsequent rows, the equity is calculated as the previous month's equity increased by 1/12 of the projected annual return plus the difference between the mortgage and rent payments:

```
=L4*(1+'Rent versus Buy'!$G$10/12)+(G5-K5)
```

The Hidden Columns

Columns O through S in the Output worksheet are hidden because there's no real need for you to see them. Columns O and P hold intermediate calculations that are used in other calculations, as detailed earlier. Columns Q through S are not used in calculations but rather organize data from other parts of the worksheet to make it easier to chart. These columns are shown in Figure A.23.

Figure A.23

These five hidden columns provide intermediate data for the Output worksheet and organize results for charting.

	Tax Value	Appr Value	Month	Buying Equity	Renting Equity
3					
4	$ 225,000	$ 245,000	1	$15,226	$ 25,000
5	$ 225,000	$ 245,613	2	$16,116	$ 25,560
6	$ 225,000	$ 246,227	3	$17,009	$ 26,122
7	$ 225,000	$ 246,842	4	$17,905	$ 26,686
8	$ 225,000	$ 247,459	5	$18,803	$ 27,253
9	$ 225,000	$ 248,078	6	$19,704	$ 27,822
10	$ 225,000	$ 248,698	7	$20,607	$ 28,393
11	$ 225,000	$ 249,320	8	$21,514	$ 28,966
12	$ 225,000	$ 249,943	9	$22,423	$ 29,541
13	$ 225,000	$ 250,568	10	$23,335	$ 30,119
14	$ 225,000	$ 251,194	11	$24,249	$ 30,700
15	$ 225,000	$ 251,822	12	$25,166	$ 31,282
16	$ 231,750	$ 252,452	13	$26,087	$ 31,851
17	$ 231,750	$ 253,083	14	$27,009	$ 32,423
18	$ 231,750	$ 253,716	15	$27,935	$ 32,997
19	$ 231,750	$ 254,350	16	$28,864	$ 33,573
20	$ 231,750	$ 254,986	17	$29,795	$ 34,152
21	$ 231,750	$ 255,623	18	$30,729	$ 34,733
22	$ 231,750	$ 256,262	19	$31,666	$ 35,316
23	$ 231,750	$ 256,903	20	$32,606	$ 35,902
24	$ 231,750	$ 257,545	21	$33,548	$ 36,489
25	$ 231,750	$ 258,189	22	$34,494	$ 37,080
26	$ 231,750	$ 258,835	23	$35,442	$ 37,672
27	$ 231,750	$ 259,482	24	$36,394	$ 38,267
28	$ 238,703	$ 260,130	25	$37,348	$ 38,849
29	$ 238,703	$ 260,781	26	$38,305	$ 39,432
30	$ 238,703	$ 261,433	27	$39,265	$ 40,019

Column O calculates the assessed tax value of the home based on information entered on the input worksheet. This value increases at the first month of each year using the formula

```
='Rent versus Buy'!$C$6*(1+'Rent versus Buy'!$C$10)^
    INT((B4-1)/12)
```

Column P calculates the appraised value of the house on a month by month basis:

```
='Rent versus Buy'!$C$5*(1+'Rent versus Buy'!$C$10/12)^(B4-1)
```

If you want to display the hidden columns in your workbook, select Format, Column, Unhide.

The Chart Worksheet

The third and final worksheet in the Rent versus Buy workbook displays a graphical representation of the results. Specifically, it charts the equity you could expect to have if you keep renting and the equity you could expect to have if you buy. This is shown in Figure A.24. Where the lines cross is the breakeven point—where you start coming out ahead if you buy. Of course, the lines will not cross in all scenarios, and in some scenarios—unlikely but possible—the buying equity will be above the renting equity from the very start.

A

Figure A.24

The Chart worksheet in the Rent versus Buy Calculator plots the renting and buying equity results.

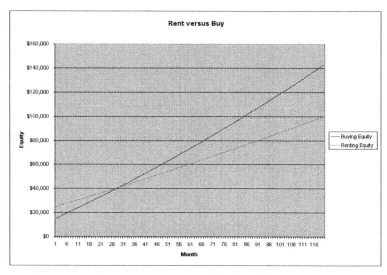

Chapter 13: Lease Payment Calculator

The Lease Payment Calculator is used to determine what the lease payment will be for an auto lease. It is shown in Figure A.25.

Figure A.25

Use the Lease Payment Calculator to determine an auto lease payment.

The Net Capital Cost field in cell C7 is calculated as the capital cost minus the capital cost reduction and trade in value:

```
=C4-C5-C6
```

The interest rate in cell C10 is calculated at 24 times the money factor (as was explained in Chapter 13, "Your New Car—Buy or Lease?"):

```
=C9*24
```

Finally, the lease payment is calculated as the vehicle depreciation over the life of the lease with the money factor and sales tax applied:

```
=(1+C12)*(((C7-C11)/C8)+((C7+C11)*C9))
```

Chapter 13: Lease or Buy Calculator

The Lease or Buy Calculator, shown in Figure A.26, helps you determine if leasing or buying a car makes the most sense financially.

Figure A.26

The Lease or Buy Calculator.

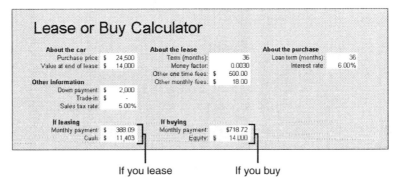

The input fields were explained in the chapter. Note that the term of the loan (cell H5) is assumed to be the same as the term of the lease because comparing different terms would not provide the desired information.

For leasing, the monthly payment is calculated as the depreciation over the life of the lease with the money factor and sales tax included:

`-(1+C11)*(((((C5-C9)-C6)/E5)+(C5+C6)*E6+E8)`

The Cash field is calculated as the sum of the monthly savings (buying payment less leasing payment) minus any one-time leasing fees.

For buying, the monthly payment is calculated using the PMT function and applying the sales tax to the price of the car:

`=-PMT(H6/12,H5,(1+C11)*(C5-(C9+C10)))`

The equity is simply the value of the car at the end of the term, copied from cell C6.

Chapter 15: Investment Portfolio Workbook

The Investment Portfolio workbook, shown in Figure A.27, enables you to maintain a list of your stock and mutual fund investments. It downloads current share price information from the Internet and displays them along with your gain or loss.

Names of stocks and funds you own

Total value of your investments

Your gain or loss

Figure A.27

The Investment
Portfolio
workbook.(Sample
data used for illustra-
tive purposes only.)

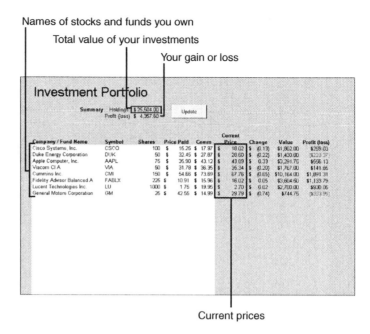

Current prices

On the Holdings worksheet, shown in Figure A.27, you enter the name
and symbol of each holding as well as the number of shares you own,
the price paid, and the commission (if any). The price and change
information in columns G and H are obtained from the Internet (I'll
explain how in a moment). The value in column I is calculated by multiplying the current price by the number of shares. The IF function is
used to display a result only when the row contains a holding name in
column B:

```
=IF(B9<>"",D9*G9,"")
```

The profit or loss in column J is calculated by subtracting the price
paid, plus any commission, from the current value. Again, the IF function is employed:

```
=IF(B9<>"",I9-(D9*E9)-F9,"")
```

Current prices are downloaded from the MSN Money website using an
Excel feature called a web query. You can define a web query using
menu commands, but for the purposes of this workbook, it is done
using a macro. There are three steps involved; the first two relate to the
web query itself and the third relates to transferring the data to the
Holdings worksheet:

1. Create a query file that contains the details of the query, including
the symbols of the stocks and funds to retrieve.

2. Execute the query and place the query results on the Query worksheet.

3. Transfer the stock price and change from the Query worksheet to the Holdings worksheet.

When you click the Update button, the macro shown in Listing A.12 is run:

Listing A.12   The Update Button Macro

```
Sub GetStockPricesFromMSN()

MakeQueryFile
ExecuteQuery
TransferDataToHoldings

End Sub
```

You can see that this macro calls three other macros, one for each of the three steps listed above. Note that the macros make use of two global variables declared as follows:

```
Dim QueryFileName As String
Dim Query As QueryTable
```

The first step is to make the query definition file. The template for this file is provided as part of the Excel installation. This macro simply reproduces that template while inserting the symbols of the stocks and funds from column C of the Holdings worksheet. The MakeQueryFile macro is shown in Listing A.13.

Listing A.13   Creating a Web Query File Containing the Stock Symbols

```
Sub MakeQueryFile()

' Create the web query file from the stocks list.

Dim fso As New FileSystemObject
Dim ts As TextStream

' This is a global
QueryFileName = ThisWorkbook.Path & "\stocksquery.iqy"

' Create the file
Set ts = fso.CreateTextFile(QueryFileName, True)
ts.WriteLine "WEB"
ts.WriteLine "1"
ts.WriteLine "http://investor.msn.com/external/excel/quotes.asp?SYMBOL=" _
    & MakeSymbolString
ts.WriteLine "Selection = EntirePage"
```

A

Listing A.13 Continued

```
ts.WriteLine "Formatting = All"
ts.WriteLine "PreFormattedTextToColumns = True"
ts.WriteLine "ConsecutiveDelimitersAsOne = True"
ts.WriteLine "SingleBlockTextImport = False"

ts.Close

End Sub
```

You can see that the MakeQueryFile macro calls another macro, MakeSymbolString, to retrieve the stock symbols from the worksheet. This macro is shown in Listing A.14.

Listing A.14 Retrieving the Stock Symbols

```
Function MakeSymbolString() As String

' Goes thru the list on the Symbols worksheet and makes a string
' containing all the symbols, comma delimited.

Dim buf As String
Dim temp As String
Dim r As Range

' First symbol is in C3

Set r = ThisWorkbook.Worksheets("Holdings").Range("C9")
temp = r.Value
' An empty cell marks the end of the list.
Do While temp <> ""
    buf = buf & temp & ","
    Set r = r.Offset(1, 0)
    temp = r.Value
Loop

' Remove trailing comma.
If Len(buf) > 0 Then
    buf = Left(buf, Len(buf) - 1)
End If

MakeSymbolString = buf

End Function
```

The MakeSymbolString macro works by starting at cell C9 where the first symbol will be found. It then goes down a row at a time, adding each symbol to the string (separated by commas) until an empty cell is found. The resulting string is returned to the MakeQueryFile macro where it is included in the query file.

What exactly does a query file look like? Listing A.15 shows an example. The string of symbols—CSCO, DUK, AAPL, VIA, CMI, FABLX, LU, and GM in this example—was generated from the stock symbols in the worksheet. The remainder is simply copied from the template installed with Excel.

Listing A.15   An Example Query File to Retrieve Stock Prices

```
WEB
1
http://investor.msn.com/external/excel/quotes.asp?SYMBOL=CSCO, _
    DUK,AAPL,VIA,CMI,FABLX,LU,GM
Selection = EntirePage
Formatting = All
PreFormattedTextToColumns = True
ConsecutiveDelimitersAsOne = True
SingleBlockTextImport = False
```

After the query file has been created and saved to disk, the next step is to execute the query. This is done by the ExecuteQuery macro, shown in Listing A.16.

Listing A.16   Executing the Query and Placing the Results in the Query Worksheet

```
Sub ExecuteQuery()

' Clear spreadsheet for web query
Worksheets("Query").Columns("A:CV").Clear

' Do web query
Set Query = ThisWorkbook.Worksheets("Query").QueryTables.Add _
    (Connection:="FINDER;" & QueryFileName, _
    Destination:=Worksheets("Query").Range("A1"))
With Query
    .Name = "Microsoft Investor Stock Quotes"
    .FieldNames = True
    .RowNumbers = True
    .FillAdjacentFormulas = False
    .PreserveFormatting = False
    .RefreshOnFileOpen = False
    .BackgroundQuery = True
    .RefreshStyle = xlInsertDeleteCells
    .SavePassword = False
    .SaveData = True
    .AdjustColumnWidth = True
    .RefreshPeriod = 0
    .WebSelectionType = xlEntirePage
    .WebFormatting = xlWebFormattingAll
    .WebPreFormattedTextToColumns = True
    .WebConsecutiveDelimitersAsOne = True
    .WebSingleBlockTextImport = False
```

A

Listing A.16 Continued

```
      .WebDisableDateRecognition = False
      .Refresh BackgroundQuery:=False
End With

Do While Query.Refreshing
    DoEvents
Loop

End Sub
```

This macro does the following:

1. Clears the range of columns A to CV to delete any previous query results.

2. Adds a query to the workbook's QueryTables collection based on the query file created earlier and located in the Query worksheet starting at cell A1.

3. Sets a number of properties of the query.

4. Enters a loop that executes until the query is complete.

When the query has completed, it will have inserted its results on the Query worksheet, as shown in Figure A.28.

Figure A.28

The results of the web query. (Sample data used for illustrative purposes only.)

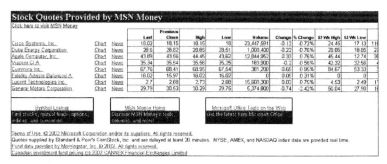

The final step is to transfer the price and change data for each holding from the query to the Holdings worksheet. This makes use of the fact that the results of the web query are in the same order as the holdings are listed. All the macro needs to do is transfer data from the first row of the web query to the first row of the holdings and so on, a row at a time, until a blank row is found. The transfer is accomplished by the TransferDataToHoldings macro, shown in Listing A.17.

Listing A.17   The TransferDataToHoldings Macro

```
Sub TransferDataToHoldings()

' Transfers data from the web query results to the Holdings worksheet.

Dim r1 As Range, r2 As Range
Dim wsh As Worksheet
Dim wsq As Worksheet
Dim HoldingName As String
Dim symbol As String
Dim found As Boolean

Set wsh = Worksheets("Holdings")
Set wsq = Worksheets("Query")

' Web query results will be in the same order as holdings.

' Start in cell C9 where the first symbol is listed.
Set r1 = wsh.Range("C9")
symbol = r1.Value
' If it's empty then there are no holdings.
If symbol = "" Then Exit Sub
' Point r2 at the cell above the first company name in the query.
Set r2 = wsq.Range("A3")
'Loop for each holding.
Do While symbol <> ""
    ' Move r2 down a row
    Set r2 = r2.Offset(1, 0)
    ' Copy company name to holdings.
    r1.Offset(0, -1).Value = r2.Value
    ' Last price
    r1.Offset(0, 4).Value = r2.Offset(0, 3).Value
    ' Change
    r1.Offset(0, 5).Value = r2.Offset(0, 8).Value
    ' Move r1 down a row
    Set r1 = r1.Offset(1, 0)
    symbol = r1.Value
Loop

End Sub
```

The operation of this macro is simple in concept. It starts in row 9 of the Holdings worksheet where the first holding is located. Because the query results are in the same order, it can retrieve the data from this holding from the third row of the Query worksheet. The company name, current price, and change are copied from the Query worksheet to the Holdings worksheet. The process repeats, moving down a row each time, until the end of the holdings is reached.

Chapter 16: Mutual Fund Comparator

The Mutual Fund Comparator workbook enables you to compare the hypothetical investment results of two mutual funds that differ in their loads and annual operating fees. It is shown in Figure A.29.

Figure A.29

The Mutual Fund Comparator.

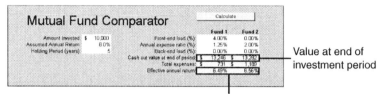

Value at end of investment period

Effective annual investment return

The workbook assumes the same initial investment, annual return, and holding period for both funds. The assumed annual return is the return of the fund's underlying investments, not of the fund itself (that is, after all, what this workbook calculates). The front-end load, annual expense ratio, and back-end load are entered in cells F4:G6. The calculations required by the workbook are not amenable to in-cell formulas, but are accomplished with macros that are called when the Calculate button is clicked. The code is shown in Listing A.18.

Listing A.18 The Mutual Fund Comparison Calculations Code

```
Sub Calculate()

Dim ws As Worksheet
Dim i As Integer, years As Integer
Dim expenses1 As Single, expenses2 As Single
Dim value1 As Single, value2 As Single
Dim initialAmount1 As Single, initialAmount2 As Single

Set ws = Worksheets("Fund Comparator")

If ws.Range("C4").value <= 0 Or ws.Range("C5").value <= 0 Or _
    ws.Range("C6").value <= 0 Then
        MsgBox "You must enter values for Amount Invested, _
            Assumed Annual Return, and Holding Period"
    Exit Sub
End If

years = ws.Range("C6").value
initialAmount1 = ws.Range("C4").value * (1 - ws.Range("F4"))
initialAmount2 = ws.Range("C4").value * (1 - ws.Range("G4"))

expenses1 = 0
expenses2 = 0
value1 = initialAmount1
value2 = initialAmount2
```

```
For i = 1 To years
    ' Calc investment gain.
    value1 = value1 * (1 + ws.Range("C5").value)
    value2 = value2 * (1 + ws.Range("C5").value)
    ' Subtract expenses.
    value1 = value1 - (value1 * ws.Range("F5").value)
    value2 = value2 - (value2 * ws.Range("G5").value)
    ' Total expenses.
    expenses1 = expenses1 + value1 * ws.Range("F5").value
    expenses2 = expenses2 + value2 * ws.Range("G5").value
Next i

' Deduct back end load
value1 = value1 * (1 - ws.Range("F6").value)
value2 = value2 * (1 - ws.Range("G6").value)

' Put final value in sheet
ws.Range("F7").value = value1
ws.Range("G7").value = value2
' Put expenses in sheet
ws.Range("F8").value = expenses1
ws.Range("G8").value = expenses2

Worksheets("Fund Comparator").Range("F3:G3").Font.Color = _
    RGB(0, 0, 0)

End Sub
```

The code performs the following actions:

1. Verifies that you have entered the required input data and, if not, displays a message.

2. Calculates the initial amount invested for each fund as the amount in cell C4 less any front-end load.

3. Loops once for each year of the holding period. For each year, it does the following for each of the two funds:

    - Increases the value by the annual return amount
    - Decreases the value by the expenses ratio
    - Adds the current year's expenses to the total expenses

4. Finally, the code deducts any back-end load.

The final value for each fund is displayed in the worksheet, along with the total expenses that will be paid over the term of the investment. The effective annual return is calculated in cells F9 and G9 with this formula (from F9):

```
=(F7-$C$4)/$C$4/$C$6
```

The formula subtracts the initial investment from the final value to get the gain, divides the original investment to get the overall percentage gain, and then divides by the term of the investment to get the overall annual return.

```
=(G7-$C$4)/$C$4/$C$6
```

Note the last line of the code in the macro:

```
Worksheets("Fund Comparator").Range("F3:G3").Font.Color = RGB(0, 0, 0)
```

This code sets the font color of cells F3:G3 to black, signaling to you that the calculations are up to date. If these cells display red, it indicates that the input data has changed but the calculations have not been run. This change in color is accomplished in the workbook's SheetChange event procedure. This procedure fires automatically whenever there is any change in one of the worksheets. The single line of code sets cells F3:G3 to red, as shown in Listing A.19.

Listing A.19   Changing Cells to Red with a Workbook Change

```
Private Sub Workbook_SheetChange(ByVal Sh As Object, ByVal Target As Range)

Worksheets("Fund Comparator").Range("F3:G3").Font.Color = RGB(255, 0, 0)

End Sub
```

Chapter 17: Inflation Effects Calculator

The Inflation Effects Calculator calculates the effect of inflation on your purchasing power in the future. It is shown in Figure A.30.

Figure A.30
The Inflation Effects Calculator.

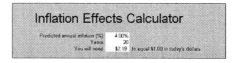

The single calculation in this workbook is simple. It adds one to the projected inflation rate and then raises it to the power of the number of years:

```
=(1+C4)^C5
```

Chapter 17: College Cost Calculator

The College Cost Calculator is one of two related calculators found in the College Costs workbook. It is shown in Figure A.31.

Annual college cost today

Figure A.31

The College Cost Calculator.

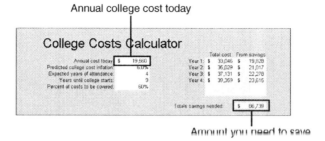

Amount you need to save

The purpose of this calculator is to give you a handle on what college costs will be at some time in the future. The most important input is the current costs for the college or university, obtained from its literature or website and entered in cell C4. After the other input information is entered, the calculator displays the total amount needed for each year of college, as well as the amount you will need to provide based on the percentage entered in cell C8.

The total cost for year 1, in cell F4, is obtained by applying the projected inflation rate to the current cost:

```
=C4*(1+C5)^C7
```

Subsequent years' costs are determined by applying one year's worth of inflation to the previous year's cost. In cell F5, for example, the second year's cost is calculated as

```
=F4*(1+$C$5)
```

The same formula is used for years 2–6. For years 3–6, the IF function is also included to display a result only for the relevant years (based on the Years of Attendance value from cell C6). Here's the formula for year 3 total costs:

```
=IF($C$6>2,F5*(1+$C$5),"")
```

The values in column G are simply calculated by multiplying the associated value in column F by the percentage value in cell C8 Total savings in cell G11 is the sum of all values in column G.

A

Chapter 17: College Savings Calculator

The College Savings Calculator is an adjunct to the College Costs Calculator and is located on a separate worksheet in the same workbook file. It is shown in Figure A.32.

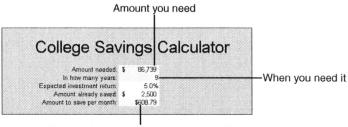

Figure A.32

The College Savings Calculator.

The purpose of this calculator is to determine how much you will have to put away on a monthly basis to meet your college savings goals. The amount needed and the years to save in cells C4 and C5 are carried over from the College Costs worksheet. When you enter the assumed investment return and the amount already saved, the monthly amount to save is calculated in cell C8 using the PMT function:

```
=-PMT($C$6/12,$C$5*12,-$C$7,C4)
```

Column D provides the opportunity to shoot for a specific money goal that is not carried over from the College Costs worksheet. Enter this amount in cell D4 and the required monthly savings is calculated in cell D8, again with the PMT function, using the data for years, return, and amount already saved from column C:

```
=-PMT($C$6/12,$C$5*12,-$C$7,D4)
```

Chapter 17: Retirement Planner Workbook

The Retirement Planner workbook is designed to help people evaluate their retirement savings goals and plans and to see if their current and planned savings are in line with their financial goals for their retirement years. This calculator is shown in Figure A.33.

A

Figure A.33

The Retirement Planner Calculator.

Information about you

Information about your retirement savings

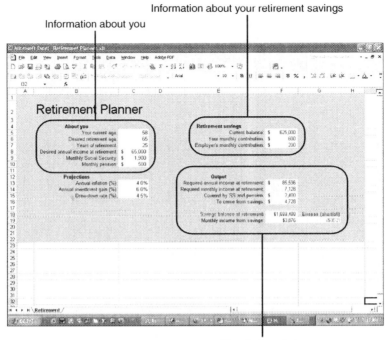

Result of analysis

As I discussed in the chapter, retirement planning is fraught with uncertainties, and even the most qualified experts often differ in their suggestions for crunching your retirement numbers. For these reasons, any retirement planner can at best be a rough guide that can help you to see if your plans are at least "in the ballpark." Neither this retirement planner nor any other should be taken as providing precise predictions.

The required annual income at retirement in cell F13 is calculated by taking the desired annual income from cell C8 and adjusting it for inflation based on the predicted inflation amount in cell C13 and the number of years until you retire:

`=C8*(1+C13)^(C6-C5)`

The required monthly income is simply the required annual income divided by 12:

`=F13/12`

The amount to come from retirement savings is this required monthly amount less what you expect to receive from Social Security and pensions:

`=F14-F15`

The savings balance at retirement is calculated by taking your current savings (cell F5), along with the projected monthly additions (cells F6 and F7), and calculating the future value when you retire based on the projected investment return in cell C14. The FV function is used for this calculation:

```
=FV(C14/12,(C6-C5)*12,-(F6+F7),-F5)
```

The projected monthly income you might expect from the savings in cell F18 are calculated using the draw-down rate from cell C15, as was explained in the chapter. The monthly income in cell F19 is simply the draw-down rate times the anticipated savings divided by 12:

```
=C15*F18/12
```

The excess or shortfall in cell G19 is calculated by subtracting the amount needed in cell F16 from the projected available income in cell F19.

A

B

Glossary of Financial Terms

adjustable rate mortgage (ARM) A mortgage whose interest rate, and hence its monthly payments, can change over the life of the mortgage. The rate is based on some independent index, such as the prime interest rate. The rate is adjusted annually or at some other period specified in the mortgage terms.

alpha A measure of mutual fund performance that compares a fund's beta value with its actual performance. Alpha values above and below zero mean that a fund returned more or less than expected, respectively, based on its beta value.

annual expense ratio The amount a mutual fund charges to manage and maintain your account. Expressed as a percentage.

back-end load A mutual fund sales charge imposed when you sell your shares.

bear market An extended period during which the stock market declines.

beta A measure of mutual fund performance that compares the fund to some benchmark, such as the Standard & Poor's 500. A beta of 1.00 means that the fund goes up and down in lockstep with the benchmark. A beta of 1.15 means that if the benchmark goes up or down by a certain amount, the fund goes up or down by 15% more.

B

blue chip stock   Stock in a large, established, and consistently profitable company. Which stocks are considered to be blue chip stocks change over time.

bond   An investment vehicle that consists of money loaned to a corporation or governmental body. Bonds are considered to be an income investment.

broker   Can refer to an individual who oversees your investment account and provides investment advice. Can also refer to a firm (a brokerage) that provides these services.

bull market   An extended period during which the stock market shows a greater than usual upswing in prices.

capital cost   In auto leasing, the price of the vehicle.

capital cost reduction   In auto leasing, a down payment or trade-in.

capital gain   Profit from selling an investment, such as a stock, at a higher price than you paid for it.

closed-end lease   In auto leasing, a lease in which the value of the car at the end of the lease is set at the start of the lease.

commission   A fee you pay to a brokerage for buying or selling shares of stock for you.

common stock   A share of ownership in a company. The price of common stock shares rises or falls depending on the fortunes of the company and the demand for the stock on the market.

corporate bond   A bond issued by a corporation.

coupon   Refers to the amount of interest paid by a bond.

debit card   It looks and works much like a credit card, but the amount of each purchase is deducted immediately from your checking account.

dividend   Income paid by a company to owners of its stock. Not all stocks pay dividends.

Dividend Reinvestment Plans (DRIPs)   An investment plan, usually run by a company, that lets you buy shares in the company without going through a broker and usually with reduced or no fees.

equity   In real estate, the difference between the value of a property and the amount owed on it. In the world of investment, stocks are sometimes referred to as equities.

exchange traded funds (ETF)   A type of mutual fund that trades on the market just like stocks. Sometimes called closed-end funds.

excess mileage fee   A fee you pay at the end of an auto lease if you have driven more miles than permitted in the lease agreement.

fixed rate mortgage   A mortgage whose interest rate and payments remain constant for the entire life of the mortgage.

front-end load   A mutual fund sales charge you pay when you buy shares.

holding period   The amount of time you own an investment.

home equity loan   A loan that is backed by the equity in your house. Sometimes called a second mortgage.

income investment   An investment, such as bonds, that is purchased more for the regular income it produces (in the form of interest or dividends) and less for the change of capital appreciation.

index fund   A mutual fund that does not actively select stocks but rather invests in a broad market index of stocks.

inflation   A general, society-wide increase in prices and wages for the same underlying product or service.

junk bond   A bond issued by a company with a relatively poor credit rating. Junk bonds pay higher interest rates than nonjunk bonds, but carry a greater risk that the company will be unable to make payments or return principal.

load mutual fund   A mutual fund that charges a commission, or load, when you purchase shares of the fund.

marginal tax rate   The income tax rate you pay on the last dollar of your income.

market capitalization   The total value of a company's stock (number of shares times current share price).

market index   Any one of many measures, such as the Dow Jones Industrial Average or the S&P 500, that combines the prices of a basket of stocks in a single number that acts as a summary of market changes.

maturity   The time until a bond becomes mature and is paid off.

money factor   The way the effective interest rate is expressed in auto leasing.

municipal bond   A bond issued by a governmental agency to fund public projects such as highways and schools. The income from municipal bonds is tax-exempt for many taxpayers, unlike income from corporate bonds.

mutual fund   An investment vehicle that consists of stocks and/or bonds from various companies that is managed by an investment company. Shares in this pool of stocks or bonds are sold to individual investors and represent a fractional ownership of the underlying investments.

no-load mutual fund   A mutual fund that does not charge a sales commission when you buy or sell shares.

open-end lease   An auto lease in which the value of the car is determined at the end of the lease.

P/E (price earnings) ratio   The price of a share of stock divided by the per-share earnings of the company. Can also be looked at as representing the price investors are willing to pay for $1 of earnings from a company.

PI   Stands for principal and interest. Refers to the portion of the monthly mortgage payment that goes toward principal and interest (omitting escrow).

PITI   Stands for principal, interest, taxes, and insurance. Refers to the sum total mortgage payment due each month.

preferred stock   A share of ownership in a company that pays a fixed dividend. The dividends of preferred stock are paid before any dividends are paid on common stock, and they receive priority over common stock in the event of a liquidation. Unlike most common stock, preferred stock does not confer voting rights.

principal   The amount you borrow on a loan.

REIT (Real Estate Investment Trust)   A company that owns and manages real estate, such as apartment buildings or shopping malls.

sector   A group of corporations that are in similar lines of business, such as petroleum, automobiles, or energy.

sector funds   A mutual fund that limits its investments to companies in a particular sector.

stock   A share of ownership in a company.

treasury bill   A short-term loan to the Federal government that matures in less than one year.

zero-coupon bond   A bond that does not pay regular interest but is sold at a discount and increases to its full face value at maturity.

B

INDEX

reward cards, 87-89
transaction fees, 82
transaction protection, 85
when to use, 88-89
debit cards, 70-71, 86

cars
leasing
advantages and disadvantages, 151-153
analyzing your needs, 149-150
closed-end leases, 153
how it works, 150-151
lease conditions, 153-154
Lease or Buy Calculator, 155-157, 245
Lease Payment Calculator, 154-155, 244
open-end leases, 153
valuing, 46

Cash Advance Cost Calculator (credit cards), 96-97, 225-226

cash advances (credit cards), 95-97

cash flow, 25

CDs (certificates of deposit), 171

cells
active cells, 18
definition of, 10
editing, 20
entering data into, 20
formatting, 20-23
money values, 25-26
percentage values, 25-26
multiline text, 22
pointers, 18
protection, 22
ranges
defining, 20
selecting, 19
selecting, 19-20

certificates of deposit (CDs), 171

Chart Wizard, 27-30

Chart worksheet (Rent versus Buy Calculator), 146, 243

charts, creating, 27-30

Checkbook Register, 73
CreateMenu macro, 218
DeleteMenu macro, 219
EnterTransaction macro, 221

headings, 78-79
how it works, 74
ProcessTransactionData macro, 219-220
reconciling, 79-80
Register menu, 217-219
setting up, 74-75
SortByCheckNum macro, 221
SortByDate macro, 222
SortByTo macro, 222
totals, calculating, 222
transactions
editing, 77-78
entering 75-77, 219-221
sorting, 77, 221-222
types, 76

checking accounts. See also Checkbook Register
account services, 72
ATM cards, 71
ATM transactions, 71
checks, purchasing, 71-72
debit cards, 70-71, 86
do's and don'ts, 72
fee accounts, 67
fee-free accounts, 67, 73
float, 70
interest rates, 68
money market accounts, 68, 171-172
overdraft fees, 69
overdraft protection, 69
teller fees, 73

checks, purchasing, 71-72

Class A shares (mutual funds), 170

Class B shares (mutual funds), 170

Class C shares (mutual funds), 170

closed-end funds, 165, 170

closed-end leases, 153

closing costs, 141-142

College Cost Calculator, 195-196, 255

College Savings Calculator, 196-197, 256

college, saving for, 193-195
College Cost Calculator, 195-196, 255
College Savings Calculator, 196-197, 256
inflation, 191-192, 254
Inflation Effects Calculator, 192, 254
over-saving, 193

predicting needs, 192
tax-advantaged college savings, 194

corporate bonds, 164

correlation (mutual funds), 173

costs. See expenses

coupons, 163

CreateMenu macro, 210-211, 218

credit cards, 81
advantages of, 85
balances
cash advances, 95-97
costs of, 84, 92
paying off, 92-94
Cash Advance Cost Calculator, 96-97, 225-226
compared to debit cards, 86
credit limits, 90
fees, 84-85
fraud protection, 85
grace period, 86-89
how they work, 81-83
insurance, 85
interest rates, 83-84
online account access, 90
payments, making on time, 89
Payoff Calculator, 94, 224-225
Real Cost Calculator, 91, 223
responsible use of, 88-90
reward cards, 87-89
transaction fees, 82
transaction protection, 85
when to use, 88-89

credit limits, 90

Currency format, 26

Current Mortgage section (Mortgage Refinance Breakeven Calculator), 130

D

debit cards, 70-71, 86
defined benefit plans, 197
defined contribution plans, 197
Delete key, 20
DeleteMenu macro, 211, 219
DIA (Dow Diamonds), 170

How can we make this index more useful? Email us at indexes@quepublishing.com